British Asian Theatre

THE UNIVERSITY OF
WINCHESTER

British Asian Theatre

Dramaturgy, Process and Performance

Dominic Hingorani

© Dominic Hingorani 2010

First published 2010 by
PALGRAVE MACMILLAN

Palgrave Macmillan in the UK is an imprint of Macmillan Publishers Limited, registered in England, company number 785998, of Houndmills, Basingstoke, Hampshire RG21 6XS.

Palgrave Macmillan in the US is a division of St Martin's Press LLC, 175 Fifth Avenue, New York, NY 10010.

Palgrave Macmillan is the global academic imprint of the above companies and has companies and representatives throughout the world.

Palgrave® and Macmillan® are registered trademarks in the United States, the United Kingdom, Europe and other countries.

ISBN-13: 978–0–230–21138–4 hardback
ISBN-13: 978–0–230–21139–1 paperback

This book is printed on paper suitable for recycling and made from fully managed and sustained forest sources. Logging, pulping and manufacturing processes are expected to conform to the environmental regulations of the country of origin.

A catalogue record for this book is available from the British Library.

A catalog record for this book is available from the Library of Congress.

10   9   8   7   6   5   4   3   2   1
19   18   17   16   15   14   13   12   11   10

Printed in China

For Mandy Tate and Daisy

Contents

List of Illustrations   viii

Acknowledgements   ix

1   Introduction: British Asian Theatre on the Map   1

2   Tara Arts 1977–1984: Creating a British Asian Theatre   18

3   Tara Arts 1984–1996: Creating a 'Binglish' Theatre   45

4   Tamasha Theatre Company 1989: Authenticity and Adaptation   71

5   Tamasha Theatre Company 1989 – *East is East*: From Kitchen Sink to Bollywood   95

6   Kali Theatre Company 1990–2007: Producing British Asian Women Playwrights   120

7   Tara Arts 1997–2007: Mapping a 'Binglish' Diaspora   143

8   New Writers from 1977: Kureishi, Bancil, Bhatti and Khan-Din   166

Conclusion   188

Notes   192

Bibliography   196

Index   215

List of Illustrations

Sacrifice Rehearsal (1977) © Tara Arts   21
Yes, Memsahib (1979) © Tara Arts   25
Chilli in Your Eyes (1984) © Chris Ha 1984   40
Chilli in Your Eyes (1984) © Chris Ha 1984   42
Miti Ki Gadi Publicity Flyer © Tara Arts   49
Miti Ki Gadi (1984) © Tara Arts   52
Untouchable (1989) © Jenny Potter   74
A Fine Balance (2006) © Robert Day   79
Balti Kings (2000) © Jenny Potter   85
Women of the Dust (1992) © Jenny Potter   91
East is East (1996) © Robert Day   96
Fourteen Songs, Two Weddings and A Funeral (2000)
   © Tamasha Theatre Company   102
The Trouble with Asian Men (2007) © Robert Day   108
Lyrical MC (2008) © Robert Workman   115
Song for a Sanctuary (1991) © Kali Theatre Company   125
Calcutta Kosher (2004) © Robert Day   134
Deadeye (2006) © Robert Day   142
Exodus (1998) © Tara Arts   147
Journey To The West Part I (2002) © Stephen Vaughan   149
Journey To The West Part II (2002) © Stephen Vaughan   151
Tara-In-The-Sky (2007) © Claudia Mayer   162
Behzti (2004) © Robert Day   179

Acknowledgements

The author and publishers wish to thank the following for permission to reproduce copyright material:

I would particularly like to thank Dan Rebellato who has provided me with great guidance, encouragement and insight in researching this subject from the outset. I would also like to thank Graham Ley and Sarah Dadswell at Exeter University who have been instrumental in driving forward research in this area for their tremendously collegiate approach, unstinting support and encouragement for my own research. I would also like to thank my colleagues at IPAD – Institute for Performing Arts Development – at the University of East London for their support and to the University for their kind contribution towards the production costs. At Palgrave Macmillan, Jenni Burnell, Kate Wallis and Felicity Noble who have supported and guided me throughout all the work on this project.

The author would like to thank the theatre companies featured in the book for their kind help and generous access to their archival material; Jatinder Verma and Jonathan Holloway at Tara Arts, Kristine Landon-Smith, Sudha Bhuchar, and Julia Good at Tamasha, Janet Steel and Chris Corner at Kali and Parv Bancil. I would also like to thank the numerous artists involved in British Asian theatre who have given their time to talk and their insightful reflections on their work and experiences. I would also like to say a special thanks to Ann Jefferson who made the time possible for me to write this book.

I am indebted to the following playwrights and their publishers for allowing me to reproduce extracts from their work; Aurora Metro Press, Rukhasana Ahmad, Parv Bancil, Gurpreet Kaur Bhatti, Sita Brahmachari, Faber and Faber, Nick Hern Books, Ayub Khan-Din, Hanif Kureishi, Amber Lone, Methuen Drama (an imprint of A & C Black), Oberon, Shelley Silas' *Calcutta Kosher* first published by Oberon reproduced by permission of The Agency (London) Ltd all rights reserved and enquires to the agency (London) Ltd 24 Pottery Lane, London W11 4LZ, and Louise Wallinger. I would like to thank Cambridge Scholars Publishing for their permission to reproduce elements of Tara and Tamasha: Producing Asian Performance – Two Approaches, from *Alternatives In the Mainstream: British Black and Asian Theatres* and Taylor and Francis (www.tandf.co.uk) for 'Binglishing Britain: Tara Arts Journey to the West Trilogy' in *Contemporary Theatre Review 14.4* (2004).

I would like to thank the following photographers for their kind permission for use of their production images; Robert Day, Claudia Mayer, Jenny Potter, Stephen Vaughan and Robert Workman.

I would like to thank the following newspaper publications for permission to use reviews; *The Birmingham Post, British Theatre Guide, The Daily Telegraph, The Guardian, The Independent, The Morning Star, The New Statesman, The Observer, The Stage, Time Out, The Times, The Times Educational Supplement* and *The Financial Times*.

While every effort has been made to trace the copyright holders but if any have been inadvertently overlooked the publishers will be pleased to make the necessary arrangement at the first opportunity.

Finally, a huge thank you to my mum and dad, Kate and Kishin Hingorani, for their constant love and support.

1
Introduction: British Asian Theatre on the Map

British Asian theatre from 1976

This book takes as its historical starting point the publication of the Arts Council sponsored report by Naseem Khan, *The Arts Britain Ignores: The Arts of Ethnic Minorities in Britain* (1976), which was the first official sign that the theatrical work by practitioners from ethnic minority communities in Britain was to be considered a part of British culture. While there was, of course, a great deal of theatrical activity from the Asian community prior to this date, the report heralded a radical reconceptualisation of the relationship between Asian practitioners positioned on the 'margins' and the 'centre' of British theatre.

If we look at the historiography of British theatre from that time, the presence of Asian artists and their contribution to that tradition has largely ignored. It is only recently that a number of excellent works specifically exploring Black and Asian theatre have been published, including Gabrielle Griffin's *Contemporary Black and Asian Women Playwrights in Britain* (2003), *Alternatives Within the Mainstream* (2006), edited by Dimple Godiwala, *Staging New Britain* (2006), edited by Geoffrey Davis and Anne Fuchs, and *British South Asian Theatres: A Documented History* (2010) and *Critical Essays on British South Asian Theatre* (2010), both edited by Graham Ley and Sarah Dadswell. It should also be noted that Jen Harvie's *Staging the UK* (2005) contains a fascinating discussion of 'Bollywood in Britain', focusing on the work of Tamasha.

Although there is an increasing wealth of published works by British Asian writers, there is no doubting the key role played by pioneering anthologies in those early years such as *Black and Asian Women Writers* (1993), edited by Kadija George and *Black and Asian Plays Anthology* (2000), with an appendix of published plays by Black and Asian

1

playwrights compiled by Susan Croft of the Theatre Museum[1] as well as the Salidaa[2] (South Asian Diaspora Literature and Arts Archive) archive in bringing visibility to the work; indeed it is worth noting that of the more than 100 plays produced by Tara Arts since 1977 only three have been published, none of which include their pioneering 'Binglish' work at the National Theatre. I am delighted that electronic access to the scripts of the productions discussed in this book, and relevant archival material relating to those productions are now available through the Tara Arts website.[3] The publication of these scripts not only provides a vital resource for playwrights and practitioners but also for those wishing to study, critique and evaluate the cultural, sociopolitical and theatrical impact of British Asian theatre on British theatre and beyond.

This book focuses on the three major British Asian theatre companies over the past 30 years; Tara Arts, Tamasha and Kali with a further chapter devoted to British Asian playwrights. It will not only examine the key productions of those producing companies and writers but crucially pay attention to *how* and *why* the work was made by examining the dramaturgies, rehearsal processes, productions and critical receptions as well as the social, cultural and political contexts. In short, this book will ask whether British Asian theatre over the last 30 years amounts to more than just 'a bunch of darkies on stage?' (Verma 1994b: 2), as Jatinder Verma, Artistic Director of Tara Arts, has provocatively conjectured.

'The arts Britain ignores'

Naseem Khan's groundbreaking report, *The Arts Britain Ignores: The Arts of Ethnic Minorities in Britain* published in 1976, for the first time officially recognised that a cultural incursion located on the borders of British theatre was taking place, an incursion that included the performance practices of the South Asian community in Britain. The report's official recognition not only served a valuable postcolonial purpose in providing visibility and documentation for the artistic endeavours of ethnic minority groups but also attempted to overturn the actual position of those marginalised groups in relation to the 'centre'. For the first time this document contained the view that 'ethnic arts' should not be regarded as an *exotic extra* outside of British theatre but should be understood, funded and fostered as though they were *part* of British theatre – not, of course, that these things necessarily occurred (my italics).

Before 1976, theatre companies from minority communities in Britain were classed as 'ethnic theatre', a term derived from 'ethnic minority communities' theatre' and a category that was criticised as it 'diminishes the work to the level of exotica and pushes it out onto the peripheries of British life' (Khan 1980: 69). Indeed, the report criticised not only the conceptual approach to 'ethnic minority' arts but also the funding strategy. Most local authorities were found to make no separate provision for 'ethnic minorities' in a 'colour blind' approach to funding, which led to 'effective discrimination' (Khan 1976: 6) as those communities had little or no knowledge of the possible availability of such funding. The report also crucially insisted on the recognition of the creative potential inherent in cultural difference as well as the heterogeneity of different ethnic communities that 'have certain talents, tastes, traditions that need consideration for them to develop' (Khan: 6) in relation to arts funding.

Critics of the report pointed to the fact that it did not recognise a 'crucial distinction [...] between Black and white immigrant communities whose creative abilities were perceived very differently by British society [...] Black creativity is underlined by a racism that is historically specific' (Owusu 1986: 56). Although grouping ethnic minority communities together in the report was intended to engender a sense of solidarity between them it was also criticised as it 'contributed [...] to the formulation of a blanket category of "deprived people" which allowed members of funding bodies [...] to add women, gays, disabled people and the unemployed to the melting pot' (Owusu: 56) which continually locates and positions these groups on the margins. Indeed, these criticisms are still the subject of debate in current funding that has the effect of annexing them and creating internal competition for limited resources. Furthermore, theatre companies from minority groups have also been charged with the job of bringing in a 'new audience', an Asian one in respect of the companies we are discussing, a role that in some respects conflates their function with an element of social work.

The report called for positive steps such as the creation of a Minority Arts Agency to be established as a service agency and funded by the Arts Council and Race Relations Commission so that it could:

a) maintain an up-to-date register of groups and individuals
b) advise groups on venues, grant sources, possible personnel
c) publicise the activities and needs of minority groups amongst local authorities, regional arts associations and all other bodies covered in these Recommendations
d) give general advice to ethnic minorities arts groups and organisations and to individual artists (Khan 1976: 143).

While these tangible practical measures were taken to record and facilitate minority groups' access to the arts and arts funding, it must also be recognised that the report did not articulate the ways in which minority groups would engage with funders. However, the Minority Art Advisory Service (MAAS) committee did come into being with Khan at its head and the report was rightly credited for making 'African, Asian, Caribbean and other ethnic artists and arts organisation around the country [...] an incontrovertible fact' (Verma 2003).

In this way, *The Arts Britain Ignores* recognised that in the 1970s the historical disadvantages faced by 'ethnic minority arts... [were]... lack of premises to rehearse, lack of comparable back up that is afforded to equivalent native British groups, lack of acceptance within the arts structure' (Khan 1976: 5). The repositioning of 'ethnic arts' such as Asian theatre in Britain as part of British theatre had direct political and practical implications in beginning to destabilise these funding boundaries. The report realised that, beneath the seemingly egalitarian approach of local authorities not making dedicated provision for ethnic artists, was the fact that they were ignored.

The exposure of this wilful 'ignorance' by funding bodies such as the Arts Council paved the way for British Asian theatre companies, especially those trying to 'find local writers and sometimes look at the British setting' (Khan 1976: 71) such as Tara Arts, to access funding for the first time. Indeed, it is worth noting the paradox that grew up in the 1980s and 1990s as the Arts Council and other funding bodies such as the Greater London Council and other Metropolitan County Councils 'made a virtue of Ethnicity: the more "different" you were, the more likely you were to gain funds' (Verma 1989b: 773). This meant that while there was a positive benefit in the recognition of Asian theatre in Britain with funding set aside for it, this also had the paradoxical effect of keeping that work marginalised and corralled in an ethnic ghetto.

Since the Khan report there have been a great number of Arts Council initiatives and conferences to promote diversity in the British theatre, key among them being the *Eclipse Report* that gave rise to the *Decibel* initiative. The catalyst for *The Eclipse Report – Developing Strategies to Combat Racism in Theatre* (2002) developed from the conference held on 12–13 June 2001 at Nottingham Playhouse was the Macpherson[4] report of 1999. The Macpherson report was a response to the police's handling of the murder inquiry into the death of Steven Lawrence, a black teenager stabbed to death in 1993 in an unprovoked racist attack while waiting for a bus in Eltham, south-east London. The report damningly concluded that the failure of the police was largely due to 'institutional racism':

> Institutional Racism consists of the collective failure of an organisation to provide an appropriate and professional service to people because of their colour, culture or ethnic origin. It can be seen or detected in processes, attitudes and behaviour which amount to discrimination through unwitting prejudice, ignorance, thoughtlessness and racist stereotyping which disadvantage minority ethnic people.
> The Stephen Lawrence Inquiry (1999)

The aims of the Eclipse conference were:

- to discuss and devise strategies to combat racism in theatre
- to explore ways of developing our understanding and knowledge of African, Caribbean and Asian theatre (Arts Council 2001: 4).

The relevance of the conference is amply demonstrated by reproducing some of the (limited) evidence put to the conference:

- Out of 2,009 staff employed in English theatre only 80 (4 per cent) are African Caribbean and Asian (The Arts Council of England Annual Statistics 1999/2000)
- The Boyden Report found that only 16 out of 463 (3.5 per cent) board members of English producing theatres were African Caribbean and Asian (The Boyden Report on the Review of Theatre in the English Subsidised Sector 1999)
- An Arts Council of England survey of 19 arts organisations found that out of 2,900 staff, 177 (6 per cent) were either African Caribbean, Asian or Chinese, with 100 of those staff working in the area of catering or Front of House. One was employed at senior management level (The Arts Council of England 1998). The African Caribbean and Asian artists' workshops, however, fully endorsed the definition of institutional racism as being relevant to the theatre sector in this country (Arts Council 2002: 9).

Peter Hewitt, chief executive of the Arts Council at that time, said the report recognised that institutional racism in the theatre was endemic with a 'distinct lack of representation of Black and Asian communities at board level, on the staff, in the programming and in the audiences of regional theatres' (Hewitt, quoted in Akbar 2002). A number of recommendations were made in order to address these issues, from confronting stereotypes, recognising the existing skills of ethnic minority artists and providing training for development, recruitment policies and recognising the fact that at that time there was no artistic director from an ethnic minority running a building.

The aim of the *Decibel* initiative that grew out of *Eclipse* was to 'promote and strengthen the infra structure of culturally diverse arts in England' (Arts Council 2003), that included profiling and showcasing the work of culturally diverse companies and artists, both established and emerging, in order to promote work that 'reflects the cultural society of this country in the 21st century' (ibid.). However, while there was no doubting the good work such initiatives have done, the latest Arts Council report from Sir Brian McMasters clearly shows that there is still a great deal of progress to be made.

In his report *'Supporting Excellence in the Arts – From Measurement to Judgement'* (2008) McMasters was asked to consider how 'public subsidy can best support excellence in the arts' (5). It was a wide-ranging report that had many positive recommendations concerning the 'Arts' in their widest sense in relation to encouraging excellence, engaging audiences and limiting funding bureaucracy. However, I would highlight his key finding in the section on 'Diversity' in the report that states that 'we live in one of the most diverse societies the world has ever seen, yet that is not reflected in the culture we produce, or in who is producing it' (11). Indeed, while the report recognised that some improvement in the support of BME (Black Minority Ethnic) companies had occurred it recommends that funding bodies should not only prioritise diverse work but also 'act as the guardians of artists' freedom of expression, and provide the appropriate support to deal with what can be a hostile reaction to their work' (ibid.); particularly pertinent in respect of the reaction that greeted Gurpreet Kaur Bhatti's play *Behzti* (2004) discussed in Chapter 8.

'Race', ethnicity and hybridity

Any discussion of British Asian theatre has to recognise that it takes place within the context of a range of cultural issues relating to 'race', identity and representation. Naseem Khan's report recognised that culture is dynamic and processual rather than fixed and static since 'cultural expressions spring out of social conditions, they should change with conditions otherwise merely the effect is preserved without the cause' (Khan 1976: 8). As we shall see, British Asian theatre has not only been concerned with the reproduction of culturally 'traditional' forms from the South Asian subcontinent such as Kathakali[5] but has also focused on the contemporary frame and the emergence of new and dynamic forms as a result of this hybrid cultural location.

British Asians in Britain belong to what Stuart Hall describes as 'cultures of hybridity' that are defined as such because they have had 'to renounce the dream or ambition of rediscovering any kind of "lost" cultural purity or ethnic absolutism' (Hall 1992b: 310). In response to the need for the postwar[6] reconstruction of Britain during the 1950s there was a rapid rise in the number of immigrants from Commonwealth countries, in particular from the Caribbean and the newly partitioned India and Pakistan that came to be symbolised by the arrival of the *Windrush*[7] in 1948. As a result of this the 1970s saw the emergence of a 'second generation' of 'British Asians', those of Asian heritage born or largely brought up and schooled in Britain.

While much is made of the perceived 'culture clash' for young Asians growing up in Britain it is important to remember that the term 'Asian' describes a heterogeneous membership differentiated according to class, caste, region, religion and gender. This as Avtar Brah points out could create 'as many possibilities of intra-ethnic as of inter-ethnic "clashes of culture"' (1996: 41) and also rather underplays the possibilities of cultural fusion, as described in the following chapters. In this respect British Asian theatre also undermines the concept of 'cultural diversity' as a societal model because it insinuates separate and discreet categories of cultural designation that remain fixed and intransigent, impervious to time and circumstance, and disavows notions of fusion, syncretism and hybridity.

The hybrid provenance of British Asian theatre is realised in its content and form because the work is made by those who 'bear upon them the traces of the particular cultures, traditions, languages and histories by which they were shaped' (Hall: 310) and these 'traces' are *both* British and Asian. Indeed, it is because British Asian theatre is a product of the syncretic notion of a 'culture of hybridity' that it contests the construction of the nation as a culturally homogeneous space. It is the insistence of theatre companies such as Tara Arts, Tamasha and Kali that they are a part of British theatre while simultaneously performing what is perceived as their 'difference' or 'Asianness' within their work that is 'provocative' in this respect.

It must be made clear at this stage that in using the term 'Asian' in a specifically British context, I am referring to work performed in Britain by companies, writers and performers of South Asian descent with their attendant range of diasporas, histories, religions, customs, practices and experiences. This definition is derived from the particular history within which the signifier 'Asian' came into operation in the postwar British context as it was applied by British administrators in colonial Kenya to describe citizens of newly independent India and Pakistan. Indeed, the postcolonial history and diaspora of the Kenyan Asians who arrived in Britain in the 1960s was dramatised in *Part II* of Tara Arts' *Journey to the West* trilogy, and is discussed in Chapter 7.

Hall rightly emphasises that 'race' is a constructed discourse rather than one built on 'essential' characteristics. However, while the discourse of 'race' is often mobilised as a discriminatory practice it can also be a locus of resistance for those on the receiving end. This was the case with adoption of the term 'black' in the 1970s as a positive signifier for both the Asian and Afro-Caribbean communities in Britain. Historically, in contrast to the 'United states, black theatre in Britain did not evolve alongside fringe theatre during the protest years of the 1960s largely because there was no strong "Civil Rights" or "Black Power" movement to which it could attach itself to offer a public voice and gain an audience' (Peacock 1999: 173).

However, in the late seventies and early eighties marginalised non-white ethnic groups coalesced behind the political signifier 'black' to create a *new* identity. The very act of creation and operation of a 'black' identity was predicated on the fact that Afro-Caribbean and Asian communities were 'not [....] culturally, ethnically, linguistically, or even physically the same but that they are treated as "the same" (i.e. non-white, "other") by the dominant culture' (Hall 1992b: 308) in order to provide a locus of cultural resistance and the collective solidarity. However, this political solidarity fragmented in the 1990s precisely because it homogenised the very different ethnic groups contained within it and therefore disavowed their particular cultural differences.

If ethnicity is the term that denotes a group of people with a common set of cultural markers such as language, custom, religion and tradition then ethnic minority groups are so termed because they are a distinct population in a larger society whose culture is different from their own. However, as Naseem Khan's report pointed out these groups are still 'part of' British theatre and by extension Britain and therefore their difference, as well as 'sameness', should be inscribed within it.

Ethnic minorities in Britain are, of course, a focus for a

> racism which has taken a necessary distance from the crude ideas
> of biological inferiority and superiority [and] now seeks to present an

imaginary definition of the nation as a unified cultural community. It constructs and defends an image of national culture – homogeneous in its whiteness yet precarious and perpetually vulnerable to attack from enemies within and without.

(Gilroy 1992: 87)

It is this imaginary claim to homogeneity that British Asian theatre also contests.

Racist discourse attempts to stereotype the 'other' in a way that *'reduces, essentializes, naturalises and fixes difference'* (Hall 1997: 258), in this case utilising the power of the white ethnic majority to exclude, marginalise and oppress the Asian ethnic minority. This discourse is heavily imbricated in British colonial history especially in relation to the Indian subcontinent and the British Raj.[8] British colonialism involved the cultural as well as economic oppression of India exemplified by Thomas Macaulay's infamous 'Minute on Indian Education' (1835) in which he declared an intention to create a 'class of persons, Indian in blood and colour, but English in taste, in opinions, in morals, in intellect' (Macaulay quoted in Ashcroft et al. 1995: 429). Benedict Anderson in his seminal work *Imagined Communities* (1983) points out that the significance of Macaulay's intention was of a 'long range (30 year!) policy, consciously formulated and pursued, to turn "idolators", not so much into Christians, as into people culturally English' (1983: 91). It is this historical disavowal and denigration of Asian cultural difference as a result of this lengthy phase of cultural imperialism that British Asian theatre attempts to redress.

Edward Said describes in his book *Orientalism* (1978) how the West created, through a range of discourses, a conception of the Orient that was profoundly racist in character and concerned with maintaining the superiority of the Occident to the Orient. Said's powerful critique of the West was itself criticised by postcolonial theorists for failing to recognise indigenous rebellion to this totalising western discourse or to provide a site of agency from which it might be contested by subjugated peoples. One of the reasons that British Asian theatre has such an important postcolonial role to play is precisely because it does perform *back*.

It is the insistence on the representation of 'other' ethnicities on stage by companies such as Tara Arts, Tamasha and Kali that means they eschew a 'colour blind' approach to casting. In spite of the range of Arts Council initiatives discussed earlier there remains a general lack of representation for minority ethnic groups in the arts and the British stage in particular. In the theatre this seems to have stemmed from a mistaken desire, outside BME companies, to wilfully ignore, or be 'blind' to, the ethnicity of the actor.

While there have been a number of recent instances of high profile non-white performers playing lead roles[9] these were largely straight-forward examples of 'colour blind' casting. This principle may appear laudable but it fails on two significant levels; it attempts to disavow the ethnicity of the performer and refuses to acknowledge the cultural difference between the performers, and it does not begin to address the causes that lead to the discriminatory practices against actors from minority communities.

Indeed, 'colour blind' casting examples are remarkable because of their infrequency and paradoxically the critical reception tends to fore-ground and problematise the ethnicity of the (non-white) performer. In contrast Tara Arts' casting policy is to have all-Asian casts while Kali and Tamasha insist on Asian actors playing Asian roles. They actively fore-ground the non-white 'difference' of the performer and insist on the presence and representation of the Asian actor on the British stage.

In recent times religion has come to the fore in relation to ethnicity, starkly exemplified in the response of the Sikh community to Gurpreet Kaur Bhatti's play *Behzti* (2004), which was cancelled as a result of vio-lent protests before the end of its run at Birmingham Repertory Theatre because it was felt to be disrespectful to Sikh religious beliefs. This fore-grounding of the religious aspect of ethnicity led one commentator to ask:

> is this new religious identity part of an overarching plural identity, or is it exclusive and separate? Put more bluntly it is a choice between either wanting religion to be a part of an identity or only being defined by religion and arguing that it is more important than any national identity.
>
> (Manzoor 2005: 22)

It should also be remembered that the construction of an overarch-ing allegiance to religion can also be *placed on* the Asian community. After the events of September 11 2001[10] in America and more recently attacks in London[11] on 7 July 2005, racism towards Asians in general has become driven by religion rather than race.

It is important that we remember in any discourse on the nation – especially because we are examining that discourse from the point of view of a minority community, in this case a British Asian one – that it equally effects the construction of the indigenous white population in Britain. As the British Asian playwright Hanif Kureishi explored in *Borderline* (1982) and makes clear in *The Rainbow Sign*:

> It is the British, the white British, who have learnt that being British isn't what it was. Now it is a more complex thing, involving new elements. So there must be a fresh way of seeing Britain and the choices it faces; and a new way of being British after all this time. Much thought, discussion and self examination must go into seeing the necessity for this, what this 'new way of being British' involves and how difficult it might be to attain.
>
> (Kureishi 1986: 38)

Kureishi's belief that there must be a 'new' construction of national identity is supported by Avtar Brah's concept of 'diaspora space' that emphasises that the British site is 'inhabited not only by those who have migrated and their descendents but equally by those who are constructed and represented as indigenous' (Brah 1996: 181). In this way British Asian theatre should be read as an indigenous rather than intercultural theatre practice for the reasons eloquently set out by Jatinder Verma below:

> Christiane Scholte: How, if at all, would you position yourself within the group of Western proponents of intercultural theatre directors such as Peter Brook or Richard Schechner?
>
> Jatinder Verma: I do admire their work and I follow their work. But I suppose if I positioned myself, then my journey is a contrary one. With Brook and Schechner, if you like, they were part of a mainstream, part of a dominant culture to be more specific, who brought into it some questions to what that dominant culture meant. So they brought into it influences from outside. I start from a position where I'm not in a dominant culture. If anything I have a kind of vexed relationship between the centre and the margin. So I am starting from the margin. So inevitably, my concern shifts in terms of its angle of vision. Plus, of course, added to that is that if I start from the margins, I'm also working with people who are on the margins. It's not as if I am bringing in actors from India or Africa as such. I'm actually working with actors here who in their existence represent this kind of marginality. And so the dialogue is not, if you like, a configuration of outsiders who are commenting on the dominant. It's *insiders* who are looking at the dominant from another perspective.
>
> (Davis & Fuchs 2006: 317; italics mine)

Asian language on the British stage

When Asian theatre companies augment English scripts with Asian languages they fracture the limit of what we understand the constituency of 'English' spoken in Britain to be. The sound of Asian languages on the British stage is politically potent as a means of amplifying 'marginal' voices and insisting on their acceptance especially if we accept the reasonable democratic rationale that Asian languages 'form part of the linguistic map of modern Britain [...]. and cannot be expected to be absent from modern British theatre' (Verma 1996: 198). Their theatrical representation therefore has political implications as it gives a voice to a previously silenced constituency. Jatinder Verma recognised in his recent interview with *Contemporary Theatre Review* that in the early years of Tara the languages utilised in the rehearsal room did not manifest themselves on the stage and responded with 'Binglish', discussed in Chapter 3, while Kristine Landon-Smith at Tamasha directly addressed this by drawing on the 'cultural context' of the actor, discussed in Chapter 5.

It can be seen in the work of British Asian theatre that the use of Asian languages within performance contests the 'centrality' of English in British theatre. It will be seen in the 'Binglish' texts of Tara Arts that the non-Asian speaking audience are purposefully 'left out' or at least behind the Asian speaking audience at times throughout the performance. However, it should be remembered that these Asian languages are structurally supplementary to the performance because ' "the word" in theatre is never entirely literary, but mediated through the bodies and voices of the actors in a specific mise-en-scène wherein the meaning of a particular theatrical representation is shaped enunciated and embodied' (Bharucha 2000: 68).

This means that while the words may not be understood by a non-Asian speaking audience the 'sense' may still be conveyed through the signs described above. Furthermore, the employment of a range of Asian languages exemplified in the work of Tara Arts, Tamasha and Kali, such as Hindi, Punjabi, Gujarati and English demonstrates the plurality of the signifier Asian and inscribes difference *within* it. This theatrical performance of difference destabilises homogeneous notions of the 'Asian' that can lead to stereotype and reflects the fact that 'postcolonial literatures are cross-cultural because they negotiate a gap between "worlds" a gap in which the simultaneous process of abrogation and appropriation continually strive to define and determine their practice' (Ashcroft et al. 2002: 38). This play between abrogation and appropriation, the rejection of English and the remoulding of English, can be seen clearly in the practice of British Asian theatre. This is one of the ways in that the hybrid form of British Asian theatre demonstrates that as a result of 'postcolonial experiences... [it]... refutes the privileged position of a standard code in the language and any monocentric view of human experience' (Ashcroft et al.: 40).

Although the performance texts contain a range of Asian languages as well as English they have all been transliterated into roman script, obviously in some measure because of the unavailability of the technological means to print scripts in the *Devanagari* or Arabic script, but also because while British Asian actors may understand and speak Asian languages they may not necessarily be able to read them. Some of the phonetic sounds that make up Hindi and Urdu have no equivalent in English and therefore the literary replication of these sounds in roman script has a recognised degree of imprecision.

The majority of South Asian languages – Bengali, Gujarati, Punjabi, Urdu, Hindi – derive from 'Sanskrit, the classical language of Ancient India' (Snell 2004: x) which is also related to the root of European languages. While Hindi and Urdu are both influenced by Persian they have very different scripts, the Urdu based on Persian and the Hindi on *Devanagari* inherited from the Sanskrit. Indeed, the representation of the Asian languages in scripts for performance is understandably more focused on reproducing the phonetic sounds for the actor than in technical accuracy in rendering an Asian word into roman script with literary accuracy.

It should also be remembered that India is a diaglossic society in which 'a majority of people speak two or more languages' (Ashcroft et al. 2002: 38) and this facility pertains not only to Asian languages but also of course to English as well as a result of colonialism, diaspora and more recently globalisation. It is worth noting that on the British site these languages are also intersected by English accent and dialect so that in plays such as *East as East* written by Ayub Khan-Din the cultural hybridity of the characters is performed as these Asian characters not only speak English with Asian accents but Urdu with northern accents. British Asian theatre also performs new grammatical particularities that apply to Asian languages when spoken that have not been present in English. An example of this is the use of echo words to generalise meaning so that while *pani* means water in Hindi, if a speaker says *pani-vani* the meaning changes from water to more generically 'something to drink'.

The importance of language in this context is perhaps best revealed by an anecdote told by Jatinder Verma that illustrates the repercussions of its disavowal. In this speech made at Brunel University entitled 'Braids and Theatre Practice' (2001) we see the impact that the rupture of language can have on the diasporic subject. When he first came to Britain aged 14 he wanted to write to his father who had remained in Kenya. The difficulty in this lay in finding an appropriate way to address his father in the letter in English. While the first line 'Dear Papaji' that started the letter was straightforward the second line in which he wanted to say 'How are you?' was more problematic. In Hindi there are two words for 'you', the honorific *aa*' and the more informal *tum* but of course in English there is only one. If he addressed his father with the English 'you' it would 'reduce' his father to equal status to that of his son; this would have constituted an unintended insult. The upshot of this linguistic difference was that he did not write to his father for six months.

Tara Arts Theatre Company (1997–present)

The catalyst that led to the formation of Tara Arts was the murder of an Asian youth, Gurdip Singh Chaggar, killed in a racially motivated attack by whites in Southall, West London on 4 June 1976. Jatinder Verma, in his final year of university at that time, described how the 'mixture of anger and of trying to understand what's happened and of trying to say something, led us to make our theatre' (Verma 1996a: 284). This political imperative has consistently manifested itself in the work of Tara Arts underpinned by the company's insistence on looking at the world from a marginal position with a desire to speak for the 'migrant' (Verma 2004: 84) and the 'outsider' (Verma 1996a: 285).

Since the inception of Tara Arts in 1977 there have been three major theatrical movements in the company's history that are mapped in this book. Chapter 2 examines their early work from 1977 to 1984 that concerned itself with a range of subjects including the postcolonial reworking of historical events on the Indian subcontinent in *Inkalaab, 1919* (1980), the presence of Asians in Britain long before post-war immigration in *Vilayat or England Your England* (1981), to young Asians growing up in contemporary Britain in *Chilli in Your Eyes* (1984) but all primarily underpinned by a theatrical methodology of text-based realism.

Chapter 3 examines the period dating from the first production of the *Miti Ki Gadi [The Little Clay Cart]* in 1984 that heralded the creation of Jatinder Verma's unique hybrid performance methodology 'Binglish' and led the company to the 'centre' of the British theatre establishment at the National Theatre in the early 1990s with adaptations such as Moliere's *Tartuffe* (1990) and Rostand's *Cyrano* (1995), transposed to an Asian setting. Chapter 7 looks in detail at the creation and performance of the epic *Journey to the West* trilogy (2002) that married the 'Binglish' performance methodology to an overt postcolonial mission to document and dramatise the stories of the Asian diaspora from India to Kenya and then to Britain over the course of the last century as well as the company's subsequent work and direction. Tara's return to a scaled-down approach to 'binglishing' European classics after the trilogy is briefly discussed alongside new artistic forays such as *A Taste for Mangoes* (2003) at Wilton's Music Hall and *Tara-in-the-Sky* (2007) in Trafalgar Square.

Tamasha Theatre Company (1989–present)

Kristine Landon-Smith and Sudha Bhuchar formed Tamasha Theatre Company in 1989 to mount *Untouchable*, which, alongside their other adaptations of Indian novels, *House of the Sun* (1991) and *A Fine Balance* (2006), will be discussed in Chapter 4. The chapter will also examine their experimentation with intercultural performance in *Women of the Dust* (1992) and the company's research-based methodology exemplified in *Balti Kings* (2000).

Chapter 5 begins with *East is East* (1996), Tamasha's popular and critical success, which realised the intracultural aims of the company by 'opening the door to the crossover of Asian culture into the British mainstream' (Bhuchar and Landon-Smith 2004b). We shall see how Tamasha draws on the term *intra*cultural defined by Rustom Bharucha as concerning itself with the 'dynamics between and across specific communities and regions *within* the boundaries of the nation state' (Bharucha 2000: 6) in the context of the regional differences within India. Tamasha are applying the term in the British context to the 'dynamics' between different ethnic communities as opposed to geographical regions. This chapter will also detail Tamasha's experiments in form with the staging of a Bollywood film in *Fourteen Songs, Two Weddings and A Funeral* (1998, 2001), the *West Side Story*-inspired dance-led drama *Strictly Dandia* (2004) as well as the exploration of verbatim theatre in relation to the Asian experience in *The Trouble with Asian Men* (2005). It will also examine the unique methodology developed by Kristine Landon-Smith drawing on the 'cultural context' of the actor utilised in the creation of *Lyrical MC* (2008).

Kali Theatre Company (1990–present)

The catalyst for the creation of Kali Theatre Company was the murder of Balwant Kaur who was killed at the Asian Women's refuge in Brent, West London on 22 October 1985 and led to Rukhsana Ahmad writing *Song for a Sanctuary*. The politics behind the foundation of Kali by Rukhsana Ahmad and Rita Wolf shared many parallels with Jatinder Verma beginning Tara Arts in response to the racist murder of Gurdeep Singh Chaggar in 1976; in the case of Kali it focused specifically on South Asian women writers.

The influence of Kali Theatre Company since its inception in 1990 is clear from its verifiable claim that of 'all the new plays by British Asian woman playwrights presented since 1988 in the UK, nearly a third have been presented by Kali and of the plays by new writers, over 75 per cent were presented by Kali' (Kali 2009). Chapter 6 begins with an examination of the inception of the company and the inaugural production of *Song for a Sanctuary* by Rukhsana Ahmad. In 1992 Rita Wolf moved to the United States and Rukhsana Ahmad became Artistic Director until 2002 at which time Janet Steel assumed control and has been in the post.

The brief of the company has not changed significantly since 1990: it is 'to create opportunities for Asian Women in the field of theatre and especially to give them a voice in the field of new writing'. Kali has not only supported and developed the work of new South Asian women writers but also produced a diverse range of work over that time. That diversity is exemplified in the three productions explored in Chapter 6; *River on Fire* (2000) by Rukhsana Ahmad that looks at issues of religious tolerance in the context of the contemporary politics of the subcontinent, *Calcutta Kosher* (2004) by Shelley Silas set in the 'dying' Jewish community of Calcutta and *Deadeye* (2006) by Amber Lone which focuses on the family pressures on British Asian women in contemporary Northern Britain.

New writing

Chapter 8 looks at new writing by British Asian writers who have been produced outside of these companies. It examines the work of four key second-generation dramatists over the past three decades, including

Hanif Kureishi's *Borderline* (1982), set during the 'Southall' riots, whose production at the Royal Court signalled the arrival of British Asian concerns on the main stage. Parv Bancil's *Crazyhorse* (1997) looks at the issues of an alienated and dramatically ignored British Asian underclass while *Made in England* (1998) examines the appropriation of Asian culture by the mainstream. This chapter will discuss Gurpreet Bhatti's *Behzti* (2004) and the reasons why it gave rise to a national debate on censorship as well as her earlier work *Behsharaam* (2001). Finally, there is a return to the work of Ayub Khan-Din's with *Rafta Rafta* (2007) a gentle Northern family comedy produced by the National that repeated the 'crossover' mainstream success achieved by *East is East* (1996).

Jatinder Verma describes finding a very obscure local history document in 1989 that recorded the appearance of an Indian performing troupe who came to England in the early nineteenth century. He wondered, justifiably in the light of the critical lack of interest at that time in postwar British Asian theatre, whether 'their history will be our history [...] unsung, unrecorded, forever trapped in the memory of those who lived at the time' (Verma 2003: 2). One of the aims of this book is to ensure that it does not.

2
Tara Arts 1977–1984: Creating a British Asian Theatre

The foundation of Tara Arts

Jatinder Verma, the Artistic Director of Tara Arts since the company's inception in 1977, was born in Dar-Es-Salaam, Tanzania on 17 July 1954 to Indian parents, grew up in Nairobi and came to live in Britain at the age of 14. His diasporic biography is worth citing as it intersects so powerfully with Tara Arts' theatrical practice that aims to 'confront ethnicity through drama' (Verma 1990b). In this respect Jatinder Verma believes that in order to culturally locate the British Asian subject 'we are not talking about the subcontinent [...] nor are we talking about Britain as it is [...] it is a peculiar mix of the two' (Verma 1984a: 9).

This 'peculiar mix of the two' eventually led Tara Arts to develop a distinct theatre praxis in the mid 1980s called 'Binglish', drawing on Eastern as well as Western dramaturgies, in response to the hybrid location of their work that is discussed in Chapter 3. However, in the early years of Tara Arts from 1977 to 1984 Tara adopted a theatrical approach of text-based realism as a means of 'trying to create a theatre tradition for Asians [...] very English in its convention but infused with stuff not of this country' (Verma 1982). In this respect the creation of Tara Arts served as a direct response to the plea of the Arts Council report *The Arts Britain Ignores* discussed in Chapter 1, for 'a brave company [that] could develop a theatre that examines the place of tradition in a new society' (Khan 1976: 71).

Tara Arts was established as a community group in 1977, garnering support in its early years from bodies such as the Arts Council of Great Britain, Greater London Arts Association, Wandsworth Borough Council, The Commission For Racial Equality and The West Midlands Arts Association; this support is perhaps indicative of the success of

Naseem Khan's report in attracting new funding to ethnic minority artists. Initially, the founding members Sunil Saggar, Praveen Bahl, Vijay Shaunak, Ovais Kadri and Jatinder Verma hosted meetings on a Wednesday evening at The Milan Centre in Tooting Bec, London, that encompassed poetry recitals, lectures and discussion as well as drama. The meetings were a valuable method of recruitment for the company exemplified in the open and inclusive programme statement that 'newcomers are always welcome' (Verma 1977b). In this way Tara Arts also provided a social as well as artistic resource for young or 'second generation' Asians primarily born or brought up in Britain, somewhere 'you could actually go and have a laugh and talk about your parents and people would understand what you mean' (Khan 2001: 2).

Tara Arts could be placed very much in the tradition of 'community theatre' that began in the early 1970s and which may be defined by a 'desire to perform to different, non-theatre-going audiences, and to engage them in a different relationship' (Khan 1980: 61). This was very much a necessity recognised by Jatinder Verma in view of the fact that 'Asians here do not, as a matter of course, have an appreciation of established theatre [in Britain] so our tours [...] have been in community centres, in homes – wherever Asians gather in large numbers' (Verma 1984a: 9). The political corollary to this determined engagement of seeking out the Asian audience meant that Tara Arts purposefully performed outside of 'mainstream' theatre venues and maintained their positions on the 'margins' in relation to critical recognition as well as public funding. However the company's growth was marked and by 1984 Tara Arts was not only running a professional group of seven actors, an administrator and director alongside the community section but had also bought their own studio rehearsal/theatre space in Garrett Lane, which they continue to inhabit today.

The plays produced by Tara Arts in these early years from 1977 to 1984 had three clear functions and this chapter will look at key productions in relation to each of these:

(i) to recover histories of the subcontinent from a subaltern perspective and make connections between those colonial histories and the contemporary British site; *Inkalaab 1919* (1980) *Yes Memsahib* (1979)

(ii) to perform the hidden histories of Asians in Britain long before postwar immigration; *Lion's Raj* (1982)

(iii) to look at the contemporary 'second generation' British Asian experience in Britain; *Diwaali* (1977), *Fuse* (1978) and *Chilli in Your Eyes* (1984).

Tara Arts' inaugural production *Sacrifice* (1977) demonstrated that the critical gaze of the company was not limited to the non-Asian community as it 'linked Race to Communalism, as being part of the same spectrum of Oppression ... [demonstrating] an uncompromisingly twin-pronged stance' (Verma 1989b: 772). This 'twin-pronged stance' has allowed the company licence to critique the Asian community from 'within' as well as the wider community from 'without' and has been a key tenant of Tara Arts' artistic stance to the present time.

Sacrifice (1977)

Set in sixteenth-century Bengal at the court of the king. The play focuses on Jaising, the daughter of the priest Raghupati. The king has banned blood sacrifices in the temple and, in response to the perceived threat to his power, Raghupati tells Jaising she must kill the king. Jaising, who agrees with the king, is morally unable to do this and torn between the duty to her father, who represents cultural tradition, and to her own beliefs, commits suicide.

Sacrifice was an adaptation from a play, *Balidaan*, by renowned Bengali playwright and poet Rabindranath Tagore (1861–1941). Tagore had translated the play, which was written in support of the pacifists of the First World War, from Bengali into English in 1917. The play was a plea against ideological extremism represented by the destructive devotion shown by the Brahmin priest to the goddess Kali, that results in the death or 'sacrifice' of his daughter, Jaising. Indeed, Jaising's rhetorical cry before her death, 'can you not rejoice in two truths – must you grant victory to one?' (Verma 1977a: 25) can be read as exemplifying Tara's mission of 'reflecting or remarking upon various aspects of Asian historical or contemporary experience [...] in an effort to provide a perspective on our lives here today' (Verma 1977b).

A second Tara commitment that has endured since this production, and which would become a key element in the 'Binglish' manifesto discussed in Chapter 3, was the use of an 'all-Asian' cast. Tara operated this strict casting policy of employing only Asian actors because 'to use a white actor means an Asian actor being left out' (Verma 1984: 10) and also Asian actors playing white roles functioned as an ironic inversion of the historically racist portrayals of black and Asian characters by white actors.

Rehearsal for *Sacrifice* (1977)

© Tara Arts.

The rehearsal photograph would seem to support the privileging of intellectual discussion in contrast to the more physical approach exemplified in the later 'Binglish' performance methodology discussed in Chapter 3.

This casting policy insisted on representing and staging 'difference' as opposed to a 'colour blind' casting policy that was predicated on 'ignoring' the race or ethnicity of the performer. For Jatinder Verma the recognition and representation of 'difference' was vital as he believed an audience cannot 'be oblivious to my colour or the colour of the actors [...] it is part of what makes me particular in the world today' (Verma 1996: 201).

Jatinder Verma's production of *Sacrifice* attempted to open a theatrical dialogue between the historical world of the play and contemporary British political issues by showing slides of the then prime minister, Mrs Thatcher, detailing her views on the virtues of the 'free market'[1]. While on an intellectual level the director was attempting to draw parallels between the 'dogma' of the individuals depicted on the stage with the contemporary figures on the slides, critics felt that theatrically 'it does not work [...] because the targets are so wide as to be either obscure or perverse' (Khan 1979).

The difficulty of addressing the contemporary experience of Asians in Britain through classical work may be the reason that the company did not attempt any further adaptations until a new theatrical form 'Binglish' was created and applied to Shudraka's *Miti Ki Gadi* (1984), discussed in Chapter 3. While there were a number of performances of *Sacrifice* from 1977 to 1981, not only in London but also at colleges and community centres in Birmingham and beyond, it must be remembered that Tara were not a professionally resourced theatre company at this time. Therefore, they could only play venues outside of London at weekends as the company members were either at college themselves or working during the week.

The post-show discussion, often a formality for theatre companies, was a vital resource for Tara Arts as it served two main purposes: first, to build a loyal audience base by encouraging a dialogue with the company concerning the work and, secondly, as a means of recruiting new members to join the acting company. It should be remembered that at this time the dearth of British Asian theatre companies or, indeed, any other visiting theatre company from a minority community, meant that Tara Arts was a role model for would-be Asian theatre makers as they attempted to close the 'extraordinary divide between studying the subject [drama] and believing the subject had anything to offer you personally' (Clarke 2001: 2). This disparity was clearly visible during Tara's tour of *Lion's Raj* (1982) when they visited a girls' school in Southall with an overwhelmingly Asian student population and found they were studying John Osborne's *Look Back in Anger* (1956).[2] Recruiting Asian actors in those early years could also be culturally problematic as Tara's first full-time administrator, Rekha Prashar, recalled 'some group members in the early days had found it hard to persuade their parents to let them come to rehearsals because the idea of Asians, particularly girls, appearing in stage productions in this country was such a new one' (Prashar quoted in Best 1982: 24).

The language of British Asian theatre

At this initial stage of Tara Arts' theatrical development their priority was to reject Asian language in favour of English to position the company *outside* of the auspices of what has been, rather pejoratively, termed 'language theatre'. It should not be forgotten that there were a number of Asian theatre companies performing in a range of Asian languages in existence in Britain at this time such as 'Leicester's Literary Arts and Lights, Birmingham's L & P Enterprises, London's Indian National Theatre, the drama section of Bharatiya Vidya Bhavan' (Khan 1980: 74). The decision Tara Arts took in relation to which language to employ for those early productions such as *Sacrifice* was 'to work in English [...] since they reject what they regard as the backward looking nature of much Asian theatre' (Khan 1980: 75); this approach was in stark contrast to their later multilingual 'Binglish' texts that will be discussed in Chapter 3. At this time Jatinder Verma was critical of the inherent insularity of 'Language Theatre' which 'almost by definition were *for* only particular language groups [...] Punjabi shows for Punjabis, Gujarati for Gujaratis, Marathi for Marathis' (Verma 1996c) as being at odds with his aim to create a theatre that reflected and included the heterogeneous constituent Asian audience as well as those beyond. It also made pragmatic sense since a large percentage of Tara's target Asian audience had been born or brought up in Britain speaking English. While this policy was driven by Tara's desire to recognise the Asian experience in Britain it did become increasingly restrictive in the expression of the heterogeneous cultural identities that are contained within the signifier 'Asian'.

The importance of working predominantly in English at this stage was fourfold for Tara: first, as has been said, to distance Tara Arts from existing Asian theatre companies who did not use English in performance; second, it made pragmatic sense as a large percentage of Tara's target Asian audience had been born or brought up in Britain; third, in order to increase the company's eligibility and access to funding bodies such as the Arts Council; fourth, and conceptually most important, they wanted to foreground the indigenous nature of the theatrical work being undertaken by 'new' Asian theatre companies such as themselves and contest their space *within* the auspices of British theatre.

Staging the Asian location

A number of the early plays of Tara Arts such as *Yes, Memsahib* (1979), *Inkalaab, 1919* (1980) and to an extent *Lion's Raj* (1982) can be grouped according to their setting on the Indian subcontinent and their shared postcolonial agenda of examining colonial relations from a subaltern[3] perspective.

Yes, Memsahib (1979)

Set in India and East Africa at the end of the nineteenth century
it follows the fortunes of Munoo, a cook, who is forced to accept
work as indentured labour for the British colonial rulers in East
Africa in order to escape the famine in his native India. He is
recruited to work on the construction of the East Africa railway
where he suffers terrible privations and attempts to organise a
strike of the indentured labourers in protest at their treatment
and the working conditions imposed by the British. As a result
he is imprisoned but manages to escape thanks to his friend Amir
and eventually became a successful trader in Nairobi. However,
with burgeoning prosperity he turns his back on his old friend,
Amir, and exploits the labour of his indigenous black worker. The
British colonisers perceive the success of Munoo and his fellow
Indian traders as a threat, so order that the bazaar from which
they trade be razed to the ground – destroying their homes and
livelihoods.

Yes, Memsahib (1979) dramatised the building of the East Africa railway
by Indian indentured labour for the British colonial power; a topic that
would be revisited in *Part 1* of The *Journey to the West* trilogy (2002).
Yes, Memsahib was first performed on 24 May 1979 at The Centre of
Indian Arts, London, and was academically informed by the MA thesis of
Jatinder Verma 'The Uganda Railway and Migrant Labour, 1895–1905.'
This manifested itself in the detailed historical information contained
in the programme that included archive pictures of the building of the
Uganda railway, excerpts from parliamentary papers and the views of
British officials in East Africa documenting the exploitation of the Asian
workforce and the racism inherent in British colonialism.

Yes, Memsahib not only fulfilled Tara's brief to make visible 'hidden'
Asian histories on the subcontinent and its diapsoras, it also placed
this story in contemporary frame in order to also make it politically
relevant for a contemporary audience. The play opens as an unnamed
white woman is addressing a contemporary meeting of the Asian British
and reassuring them that contrary to reports in the media she was not
'anti-immigration'. The action then moves to East Africa at the turn of
the nineteenth century until returning to the Asian British Association
meeting as a means of theatrically reinforcing the connection between
the politics of the two time frames.

A scene from *Yes, Memsahib* (1979)

© Tara Arts.

Poonam Trikha as Kunti appeals for work from Paul Bhatterchargee playing the British Sahib at the desk willing to exploit her labour.

In an echo of Margaret Thatcher's[4] 'powerfully sympathetic state-ment about legitimate fears among white Britons that they were being "swamped by people with a different culture"' (Young 1989: 111) the white guest speaker revealed the underlying ambivalence of the white community to immigration when she announced that 'the genuineness of our regard for our Asian citizens is in no way compromised by our pro-posal for restricting the number of immigrants into this country' (Verma 1979a: Epilogue). The play drew a parallel between the British use of labour to build the railway in East Africa and the postwar use of Asian labour in Britain inferring that the Asian workers in both cases were an unwelcome necessity, treated badly and discouraged from settling.

Politically, the production followed Tara's objective in critiquing the Asian community as well as the treatment of Asians in society. *Yes, Mem-sahib* dramatised the poor treatment of the indigenous black population by the Asian as well as white communities in East Africa. Indeed, many of the indignities visited on the Asian workers by the British, such as starvation wages and summary dismissal, are reflected in Munoo's treat-ment of his African worker whose name he has anglicised to John, or 'Johnny black man' in an unsettling act of colonial mimicry.[5]

Inkalaab, 1919 **(1980)**

Sarfraz leaves his village and joins the 8th Punjabi Regiment
to fight for the British in the First World War. While Sarfraz is
away his wife, Salma, and son, Asim, are evicted from their farm
and harassed by a local entrepreneur. On Sarfraz's return he is
employed as a bearer to General Dyer, the brigadier general in
Amritsar. The oppression suffered by Sarfraz and his brother and
the brutality of the Raj administration leads to his political awak-
ening as he recognises that 'the sahibs are no gods' (Verma 1980a:
46) He attends a peaceful protest at the Jallianwalla Bagh at which
he and his family are killed by British soldiers. In the epilogue
Asim, Sarfraz and Salma change into modern dress to draw a parallel with the racism the family experience to that which Asians are
currently experiencing from the police in contemporary Britain.

Inkalaab, 1919 [Revolution] dramatises the 'Amritsar massacre',[6] a historical event in colonial India in 1919 when a British officer, General Dyer,
opened fire on a crowd of peaceful demonstrators, killing hundreds and
injuring over a thousand. The play explored the theme of collaboration and its tragic consequences and also provided further evidence of
Jatinder Verma's increased role in all aspects of production as he not
only acted, but also directed and wrote the script. The central historical plot was placed in a contemporary frame with the aim of drawing
a parallel between the repressive legislation introduced by the Rowlatt
Act in India and the so-called 'Sus' law in Britain that gave the police
the power to stop and search anyone they believed worthy of suspicion,
which had a disproportionate affect on those from an ethnic minority
background.[7] The Rowlatt Act was the focus of protests led by Gandhi in
India in 1919 as it 'aimed at severely curtailing the civil liberties of Indians in the name of curbing terrorist violence (Chandra et al. 1988: 181).
The production programme detailed, over two pages, the great increase
in power given to the British authorities by the Rowlatt Act and the
resultant protests against it in India at that time under the slogan '*na
vakil* [no lawyer], *na dalil* [no argument], *na apil* [no appeal]' (Verma
1980b).

The prologue to *Inkalaab, 1919* in which an unnamed young Asian
returned home to face his elder brother and sister-in-law after being
picked up by the police for an alleged breach of the peace was set in

the modern day. Although the young man is reluctant to challenge his treatment and believes the police are 'only doing their duty' (Verma 1980a, 2) his family are outraged and advocate that he fight the charge since he had been the innocent victim of racist policing.

The three contemporary characters in the prologue change costume in view of the audience from modern dress into Asian dress circa 1900 in order to make the historical connection. This convention was utilised to reinforce the elder brother's point that 'two hundred years of seeing someone as a coolie and a slave does not end in forty years [...] outside you're only a Paki' (Verma 1980a: Epilogue) as the actor playing General Dyer changed his peak cap for that of a present day police inspector and produced a warrant to see their passports. While this literal connection between the brutality of colonial oppression and police harassment may have been simplistically direct it was certainly in keeping with Tara's desire to be provocative, as Fred Childerstone, the local police commander reportedly told a Wandsworth Council AGM that the play 'was not in the interests of racial harmony' (1980).

As a result of work such as *Yes, Memsahib* and *Inkalaab, 1919* the company were justifiably starting to receive attention for 'giving light to subjects, that white-oriented theatre would not feel sufficiently confident in undertaking' (Morris 1980) and providing an Asian perspective on such events. However, Tara were quick to refute charges of bias, and with no little sense of irony, insisted at post-show discussions that 'the play was not meant to be taken as anti-British, but as straightforward history' (R.L. 1980).

Inkalaab, 1919 also demonstrated how a level of intertextuality[8] – how this text connects to other texts – could be used to introduce Asian cultural references such as when the recruiting agent called on the 'would be' conscripts that it was their chance 'to become Rustoms and Sohrans and fearless Arjuns for their wives' (Verma 1980a: 6) to fight, ironically, for the British who had colonised them. The references to these iconic Asian characters, allied with the inclusion of Asian philosophical concepts such as *izzat* (honour) introduced a new and creative intersection into Tara's theatrical performance that was to be developed further in their 'Binglish' methodology discussed in Chapter 3.

Finding the Asian voice – in English

In the light of their decision to work primarily in English Tara faced a methodological problem – finding an Asian voice in English for characters from the Indian subcontinent and its diasporas. According to the realist convention, when an Asian character talked to an English character in English, it was scripted in what has become known as 'pidgin' English because it was not a first language. The signs of this were incorrect syntax and tenses, and missing indefinite and definite articles, for example Munoo in *Yes, Memsahib*, 'I coolie Sahib. Coolies say sahib not doing good – work too hard, and not good money. Then sahib takes money for fines' (Verma 1979a: 17).

As Ashcroft points out, the use of 'pidgin' English for Asian characters speaking to English ones may be 'authentic' as 'pidgin was inevitably used in the context of master-servant relationships during the period of European colonisation' (Ashcroft et al. 1989: 75). The danger being that Tara's use of 'pidgin' would unwittingly perpetuate an 'orientalist'[9] stereotype of Asians who speak English badly in the performance and linguistically rearticulate colonial power relations into the contemporary moment. A further performance question for Tara emerged when one Asian character addressed another. If an Asian character spoke in 'pidgin' English to white English characters how could this established theatrical convention be amended when Asian characters spoke to each other and still remain in line with the decision of Tara to perform in English? The danger of not finding a methodological solution to this problem becomes clear when we look at the following extract:

> MUNOO: You right, brother! I liking this country. Next year, I get my
>   wife to come here. Build own house.
> AMIR: Munoo lucky.
> MUNOO: No luck, brother. I not believe sahib when he say I a child.
>   That why I do well now.
> AMIR: Munoo give me job?
>
> (Verma 1979a: Sc. 8)

This register of speech does not suggest a colloquial or native voice as it is redolent of the incomplete grasp of language in the performance of English as a second language. It is here that the limits of the theatrical methodology become clear as Tara were unable to meet the demands of performing the Asian voice and therefore descended into stereotype.

However, this methodological limitation was also exploited by Tara to provide moments of humour. When the British recruiting officer in *Yes, Memsahib* was introduced to the 'coolies' by the Asian interpreter he looked on, none the wiser, as the Asian interpreter told the coolies 'this cow-eating sahib saying if you not listening to him, he getting his Memsahib to nag you!' (Verma 1979: 2). The convention was repeated in the following scene in which the Asian interpreter purposely mistranslated for the 'white' officer what he was saying to his Asian workers and vice versa.

> MAGISTRATE: (*to coolies*) Now listen carefully you men. You are being sent to the East African Protectorate under contract with the Imperial British East Africa Company to build a railway in this newest possession of Empire. The Government of India signified its assent, on condition that you are treated fairly, which of course you will be. I am here as a representative of Her Majesty's Government of India to ensure all the regulations are complied with. (*To Interpreter*) Translate.
> INTERPRETER: (in English) The Magistrate-sahib – who is going to jail a coolie today because he is not liking moustache, say you be quiet and government look after you well. It take you in ship to its country across sea. Maybe you meet Queen Victoria if you good. Shake your head. (*The coolies nod. To Magistrate*) They understanding sahib.
>
> (Verma 1979: Sc. 5)

The performance of the Asian interpreter, exploiting both sides in the scene, exemplified the creative possibilities that would be available to Tara if they were bold enough to employ both Asian and English languages. Indeed, the linguistic de-centring of the English voice by Asian language hinted at, but not realised in these scenes, demonstrated the way in which the linguistic borders of Tara's performance methodology needed to be expanded.

Jatinder Verma's script for *Inkalaab, 1919* addressed the problematic nature of performing the Asian voice in English that was manifest in *Yes, Memsahib* by establishing a different linguistic convention. When the Asian characters addressed each other it was in colloquial English but peppered with colloquial Punjabi terms of endearment such as *bhaijaan* [brother], *babhi* [sister-in-law] and exclamations such as *acha*, a slightly more exasperated version of 'all right'. So that when Asim tells the landowner 'Don't insult us by calling her your *babhi*' (Verma 1980a: 7) he was rebuking him for overfamiliarity.

When an Asian character speaks to an English character, such as when Asim complains to a white missionary 'but he treat me like dog' (Verma, 1980a: 25), it was scripted as a second language with none of the fluency that was present between Asian characters. In this way we can see Tara's performance methodologies starting to play and innovate at the borders of realist theatrical linguistic convention.

Hidden histories – Asians in Britain

Lion's Raj (1982)

The play opens with a brief re-enactment of Gandhi's murder, which is then framed as a play within a play by three modern Asian youths who directly address the audience. They question the application of Gandhi's legacy of non-violence in contemporary Britain. The scene then changes to Gandhi's education in England in the 1930s that involved learning social etiquette in order to behave like an 'English' gentleman as well as his academic studies. These scenes were intercut with examples of his political activity in India and South Africa against British colonial rule. The play ends with the three youths still divided over Gandhi's legacy for British Asians.

In August 1982, funding allowed Tara Arts to become Britain's first professional Asian theatre company with, however, the proviso they employ a professional director. As, unsurprisingly, no British Asian or Asian directors came forward, Jatinder Verma approached freelance director Anthony Clarke, on the advice of David Sulkin, Director of The Royal Court Young People's Theatre. Politically, the employment of Anthony Clarke demonstrated that Tara were able to put pragmatism above ideology in seeking experience from outside the Asian community in a bid to become professional.[10]

Tara's lack of administrative and artistic professional experience was evident from Anthony Clarke description of how they 'wanted very simple things, to get union membership, to learn how to rehearse... [as] they had never done a full day' (Clarke 2001). However, this lack of knowledge was not one-sided and Anthony Clarke came to Tara with, by his own admission, 'banal preconceptions' of the homogeneous nature of Asian theatre in which the actors 'would all share the same point of view about the subject, which was not true [...] and their life experience would in some way be similar, which it wasn't' (Clarke 2001). Instructively, Anthony Clarke was surprised to find that 'it wasn't as if they were bringing unique skills to the process, in that they had not been trained in any particular discipline' (ibid.). This reflected not so much the dearth of Asian performance influences on the company but the ability of the performance methodology to access them.

The decision to do *Lion's Raj*, about the life of Ghandi, arose because 'it was about the time of the Attenborough film and the company felt that it did no favours to the community. It made them appear as if they would turn the other cheek' (Clarke 2001). While Jatinder Verma was theatrically 'very wary of just following Indian tradition' (Verma quoted in Porter 1982) there were signs of greater Asian cultural influence within the realistic form of this production. Linguistically there was a far greater integration of Asian languages into this text in the form of songs, religious texts, chants, prayers and dialogue: counterpointed by Gandhi giving a very bad rendition of the English folksong 'Greensleeves'.

The following dialogue exemplifies the way in which Asian language was employed in the text. In this extract Gandhi addresses the Indian indigo growers who had come to him for help because their British planter landlords were exploiting them.

GANDHI: Can you substantiate your allegation?
(*They don't understand*)
GANDHI: What proof have you?
(*They don't understand*)
GANDHI: (*continuing*) ... Koi gaavahi hai? [Anybody else have evidence?]
SHUKLA: Haan, haan, [Yes, Yes] your honour.

(Verma 1982a: 11)

The scene above self reflexively demonstrated that in order for Gandhi to help these people he must not only use what he learnt in England studying law but also have recourse to his Asian culture in the form of language to communicate effectively. Jatinder Verma was quoted in an interview as wanting the audience, and indeed Tara's theatrical practice, to relate to Gandhi 'having to pick up English influences at times, at times having to rely on Indian influences, but constantly having to create something new' (Verma quoted in Porter 1982).

One local reviewer of the production commented that she 'couldn't translate the actual words [...] but [...] I didn't need to. I understood the feeling' (Gaier 1983). The reviewer mitigated the de-centring effect of this linguistically hybrid performance on a non-Asian speaker by emphasising that theatre, and in this case theatre language, is a multivalent system so that while the words may not be understood the performance can still give insight into the meaning. This could be read as a positive sign for Tara's theatrical practice that the de-centring of non-Asian speakers by employing Asian languages will not, ipso facto, completely alienate those members of the audience from the performance.

Jatinder Verma again mobilised the hybrid possibilities of British Asian intertextuality in *Lion's Raj* when Gandhi instructed his wife in the Christian scriptures and recited the story of the feeding of the five thousand by Christ. She tells him 'it is like Draupadi, when she fed all the thousands of Brahmin priests from one bowl of rice' (Verma 1982a: 29). The example demonstrates how the cultural authority of the Bible and Western cultural tradition can be de-centred as it is put into play with the *Mahabharata* revealing how 'hybridity is a problematic of colonial representation and individuation that reverses the effects of the colonialist disavowal, so that the other "denied" knowledges enter upon the dominant discourse and estrange the basis of its authority – its rules of recognition' (Bhabha 1994: 114).

The penultimate scene in *Lion's Raj* was the recreation of the famous march to the sea by Gandhi and his followers. In 1930 Gandhi organised a non-violent protest march to Dandi against the British Salt Tax. That tax made it illegal for Indians to buy or sell salt and so they were forced to buy it from the British at punitive prices. In the course of these protests that spread throughout the country many protesters were violently attacked by the police. In order to try and realise this epic event theatrically the company started to reach out beyond realism:

Gandhi and the marchers continue to sing. They are repeatedly hacked down as they continue their journey to the beach; only to rise up and receive further blows – all the time steadfast in their non-violent resistance. *This sequence ought to be stylised, preferably to tabla accompaniment.*

(Verma 1982a: 40)

The final scene then returned to the three youths from the opening sequence as they literally performed Tara's brief to examine the contemporary relevance of the historical element of the play. While the first youth rejected non-violence as useless against persecution in Britain, explicitly citing racial attacks in Coventry and other British cities the second wholeheartedly embraced Gandhi's vision. However, the intentions of the performance are clearly stated by the final youth when he said, 'Neither Indian nor English, more English than the English and more Indian than the Indian [...] The Asian was born with you, Bapu' (Verma 1982a: 41).

The 'second generation' – Young Asians in Britain

This section will look at how Tara addressed the concerns of the so-called 'second generation' Asians born, brought up or predominantly schooled in Britain. The productions explore the place of cultural heritage while living in a different country in *Diwaali*, look at the difficulties of life at school for a newly arrived migrant in *Fuse*, and young adulthood and unemployment in *Chilli in Your Eyes* in an increasingly hard-edged dramatic progression.

Diwaali (1980)

A group of young Asian students come together under the gaze of an autocratic director to rehearse a production of the *Ramayana* for the Diwaali festival. Diwaali is a predominantly Hindu festival – the festival of lights – that celebrates the Ramayana legend in which Rama and Sita return to Ayodha after a 14-year exile having defeated Ravana, the demon king. During the rehearsal the students balk at the authority of the director and the traditional ending of the tale by giving the myth a feminist reworking in which Sita refuses to be subject to Rama's authority.

Diwaali (1980) written by Jatinder Verma and directed by Paul Bhattacharjee was first performed on 16 November 1980 at Wandsworth Town Hall and self reflexively examined the Hindu festival's cultural relevance to the lives of 'second generation' British Asians. The plot concerned the attempts of a director who espoused a view of cultural tradition as fixed and unchanging and a sceptical young cast who acceded to doing scenes from the *Ramayana* only if they were given room to 'display them according to our ideas today' (Verma 1980d: 23). The Ramayana, an epic poem of India written in the seventh century BC is composed of seven books and concerns the life of Rama, the incarnation of the god Vishnu, and his battle with Ravana, the demon king. There are two key versions, a Sanskrit text attributed to Valmiki traditionally divided into seven books and a Hindi version by Tulsidass from the fifteenth century AD.

The play within the play, *Ramayana*, was given a more robust feminist reworking so that the actor playing Sita, in response to the director's plea that she should be 'the paragon of humility, of womanly obedience and duty' (Verma 1980d: 13) tells him 'you can stuff that' (Verma 1980d: 13). Indeed, in response to Rama who was 'portrayed as a dominating arrogant chauvinist' (Bhegani 1981) the actor playing Sita announced that 'all the lamps were lit to celebrate Raam and Sita's *life of equality*' (Verma 1980d: 22), as the play demonstrated the possibility of reinterpreting cultural traditions.

The audience were also engaged directly in this cultural debate as the production breached the 'fourth wall' and invited them to decide whether or not the character of Sita was to enter the fire; depending on the response there were three scripted alternatives. In this way the form of the performance attempted to convey its message as the cast and audience literally took control and interrogated constructions of their cultural heritage. This radical approach to content and form by Tara apparently provoked 'some opposition from older Asians who saw the play' (Best 1982); a response Tara was surely not unhappy with.

Fuse (1978)

Set in a south London secondary school. Praveen is asked to chaperone Yogesh, the new boy from India. In the course of his growing friendship with Yogesh, Praveen is forced to confront the racism of his white friends, girlfriend and teachers and recognise his own British Asian cultural identity.

Fuse was Tara's second production and the company's first original script that aimed to depict the experiences of the 'second generation' of British Asians. *Fuse* was first produced in 1978 as part of the Youth Programme of the Young People's Theatre Scheme at the Royal Court and was directed by Gerald Chapman, who was responsible for the Scheme itself. Jatinder Verma wrote the script based on the improvisations of the company who drew on their own experiences in a 'deliberate attempt on the group's part to present an Asian view of the white society we live in' (Verma 1978b). Indeed, such is the autobiographical nature of much of the experiences recounted in *Fuse* that the actor playing one of the main protagonists, Yogesh Bhatt, gives his name to his character.

The play examined a number of cultural differences through the character of Yogesh, such as eating with fingers rather than a knife and fork, being a vegetarian and attitudes to cross-gender friendship. As a result of Praveen's growing friendship with Yogesh he is forced to re-appraise the extent to which his acceptance at the school has been based on his cultural assimilation. However, Praveen's final visionary statement in *Fuse* that 'it's not a question of losing our culture, it's building a new living one' (Verma 1978a: 10) once again reflected Tara's aspiration to promote a new definition of Asian culture that was not premised on assimilation or a reversion to a lost traditional purity but on a cultural hybridity. *Fuse* also theatrically addressed Tara's didactic purpose to represent the heterogeneity of the Asian experience as it gave voices to characters from Sikh, as well as Hindu and Gujarati backgrounds. These characters came from the cities, as well as the villages, in an attempt to dispel the stereotype of the non-metropolitan Asian, as well as particularise different Asian experiences.

The script for *Fuse* was in English but there were unscripted improvisations in Gujarati between Yogesh and his father outside the deputy headmaster's office suggested by the stage directions that begin Scene Two. In the subsequent scene, the deputy headmaster tells Praveen to act as an interpreter so that he can question the prospective new boy, Yogesh, and his father. Praveen's compliance with the deputy headmaster's request to ask Mr Bhatt 'in Hindu if he has brought any references' (Verma 1978a: 2) is unscripted, but comes after he has corrected the teacher's confusion between the religion and the language. This short scene demonstrated the cast's ability to improvise fluently in Asian languages as well as representing Hindi and Gujarati on the stage, however, theatrically, the Asian language employed was limited and displaced to the margins.

There was also a second version of *Fuse* written in 1981 and although it was largely similar to the 1978 version there were some interesting developments that are worth outlining. Firstly, the character of Yogesh Bhatt was changed to Ashwin Patel who comes from Fiji, as means of introducing the wider Asian diaspora. The second version also contained a scene in which Ashwin told the class of the Asian *lascars* (sailors) in London in the nineteenth century; an early attempt by Tara to make visible the hidden histories of an Asian presence in Britain before the postwar migrations, which was to be explored more fully in subsequent plays such as *Vilayat* (1981), *Lion's Raj* (1982) and *Ancestral Voices* (1983).

While the play documented the racism that cultural difference aroused, not least when Praveen's white girlfriend decided to end their relationship because 'you babble in your lingo, you whistle your funny tunes…you…you've just changed' (Verma 1978a: 10), the company had not as yet found a way to incorporate that 'lingo' and those 'tunes' theatrically. However, Tara's theatrically groundbreaking use of all-Asian casts meant that Asian actors played the white characters that expressed racist sentiments. This casting policy subverted that racist discourse and questioned the acceptability of British theatrical practice at that time in which white actors would routinely 'black up' to play black or Asian characters.

Chilli in Your Eyes (1984)

Sonny, an unemployed Asian youth, is thrown out of home and is living rough on the streets. While Sonny and Gaz are out 'taxing' (robbing) people in the park they see an Asian girl, Rit, being attacked by two Asian boys from Bradford. Sonny intervenes to help Rit and is wrongly arrested. The police interrogate him and he is let out on bail. Sonny tries his hand at becoming a professional pool player and moves into a squat with Gaz. Sonny finally triumphs in a pool competition but returns 'home' to the squat to find he has been evicted and is once again left homeless.

One of the Asian youths interviewed in the research process for *Chilli in Your Eyes* (1984) relates how when he was attacked by some racist white youths he had attempted to throw chilli in their eyes, unfortunately he had not factored in the wind and the chilli was blown back into his face. This story recounted in the programme for *Chilli in Your Eyes* illustrates the casual racism experienced by Asians, as well as their self-deprecating humour, uncovered by the company in Newham.

While *Chilli in Your Eyes* (1984) was Tara's final engagement with realism before turning towards the 'Binglish' form discussed in Chapter 3, the desire of the company to break free of the realist conventions can be seen in the Artistic Policy set out in the programme:

> Objective (iv): 'to seek to fuse Dance, Music and other art-forms with Stage Plays'.

Although, in those early years the company had no formal theatrical training in Western conceptions of realism they 'found [themselves] slipping into a kind of convention which was the usual thing, drama and right speaking and tables and chairs and so forth' (Verma 2004: 84) and determined to consciously break from it.

Chilli in Your Eyes was based on research conducted by the company in the London borough of Newham and drew on the case of the

'Newham 8' who were tried at the Old Bailey in 1983. The eight Asian youths had been accused of assault and the trial ended with four of the defendants being acquitted and the remainder being found guilty of charges of affray. A number of reported attacks on Asian school children at the Little Ilford School in the Manor Park area of Newham by National Front sympathisers formed the backdrop to the trial. It had been rumoured that another attack was to take place on Friday 24 September and so the Asian youths in question had gathered at the school to escort the children home. However, they apparently mistook three plainclothes policemen from the District Support Unit who emerged from an unmarked car to be the racist attackers in question and were subsequently charged.

Chilli in Your Eyes was directed by Yogesh Bhatt and written by Jatinder Verma based on three weeks the company spent researching the experiences of young Asians growing up in the London borough of Newham. The play was in two acts and dramatised the conflict of 'second generation' British Asians with the 'traditional' cultural values of the older generation of their families and the unwelcoming and at times overtly racist wider community through its five main characters: Jag, Nalini, Sonny, Rit and Gaz, who were from a range of different Asian religious backgrounds, Sikh, Muslim and Hindu.

The research was geared towards not only gathering information and identifying the key issues that the company would like to address but also beginning to devise and structure the piece. The company visited a range of institutions in order to conduct research, including the police, social services, the Race Relations Unit and the Newham Monitoring Project; which aimed to monitor racism and racial attacks in Newham as it was felt that the police were not sufficiently responsive. The company also spoke to the chief superintendent of West Ham Police Station whose misunderstanding of Tara's work may be inferred from his concern that 'your not going to dance in my office, are you?' The company decided to focus on Asian youth in the borough and, ironically in the light of the policeman's comment incorporated, *Bhangra*, the Punjabi folk dance, into the production as a symbol of their 'spirit of energetic defiance' (Production Programme 1984).

The cultural negotiation of the second generation characters can be seen in the following exchange between Sonny and his mother. We learn that Sonny has anglicised his name and is deemed effete by his mother for his breakdancing. The hybrid text that integrated Asian and English languages reflected the linguistic reality behind the cultural location of the British Asian subject.

MOTHER: Vey Arvind – kithey murrandhya – ey tuu? [Where the hell are you Arvind?]

SONNY: Sonny mum.

MOTHER: (*noting Sonny's gyrations*) Laanutt hoey khas-mannu khaaldeya! Aahi reya-si meyrey buss vich? Aadmia dhey ruup vich kuldi nuu junldum? [God damn you! Was it my fate – to have given birth to a pansy]

SONNY: Sonny mum.

MOTHER: Sonny-shunny hoey ghaa bhaar! [Call yourself whatever you like outside!] Eys kaar vich tuu Arvind jummeya, Arvind marunghaa! [You were born Arvind and you'll die Arvind!]

(Verma 1984d: 2)

The exchange between the mother in Gujarati and the son in English reflected the reality of many bilingual Asian homes. However, in the following exchange the play also recognised that some second generation Asians did not speak or understand Asian languages:

NAL: (*to Jag*) Kaytla vakt ghurr ausuu? [When will you get home?]

JAG: Finish duty at 11.

NAL: Ring kurrsuu [Give me a ring]

GAZ: Talk in fucking English why don't you? You know I don't understand.

(Verma 1984d: 16)

The play also attacks the rigidly stratified caste system, which is depicted as in operation in India, but shown to be fragmenting in Britain. Nalini and Jag want to get married and while both are Gujaratis they are from different castes. Even though Jag had a good job and was shown to be caring and supportive of Nalini, the fact that she was a Patel and Jag a Luhanalda was seen as a bar to marriage by her father:

FATHER-IN-LAW: Tummey Luhanalda Chhau [You are a Luhanalda].

JAG: Both Gujarati, though, Nalini and me.

FATHER-IN-LAW: How long – meeting Nalini.

JAG: Four years. On and off.

FATHER-IN-LAW (*controlling himself*) See my daughter one more time, anney police chiko maa bundh kurri dheysi [and I will have you locked up in the police station].

JAG: She is over eighteen.

FATHER-IN-LAW: I will tell police – Nikuldhi jhaa! [Get out!]
JAG: They'll laugh at ya.
(*Jag exits pissed off with himself*)
FATHER-IN-LAW: (*calling out*) Nalini.
(*Nalini enters. Father slaps her*)

(Verma 1984d: 67)

The challenge to patriarchal authority demonstrated by Nalini and Jag's attempt to arrange their marriage, as well as their secret liaison, results in her ostracism from the family as her father informs her 'Ammare aankh bundh chhey' [My eyes are closed] (Verma 1984d: 60) and orders her from the house. Although the play dramatised the violent consequences of such a challenge it ended with Jag and Nalini still happily together in a defiant rejection of what they, and by extension the playwright, perceived as a generational disagreement over cultural practices. However, *Chilli in Your Eyes* was more nuanced than a simple 'culture clash' play. Jag and Nalini do not simply reject 'traditional' Asian cultural practices but attempted to re-inflect them and still plan to get married 'in one of the Luhanalda Community Centres' (Verma 1984d: 78).

We can see that Tara's 'twin-pronged stance' was still in operation in *Chilli in Your Eyes* with particular reference to two scenes. The first shows Sonny as the victim of racist police brutality as a white officer beats him up in custody. The second, which shows the attempted rape of an Asian woman by a gang of Asian men, was not designed or destined to court popularity within the Asian community even though it was 'based on actual testimony of people living in Newham' (Verma 1989b: 772).

FIRST LAD: Takko yarrow! Keylda phul ughda-ey es baagh-ich! [Well, well! What do we have here]
SECOND LAD: (*Obviously*) Phul nai, kuldi-a! [Not – a girl!]
FIRST LAD: Kuldai nai – rhundi-a! [No girl – a whore]
RIT: (*To lads*) Rundhi teyri maa! [Call your mother a whore!]

(Verma 1984d: 35)

When Sonny attempted to stop the men's attack he was beaten up and subsequently wrongly arrested by the police. While in custody the first police officer he encountered was sympathetic to the Asian community, albeit in a way that homogenises and stereotypes them, and he admonished Sonny 'not to go giving up your culture' (Verma

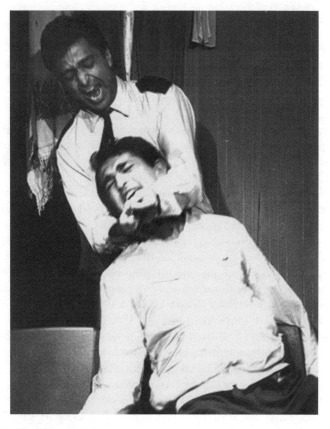

***Chilli in Your Eyes* (1984)**
© Chris Ha 1984.
A police 'interrogation' scene with Harmage S. Kalirai playing Sonny and Sheetal Verma the policeman.

1984d: 42). However, the second officer Sonny encountered was openly racist:

> POLICEMAN II: Now listen here you black scum, an' listen proper! You wanna sit in the comfort of your magic carpet you'd better come up with a name or I swear for every day that copper lies in hospital I'll knock out one of your teeth – an' I'll do it good and slow.
>
> (Verma 1984d: 44)

The portrayal of Mr Bhambra, the Asian corner shop owner who exploited his Asian workforce, in the form of Sonny, by underpaying him for his work in the shop demonstrated that Tara were also prepared to risk playing into stereotype. The dramatic irony with which Jatinder Verma attacked this character is reinforced by the director's utilisation of a direct address convention to the audience:

> MR BHAMBRA: (*To audience*) Generous – it is a fault! My wife tells me every day – people take advantage of you Bhambra [. . .] business here can only run as family. But who believes in family nowadays?
>
> (Verma 1984d: 22)

The representation of Mr Bhambra as an unashamedly unsympathetic character played with a stereotypical 'sing-song' voice and nodding head is at least mitigated by the stage being peopled with a range of positive, as well as negative, Asian characters.

Jatinder Verma's script also recognised that the British location had dislocated what was constructed as a traditional Asian 'family' in ways that had ambivalent effects. *Chilli in Your Eyes* dramatised the ambivalence of a second generation who desired greater independence and autonomy balanced by loss of security as a result of weakened community ties – reflected in the fact that Sonny is homeless. While the collapse of Rit's arranged marriage to a man from Pakistan because 'Immigration nay – entry nahi dhi' [Immigration refused entry] (Verma 1984d: 80) is a convenient outcome for her, the operation of British immigration laws is still demonstrated to be discriminatory in its operation and application to the cultural practices of those in the Asian community in Britain.

The dancing in the play functioned as a means of challenging constructions of gender roles and cultural practices. The mother's concern that Sonny's dancing made him a 'pansy', a view not shared by his friends, suggested the changing construction of acceptable cultural practices with regard to gender. Furthermore, while Nalini was considered a *rhundi* [prostitute] by her mother because of her desire to be a dancer, as that was its common cultural connotation in India, she was encouraged by her boyfriend, Jag, who promised to send her to a 'proper dancing class' (Verma 1984d: 77).

The syncretic aims of Tara's work are exemplified in the play through the dancing (see above), which was a fusion of traditional Asian dance forms and contemporary 'body popping' symbolised the cultural hybridity of the second generation. The company's success in theatrically integrating song and dance-based movement into performance was still circumscribed by the limits of the realistic form. However, Tara

***Chilli in Your Eyes* (1984)**
© Chris Ha, 1984.
Harmage Singh Kalirai playing Sonny and Sudha Bhuchar as Nalini, dancing.

attempted to challenge these realistic limits through the use of song in
Chilli in Your Eyes. The play opened with the 'Song of the Futureless' in
which the characters gave an agitprop[11] style account of the historical
and contemporary sociopolitical position of immigrants in the borough
of Newham.

Newham sits between Lea and Barking Creek
Docklands laid low
Jews came Irish too
And fled through Newham to Barking true
Leaving room for Pakis to come and lie low
Flow through Newham
Rivers of Hindustan
And in Silvertown, Paki windows are bricked
1984 and England's a place of woe
3 million unemployed, 30 million to go

2 lakh (hundred thousand), a quarter them are black
…
Buckets of shit, piss in Tesco bags
Writing on the wall says send them all back.

(Verma 1984d: 1)

While the song above and the title song *Chilli in Your Eyes* below painted a bleak picture of Britain from the perspective of the second generation British Asians:

School does you down
Jobs give you lies
Police are no fair cop
So its chilli in your eyes.
Dad's down and out
Mum's out of cheer
Skinheads come to town
So its chilli in your beer

(Verma 1984d: 45)

there are signs of optimism as the song was reprised at the end of the play with new lyrics and a dance:

we've got a home
and we're gonna live our lives
(*The five begin dancing the bhangra again – ecstatic defiant and Exit*)

(Verma 1984d: 85)

The play ends optimistically with a show of solidarity between the five second generation friends as they set up home together and organise a petition to get an inquiry into Sonny's assault in police custody. This spirit of resistance was reinforced by the final *bhangra* dance which in its 'fusion of Punjabi folk dance movements with contemporary electronic beats, gloriously symbolised' (Eccles 1984) the creative reinvention of tradition in the play.

Indeed, the final song of the play is a defiant reclamation of the term 'Paki' from a term of racist abuse to one of solidarity:

Ding dong here's a Paki
Ding dong there's a Paki

Ding dong Paki Paki everywhere you go
Oo-ah up they rises (x3)
Chilli in your eyes (*and burst into laughter*)

(Verma 1984d: 86)

There was a largely positive critical reception to the play with praise in *City Limits* for the writing of 'Verma's penetrating new play' (Eccles 1984) and the 'compassion and no sentimentality' of the acting which was, in the view of Anjana Paz of the Asian magazine *New Life*, 'brilliantly performed' (1984). These views, perhaps, reflect the ability of a company such as Tara, with its all-Asian cast, to engage theatrically with the material in a way that is 'usually described in more alienated sociological terms' (Vaughan 1984a). However, Naqi Ali of the *Asian Herald* was less impressed with the 'elementary play with no artistic guile or subtlety' (1984) and was not sympathetic to the way it 'openly mocks the taboos and traditions that drive young recalcitrant Asians to rebellion' (1984).

While *Chilli in Your Eyes* utilised direct address, song and dance and some use of Asian languages it became clear to Jatinder Verma that Tara Arts needed to go further to discover a form 'not restricted by the dead hand of naturalism' (Verma 2002). As we shall see in the next chapter, this would be premised on the ancient Indian treatise on performance, the *Natyasastra*, through which they could explore the hybrid British Asian cultural site that would lead to the creation of Tara's unique hybrid 'Binglish' form.

3
Tara Arts 1984–1996: Creating a 'Binglish' Theatre

Introduction

Jatinder Verma describes himself as a 'translated man', alluding not only to his own diasporic journey to Britain but also 'the sense in which I choose to "bear across" my ideas, my sensibility of theatre to another dominant sensibility in contemporary Britain' (Verma 1994a: 57). This 'bearing across' was initiated when Tara Arts began 'a self conscious drive to elicit the company's theatrical identity: in other words, to discover in theatrical terms that which made Tara distinctive – beyond the socio-political badges of colour, race, legal status' (Verma 1998b: 129). In 1984, they set out to create a theatre praxis that would draw on Eastern as well as Western influences and further the political aspirations of Tara Arts to contest the marginal status of the Asian in Britain and British theatre. In contrast to Tara's early theatrical approach discussed in Chapter 2, that produced a theatre rooted in realism that was 'very English in its convention' (Verma 1982) Jatinder Verma created the innovative hybrid form of 'Binglish' that was established by 'the heaping together of fragments of diverse cultures' (Verma 1998b: 131).

'Binglish' has been defined by Jatinder Verma as 'a distinct contemporary theatre praxis [...] featuring Asian and black casts, produced by independent Asian or black theatre companies [...] to directly challenge or provoke the dominant conventions of the English stage' (Verma 1996: 194). While Tara Arts were already in straightforward accordance with the first of these two tenants, in order to 'challenge and provoke' they drew on Asian as well as Western methodological sources including the *Natyasastra*, the Indian treatise on acting dating from circa 200 BC, Indian folk forms such as *bhavai* and the Bollywood film genre. This led them away from a text-based realism towards a performance methodology in which 'movement and music [...] are not ancillary to the spoken word but form an integral part of the "text" of performance' (Verma 1996: 200).

While Tara's early work consisted of 'doing worthy plays about historical and social subjects [...] the content of the work was radical but its form was the same as all other touring groups' (Verma quoted in Hiley 1989a) as we saw in the productions discussed in Chapter 2. The clear aim of the company from 1984 was to radicalise the form and through it 'attempt to demolish the white Eurocentric way of looking at the world and replace it with another' (Peacock 1999: 175).

The provenance of 'Binglish'

'Binglish' was heavily influenced by Jatinder Verma's study of the *Natyasastra*, which is attributed to Bharata Muni, is dated between 200 BC and AD 200 and gives an insight into the Sanskrit theatre tradition of Ancient India. The meaning of *Natyasastra* as defined in *The Cambridge Guide to Asian Theatre* (1993) is made up of *Natya*, meaning drama, and *sastra*, a generic term referring to any authoritative text. The *Natyasastra* consists of 36 chapters and is a comprehensive dramaturgical guide. The majority of treatise is devoted to acting but it also examines in some detail theatre architecture, costume, makeup, properties, dance, music, play construction and the organisation of theatre companies, audiences, theatre construction and even the holding of dramatic competitions.

The discussion of *Abhinaya* [acting] divides it into four key elements: *Angika* [Bodily Movement], *Vacika* [Voice], *Aharya* [Spectacle], *Sattvika* [Emotion]. The importance of the actors' physicality in the Indian tradition, in contrast to the contemporary realism of the Western stage, was evident from the fact that four chapters were devoted to it, and it was this that was to heavily influence Jatinder Verma's 'Binglish'. There are descriptions of whole body movements such as *cari* [poses] or *gati* [gaits] which were ascribed to a range of characters of different ages, genders and temperaments, even detailing specific eye or lip movements. The treatise also gave great emphasis to way in which stylised costume and makeup could be employed in the creation of characters. Music was also privileged in the *Natyasastra* as a fundamental element of performance. Songs were integrated into the performance and served a range of functions: introducing characters, marking character exits, reinforcing a dramatic mood, revealing plot and character or simply covering a costume change.

Jatinder Verma drew on the *Natyasastra*'s key dramaturgical principles such as the integration of music and song, stylised movement, non-naturalistic makeup and costume and the dismantling of the the-atrical 'fourth wall' in order to challenge 'the dominant convention of the modern English stage – the spoken word' (Verma 1998b: 129).

The 'Binglish' language

The 'Binglish' text was also to address the linguistic flaw in Tara's previous methodology, which as Jatinder Verma pointed out in an inter-view with Jane Plastow meant 'in rehearsal we negotiated across several languages, and yet none of these languages are on stage' (Plastow 2004: 91). Indeed, the performance of Asian languages alongside English as they 'form part of the linguistic map of modern Britain [...] and can-not be expected to be absent from modern British theatre' (Verma 1996: 198) was a powerful rationale for inscribing cultural difference on the British stage. This view came after a re-appraisal of the use of Asian lan-guages on stage by Jatinder Verma who had mistakenly thought that '[in the late 1970s onwards] that I was witnessing the end of an age... [and] successive generations would necessarily lose fluency in Asian languages and any sentimental attachment to them [...] I am [...] proved wrong' (Verma 1994b: 5).

Crucially, he also recognised that these were hybrid British Asian lan-guages spoken by people who 'assert themselves as Asians with the odd *ji* [honorific] or *vanga* [go away!] injected into their Cockney or Brummie or Yorkshire variants of English' (Verma 1994b: 3). Indeed, 'Binglish' responded to the fact that 'the syncretic and hybridised nature of post-colonial experience refutes the privileged position of a standard code in the language' (Ashcroft et al. 2002: 40) and so employed a range of Asian languages, accents and dialects alongside English.

The employment of a range of Asian languages, as exemplified in 'Binglish', such as Hindi, Punjabi, Gujarati and English, had the further function of performing the plurality of the signifier 'Asian'. However, while 'Binglish' performances demonstrated the difference and linguis-tic plurality of the Asian community in Britain it should be recognised that all Asian language speakers largely aurally understood those Asian languages and therefore their employment remained a locus of solidar-ity. It has been found that in Britain that 'nearly all ethnic minority persons speak a language other than English' (Modood et al. 1997: 308) and in the specific instance of the South Asian communities Punjabi is the most commonly used South Asian language among British Asians.

Modood pointed out that while Hindi and Urdu have different scripts, aurally they share a common base sometimes referred to as Hindustani which was also understood by some speakers of other Asian languages such as Punjabi; it is thus the medium that enabled the Bombay film industry or 'Bollywood' to reach such a massive audience. In this way the plurality of Asian languages utilised in the 'Binglish' performance not only performed the heterogeneity of the signifier 'Asian' but also simultaneously de-centred the usually privileged monolingual English speaker. The use of a range of Asian languages further inserted difference into the 'Binglish' performance as 'a universal theatre language will not be achieved by theatrical Esperanto but by accepting and giving voice to cultural diversity' (Verma quoted in Lewis 1991).

One of the key methodological impacts of 'Binglish' linguistically was, as suggested above, to privilege the Asian speaker at times during the performance as it did not directly translate the Asian languages employed. While the use of Asian languages clearly signified cultural difference in the performance, the purpose of 'Binglish' was to go beyond an essentialist view of language in which 'the untranslated words, sounds textures of the language can be held to have the power and presence of the culture they signify – to be metaphoric in their inference of identity and totality' (Ashcroft et al. 2002: 51). As we shall see the 'Binglish' performance highlighted the hybridity and fluidity of language by putting Asian languages, colloquialisms, prayers, songs and texts into play with British accents, dialects, registers and texts via multilingual British Asian actors.

Furthermore, the use of untranslated words in the 'Binglish' text meant the non-Asian speaking audience had 'an active engagement with the horizons of the culture in which these terms have meaning' (Ashcroft et al. 2002: 64). Crucially, however, rather than being understood linguistically as an 'other' culture the hybrid 'Binglish' performance insisted that the audience recognised those languages under the auspices of British culture and as part of the 'English' language. Jatinder Verma defended the relevance of the non-Asian speakers moments of marginalisation within the 'Binglish' performance, 'that moment of incomprehension is terribly important because that is the reality of multicultural Britain' (Verma quoted in Brace 1994).

This use of Asian languages alongside English as well as the employment of non-Western theatre forms meant that a 'modern white audience in Britain experiencing a "Binglish" production could be said to be oscillating continuously between the sense of the native, the familiar and the foreign' (Verma 1996: 200). There is a clear politics to this as the audience are constantly being made aware of their own and by extension the culturally constructed 'others' constantly shifting position of centrality or marginality. Ashcroft suggests 'in the early period of postcolonial writing many writers were forced into the search for an alternative authenticity which seemed to be escaping them' (Ashcroft et al. 2002: 40) as there was no possibility of a return to an 'original' or precolonial culture and yet there was a desire to reclaim and reanimate cultural difference. In this case the 'alternative authenticity' exemplified in 'Binglish' was predicated on the hybridity of the British Asian subject that articulates cultural difference while simultaneously insisting on the inclusion of that 'difference' in the discourse of what we understand as British theatre.

The creation of 'Binglish' in 1984 took Tara from the margins of British theatre to centre stage at the Royal National Theatre in the 1990s. I will discuss three key 'Binglish' productions from that time, *Miti Ki Gadi [The Little Clay Cart]* (1984), *Tartuffe* (1990) and *Cyrano* (1995).

Miti Ki Gadi [The Little Clay Cart] (1984)

The non-European text that began the development of Tara's 'Binglish' theatrical methodology was *Miti Ki Gadi [The Little Clay Cart]* (1984)

Miti Ki Gadi **Publicity Flyer**

© Tara Arts.

Publicity flyer for 1985 performance of *Miti Ki Gadi* at Bharatiya Vidya Bhavan, west Kensington, London. (Note the range of scripts used on the flyer: Roman, Urdu and Devenagari)

ascribed to Shudraka who was said to have written the Sanskrit drama *Mricchakatika* between the seventh and eighth centuries AD The production of *Miti Ki Gadi [The Little Clay Cart]* was first performed in 1984 at community venues, later re-staged at the Arts Theatre to open the third 'Black Theatre Season' in 1986 and then revised for a production in the Cottesloe Auditorium, at the Royal National Theatre on 5 December 1991.

The critical ramifications of Tara's new hybrid methodology 'blending conventions of Indian classical acting [...] with western realism' (Rea 1984) were swiftly recognised and lauded as 'a milestone for both Asian Theatre in Britain and for Tara whose mature, refreshing approach can only be an inspiration to others' (Kalsi 1984).

Miti Ki Gadi (1984)

Act I	The gems are left behind
Act II	The shampooer who gambled
Act III	The hole in the wall
Act IV	Mandanika and Sharvilaka
Act V	The storm
Act VI	The swapping of the bullock carts
Act VII	Aryaka's escape
Act VIII	The strangling of Vasantasena
Act IX	The trial
Act X	The end

The action is set in the city of Ujjain, central India, as the protagonist, Charudatta, a married merchant reduced to poverty, becomes involved with a wealthy courtesan, Vasantasena. The king's wicked brother-in-law, Sansthanaka attempts unsuccessfully to win Vasantasena's love but when she rejects him he strangles her and accuses Charudatta of the murder. At his trial, Charudatta is condemned to death, in no small part due to the malign and powerful influence of Sansthanaka. Meanwhile, Aryaka, a freedom fighter who has been jailed by the king, escapes. Fortunately for Charudatta, the heroine, Vasantasena, is not dead, and appears in court to save his life. There is a revolution and the popular rebel leader, Aryaka, is made king.

'Binglish' praxis

Some insight into Jatinder Verma's rehearsal methodology can be gained by examining the rehearsal notebooks for the 1984 and 1986 productions of *Miti Ki Gadi*, in which he questions 'the Asian perspective' of the play in theatrical terms.

The play as I see it in *structural* terms:

- Open stage. No sets. Minimum props. Costumes. Live music.
- All performers on stage all the time.
- No break from scene to scene or Act to Act (except interval).
- An invocation/prelude/warm up leading into the story itself.
- The *fact* of a 'performance' is clear all the time: i.e. that Yogesh [Bhatt] etc., are performing as characters.
- Audience treated *directly*: talked to, played with: i.e. performers not to hide fact that people *are* watching, and that they are performing.
- Question: How are plays represented on the stage in the West?

(According to the N-S [Natya Shastra], a play is to be represented in only 4 ways: words, gesture, make up & costume – with thought underlying all. By these 4 ways alone, the meaning of a play should be clear. Thus reducing a play to its simplicity; the performer).
(Jatinder Verma 1984b)

In *Miti Ki Gadi* the actors came into the space while the houselights were up, acknowledged the audience and, in full sight of them, organised any remaining props or articles of costume on the performance area ready for the performance. The actors then went into an inward facing circle at the perimeter of the acting area. After a group warm up they started doing their own individual stylised character gestures while remaining in the circle and then began the *alaap*. Usually the *alaap* in Indian classical music is a prelude or invocation to a *raga* and aimed to create a particular *rasa* or feeling in the audience. In the opening sequence of *Miti Ki Gadi*, when the characters moved into a circle and danced with a rhythmic stamping movement and then introduced their characters

Miti Ki Gadi (1984)

© Tara Arts.

Pictured foreground Bhaskar, stage right Nizwar Karanj and up stage left Rezaul Kabir from *Miti Ki Gadi* (1984). (Notice the stylised collective movements by the actors.)

by name in direct address to the audience *as the house lights are dimmed*, this drew on both cultural traditions.

The acting area was demarcated by a square of cloth in the auditorium that then became the centre of the playing space. In *Miti Ki Gadi* the actors remain on stage at all times – according with the second of Jatinder Verma's structural notes above – and there is no attempt to 'conceal' the actors when they are not in character.

The musician, who was also present onstage throughout the performance and clearly visible, sat on the floor in the down stage right corner of the acting area. The instruments used by Baluji Srivastav were *tabla*, *sitar* and *dilruba*; the last of which, though similar in appearance to a *sitar*, was a bowed stringed instrument. The difference in a 'Binglish' production was not only that the instruments used were non-Western but also that the South Asian tradition of musicians playing while seated on the floor was followed. The integration of the music was noted by the critics as 'every movement is punctuated or underlined' (Gilbert 1985) and also accompanied the actors during songs, underscored the action throughout the play and interacted with the performers as discussed in the scene below.

The comic 'burglary' scene in Act III in which a burglar breaks into the house of Charudatta, the impecunious merchant, and steals the jewel box entrusted to him by Vasantasena requires great dexterity in *angika abhinaya* [bodily movement] in order to dismantle an imaginary wall. Before the thief breaks in through the wall of the merchant's house he consults a robber's 'textbook' in order to ascertain the best method of entry. There are a range of options described:

SHARVILAKA: (*To the audience*) How do I get in so I don't disturb any guards? Let's see what the textbook says. (*Gets his book out and reads*) 'Four ways of breaking in. First for 'baked bricks – pull them out [...] for unbaked bricks – cut through them [...] for clay [...] soften by wetting. Fourth, for wood – saw through it.' (*Looking at the courtyard wall*) Here we have baked bricks. So pull them out! Here goes! (*He starts to work*)

(Verma 1984a: Act 1, Scene 12)

According to the textbook he must then decide which shape to make the entry hole from a range including Lotus, Lake Swastika and Water Pot. As the actor tapped the imaginary wall of the house to ascertain which type of brick it was made from, the musician synchronised the beats of the *tabla* to the action. Critics praised this physical approach whose 'movement is formal and elegant [...] derived from classical Indian dance' (Vaughan 1984b) and particularly noted that the scene discussed above 'was inspired' (Gilbert 1985). The burglary scene in the 1986 production was again recognised by critics as exemplifying the hybrid 'Binglish' performance as the character by a 'combination of Indian *abhinaya* and Western mime showed that he is cutting a hole through the wall of a house' (Hall 1986). Interestingly, while Hall demonstrated some knowledge of traditional Indian theatre from the *Natyasastra*, in actuality *abhinaya* is defined as including speech and costume as well as movement. So we can see that far from being 'a combination', *abhinaya* would totally subsume mime while mime in no way encompasses the breadth of *abhinaya*. However, the review does point to a new critical vocabulary drawn from Asian theatrical discourse being employed to analyse this piece of British theatre.

The actor's approach to characterisation in a 'Binglish' production is gestural rather than psychological so that each character exhibited a distinctive rhythm and style to their walks. The hero, Charudatta, walked with a very upright posture with his heel kicked up behind at each step while his friend Maitraya, the Brahmin, walked with a wide waddling gait constantly bent at the knee as if sitting and the Masseur had a high tempo, short-gaited, shuffling walk. The characters' movements were integrated with the music so that the musicians accentuated the different rhythm of the actors' movement. The rehearsal notes from the production detailed how Maitreya moved to a seven-beat rhythm, Sansthanaka to a two-beat rhythm and the Judge to a five-beat rhythm. A great deal of the exercises employed in the rehearsal process focused on the body, exploring posture and rhythm, and the rehearsal records showed the importance attached to the physical manifestation of character as discussed earlier. These stylised movements also facilitated the actors moving freely and recognisably through a range of characters throughout the performance.

The exercises described in Jatinder Verma's rehearsal notebook show how the rehearsal methodology was developed to further atomise and stylise the physical performance of the actors.

3. Stylization Routine:
Body Project → character names
　"　　　　　→ eyes & character names
　"　　　　　→ face & eyes & character names
　"　　　　　→ shoulder & face & eyes & character names
Walks – try different types, explore new ones. Then footwork
(7 beat – 5 beat – 3 beat)
(Verma 1985b).

While Tara's 'Binglish' performance draws on the *Natyasastra* in its codified approach to acting the actors were encouraged to create their own interpretations after working off the existing template. Indeed, as this performance methodology was unfamiliar to the actors it had to be self-consciously inculcated into the performers throughout the rehearsal especially because 'if you are going to used [sic] *stylised gestures* then ensure you spend proper time on each and that they are

constantly utilized in *every* exercise/warm up/game – leaving performers
to develop more from their own researches in *N – S* [*Natyasastra*]' (Verma
1985b).

The relatively short rehearsal time made it practically unrealistic that
any performers could give a performance in complete technical accordance with the *Natyasastra*. Hence, the director's recognition that the
performers will 'develop' their own researches *based on* rather than repli-
cating the precepts laid out in the *Natyasastra*. However, the importance
of the *Natyasastra* as a source for the performance was exemplified in
the director's admonishments to the actors to 'keep it with you always'
(Verma 1985b).

Jatinder Verma also employed Shobana Jeyasingh, whose fusion of
Indian classical dance with Western forms mirrored the aims of Tara's
hybrid form of 'Binglish', to work with the actors. Her focus was
on the physicality of the actor and on the need to provide a movement vocabulary drawn from classical Indian dance for the company,
none of whom were trained dancers. However, the aim was not to
teach the actors to master classical dance forms such as *Kathak*,[1]
nor would this be practically realistic, but rather to provide a sufficient knowledge of those forms' basic movement vocabularies in order
to find 'a new articulation of an Asian style' (Bhuchar 1999d: 3).
The methodological benefit of this physical approach developed with
Shobana Jeyasingh was that 'each character being given his or her
own dance movements and stance [...] enables instant character
identification...[and] permits considerable doubling and trebling of
roles' (Hepple 1986).

Jatinder Verma was obviously aware of the importance that this physical discipline was maintained as this rehearsal notebook entry for Day
12 demonstrates.

'what do I mean by "concentrated effort"? [...]
2 Remember the checklist of Shobana's [Jeyasingh]: Shoulders/
Back/Knees when assuming a posture [...] '
(Verma 1985b)

Even when the rehearsal emphasis was on vocalising the text the actors
were encouraged to retain the physicality of their characters.

Day Three
Script work: [...]
2.4 Telling story of *LCC* (sitting in circle, moving in stylised way
to middle & maintaining stylised posture)
(Verma 1985a)

These rehearsal notes give an insight into the privileging of the actors
physicality in building character and the way in which in a non-
naturalistic performance methodology based on the *Nayasastra* was
utilised in forming the 'Binglish' performance methodology.

In *Miti Ki Gadi* the characters spoke with a range of accents from standard English to northern English and Asian. From the notes that Jatinder
Verma made from his reading of the *Natyasastra* he drew out that
'only principle male characters to speak in Sanskrit; the rest, in *prakrits*
[dialects]' (Verma 1984b), which suggested he was trying to realise this
methodology within an English linguistic framework. The actor playing
Charudatta was Ayub Khan-Din,[2] who grew up in the north of England,
so he spoke in a Standard English accent when playing Charudatta but
a northern English accent when playing one of the gamblers. However,
the convention did not hold for Asian accents which were employed
by 'high' and 'low' characters alike so that the actor playing another
gambler in the same scene as Khan-Din spoke in an Asian accent, as did
the Brahmin, Maitreya, friend to Charudatta, and the wicked leading
character, Sansthanaka.

Asian languages peppered the production ranging from the profane,
to devotional and protest songs and to colloquial greetings. In the first
scene when Maitreya referred to the friends that deserted Charudatta
now that he was poor, he called them 'kaminey aur kamino-kay-
baap' [nasty bastards and nasty bastard's fathers] (Verma 1984c: Act 1,
Scene 2). However, the sense of this was contextualised by the previous
two speeches that introduced this theme and then explained in the line
that followed it in which he described them 'as cattle-herders that feed
on the greenest pastures'.

While a non-Asian speaking audience would not understand the literal meaning of the line they could understand the sense of it from the
surrounding text. It may also be imagined that for those who did understand, this moment may elicit laughter that for a moment privileges
the Asian speaker in the audience. In this respect, the laughter raised

through the 'Binglish' process functioned as a moment of provocation that unsettled and de-centred a non-Asian speaking audience.

Jatinder Verma's 'translation' of this classical tale was also re-inscribed with contemporary references. The effect of Sansthnaka's attempt to woo the courtesan Vasantasena by describing her as 'chicken tan doori, lamb pasanda, kashmiri tikka [...]' (Verma 1984c: Act 1, Scene 2), which 'sounds surprisingly like the menu from a North Indian Restaurant...[was to]...jerk the audience back into the twentieth century' (Baker 1984a). The contemporary reworking of *Miti Ki Gadi* also extended to giving the play a feminist reading in line with Tara's insistence that they would draw on, rather than be bound by, tradition. In the original version 'King Aryaka gave Vasantesena the status of "wife" and the kingdom to Charudatta, and everything ends well' (Varadpande 1987: 38) while at the end of the play in the 'Binglish' production a courtier tells Vasantasena that King Aryaka had conferred upon her the title of wife to Charudatta. This news is not received positively by Mandanika, Charudatta's first wife:

SHARVILAKA: (*To Vasantasena*) His Majesty, King Aryaka has asked me to confer upon you the title of Wife to Charudatta, if he consents to have you as his second wife [...]
MANDANIKA: (*entering in a fury*) No he bloody doesn't!

(Verma 1984c: Act 2, Scene 34)

The Little Clay Cart (1986)

If we look at the prologue to *The Little Clay Cart* (1986) we can see how many of the 'structural' imperatives outlined by Jatinder Verma for the 1984 production were realised by a textual development that utilised the theatrical framing device of a prologue.

PROLOGUE
MALA: I bring a story
     From the ruins of
     India's past,
     Written by one Shudraka
     Whose name is now lost.
     A story of Kings,
     Brothers-in-law, thieves,
     Lovers and gamblers
     Rising phoenix like

From an ancient splendour
To grace this cold winter of our present
Before unfolding the story of this *Little Clay
Cart* I join hands
In praise of our ancestors
Praying I may prove
Worthy of giving voice to their words
YOGESH: She's in love with her past!
MALA: We have no need of cynics!
Our actors!
(Actors introduce their characters)

(Verma 1985c: Prologue)

In order to 'frame' the story of *The Little Clay Cart* Jatinder Verma drew on Indian folk forms and designated two of the actors to play the roles of *sutradhars*: the closest equivalent in Western theatre for the role of the *sutradhar* would be storyteller or narrator. The word *sutradhar* literally means 'holder of the threads or strings that is a puppeteer, an architect or a manipulator' (Brandon 1993: 61) and was a common 'feature of all Indian theatre, whether it is the high stylised pan-Indian form or any of the populist versions that there is a story teller, the master puppeteer who holds all the strings' (Verma quoted in Lustig 1990a: 16). The wide theatrical licence given to the *sutradhar*, the antithesis of a naturalistic character of the Western tradition is evident from the definition of its function below:

He remains present on the stage throughout the performance to guide its course into a coherent theatrical pattern [...] He gives general information about the play – its story, the name of the author. He defines the time and place of the action [...] He introduces the characters of the play to the audience by announcing their entry or by taking them to it or by asking them questions leading to the revelation of their identity [...] He suggests change of scene or venue of action.

Alienating himself from the dramatic action he gives a running commentary on the scenes presented on stage [...] He takes the audience into confidence about things to come and highlights their significance [...] Sometimes he even impersonates a character in the play [...] He maintains direct contact with the audience.

(Varadpande 1979: 95)

The function of the *sutradhar* role in *The Little Clay Cart* was clearly set out in the director's notes; to 'introduce the story, push it along, commentate upon, tie up loose ends' (Verma 1985b) as well as initiating the songs. The separation of these two roles was coherently maintained but quite fluid so that 'sometimes we see Yogesh Bhatt in the traditional role of the *sutradhar* who introduces the piece and comments on it, at other times he becomes the wicked Sansthanaka' (Hall 1986).

The play was interspersed with songs, dances and music, provided by live musicians on Asian instruments. The songs were influenced and 'based on the spirit of the quwaali [...] clapping, chorus, lead singers' (Verma 1985b) except for the last song, the 'Bandera Rossa' adopted by the Italian Communist Party and included for its revolutionary connotations.

Miti Ki Gadi, unlike other Sanskrit works of this time, was peopled with 'low' characters as well as the more exalted classes. Indeed, this representation of the 'people' on stage whose political agency resulted in the subaltern being placed literally centre stage very much reflected the decentring aspirations of a 'Binglish' production as it sought to contest the political as well as theatrical marginalisation of Asians in Britain. The 1986 production of *The Little Clay Cart* also tackled the sociopolitical issue of racism directly, to the dismay of some critics who complained they could 'do without the GLC style crass overstatement which mars the conclusion [...] tragic though racial attacks are, Waltham Forest cannot have featured in the original Sanskrit' (Murdin 1986).

However, the presiding view of the critics was extremely positive from the *Daily Telegraph* praising its 'splendid vitality' (Hall 1986) and *The Times* noting the 'colourful witty language' (Kingston 1986) to *City Limits* proclaiming 'a milestone for both Asian theatre in Britain and for Tara whose refreshing approach can only be an inspiration to others' (Kalsi 1986).

The Little Clay Cart (1991)

The Little Clay Cart opened on 5 December 1991 at the Cottesloe Theatre. It heralded the return of Tara to the National Theatre after the success of *Tartuffe* (1990) and led some critics to express the hope that the 'National theatre under Richard Eyre is becoming more truly national [...] attempting to reflect the cultural variety of modern Britain' (Billington 1991). It was notably the first time in the history of the Royal National Theatre that an Indian classical play had been performed on one of its stages with an Asian director. On this production,

Jatinder Verma collaborated with Ranjit Bolt who provided additional verse and songs.

The critical reaction was cautious but on the whole positive to the 'other' content and form of *Miti Ki Gadi*. It was led by Charles Spencer in the *Telegraph* who had 'feared an inaccessible museum piece [...] but [...] turns out to be wonderfully fresh and inviting... [creating] an enchanting world of its own, full of colour, humour, amazing co-incidences and beguiling innocence' (1991).

A notable element of this production of *The Little Clay Cart* was its employment of two Irish actors, Stanley Townsend who played Sansthanaka and J. D. Kelleher who played Sharvilaka, the burglar, in the cast as well as an Irish musician. This gave rise to the rhetorical question posed in the play 'what do you get if you marry a paddy with a paki' (Verma and Bolt 1991b). The rationale given by Jatinder Verma to answer this question and justify a casting policy that was at odds with the 'all-Asian' tenant of 'Binglish' methodology was that Tara 'see ourselves in the context of a series of marginalities' (Verma quoted in Cook 1991b: 6) and therefore were happy to draw a parallel between Irish and Asian experience. Indeed, Jatinder Verma wanted to 'look for connections between the two cultures, Indian and Celtic' (Verma quoted in Lewis 1991).

The premise that justified Jatinder Verma's artistic and political analogy between the non-white and white historically marginalised minority was that 'there are many connections across the centuries [...] Indian and Irish independence movements inspired each other [...] Celtic mythology has many similarities with Indian legend' (Verma quoted in Cook 1991b: 6). However, Jatinder Verma's desire of 'transfusing the spirit of classical Indian theatre through the bodies and voices of Asian and Irish actors in Britain today' (Verma quoted in Hiley 1991) was met with one critic's response 'whatever for?' (Kingston 1991). This response may be read as a reaction against the overtly political provenance of this version of *The Little Clay Cart* that became a locus of solidarity between Asian and Irish colonial histories.

Stanley Townsend, in an interview with Jim Hiley for *The Late Show* filmed during rehearsals for *The Little Clay Cart*, talked of the difference between his own theatrical approach which he categorised as a 'theatre of language' and that of Jatinder Verma's which he saw as a 'theatre of image'. He described how the director, Jatinder Verma, was more interested in finding 'a posture for a character, he wants a physicalisation of a character [...] before you intellectually or emotionally examine a character' (Townsend quoted in Hiley 1991), in line with the 'Binglish' methodology privileging the physical over the psychological.

Jatinder Verma used the programme as a didactic tool to locate the theatrical provenance of the 'Binglish' performance in the *Natyasastra* with its 'unashamed avoidance of "realism" and [...] emphasis on weav ing speech, movement, music, narrative, costume and make-up into one syncretic "text"' (Verma 1991c). To this end the actors were again taught a classical Indian movement vocabulary by Shobana Jeyasingh, focused in this production on the form of *Bharata Natyam*, to punctu ate their movement and create characters that resulted in 'the acting [being]...uniformly stylised' (St. George 1991). This Asian movement vocabulary was effectively realised by a 'Saddam-like Stanley Townsend whose gross brutalities are expressed through a movement vocabulary of the most intricate delicacy' (Wardle 1991). However, the 'Binglish' conventions of the actors playing a number of roles and not leaving the stage did trouble some critics who noted that supporting characters were 'confusingly [...] played by principles doubling without leaving the set or changing clothes' (Hassell 1991).

The theatrical, and indeed political, problem of how a white, albeit Irish, actor plays an Asian character without being subsumed within a racist discourse was addressed by the hybrid 'Binglish' methodol ogy, which maintained the differentiation between actor and character meant that the actor is not attempting, in a Stanislavskian[3] way, to 'be' the character but rather is presenting the character. Furthermore, the hybrid 'Binglish' text incorporated not only Asian languages alongside English but also Gaelic.

The effect of incorporating this linguistic cultural difference into the text as a means of contesting the centrality of English was not wholly appreciated by some critics who found that when the Irish actors 'lapse periodically into Irish brogue [...] presumably [...] to explore the sensi bilities of marginal groups [...] the effect is cheap and irritating and fails to convey any serious purpose' (Milne 1991). However, I would dispute Michael Coveney's assessment of the 'reverse colour blind casting (i.e. a couple of whites among blacks) which suggests we are further along the road of racial integration that it is often claimed' (Coveney 1992) as the 'Binglish' performance is culturally provocative precisely because it does not ignore difference but is based on theatrically incorporating it into performance.

What is clear is that critics had begun to recognise the theatrical chal lenge of Tara's 'Binglish' productions such as *Tartuffe* and *The Little Clay*

Cart and sent out a warning that 'a few more shows like this and western linear theatre will start looking primitive' (Wardle 1991).

'Binglishing' the European classics

I have discussed *Miti Ki Gadi* at some length as it heralded the creation of a performer-training methodology as well as an innovative performance form of the 'not quite English' 'Binglish' that has subsequently underpinned the work of Tara Arts since that time. Initially, Jatinder Verma developed his 'Binglish' methodology through his work with Dr Anuradha Kapur, an Associate Professor at the National School of Drama in New Delhi, who was a specialist in Indian folk theatre, especially the Ram Lila folk form of Benares. He identified and drew upon what he saw as the four major elements common to Indian folk theatres, the chorus, the *sutradhar* [narrator], the *yavanika* [curtain] and the mask that creates a 'theatre that does not lay exclusive emphasis on spoken words as the *only* language of communication, but rather seeks to extend theatre's bounds in this country by incorporating other dramatic languages of movement, song, music, mask, mime' (Verma 1985a: 1).

From the late 1980s, Tara began to approach 'classical' European playwrights, employing their 'Binglish' methodology so that their productions were focused on 'viewing Gogol, Buchner, Molière, Shakespeare, Sophocles, Chekhov, Brecht through Asian eyes and ears' (Verma 1998b: 129).

Tartuffe (1990)

Tara Arts' production of *Tartuffe*, which was first performed on 19 April 1990 at the Cottosloe Theatre, was notable for a number of reasons not least of which were that Jatinder Verma became 'the first of the current generation of Asians to be invited to direct at The National [and that] . . . an all-Asian cast was seen for the first time at the Royal National' (Verma 1998b: 130).

Molière's *Tartuffe*

Orgon, a rich man, is duped into believing Tartuffe is a very pious and religious man and invites Tartuffe into his house and

---

becomes his patron. Orgon orders everyone in his household to obey Tartuffe as he does not realise he is a hypocrite. Orgon decides that his daughter Mariane should marry Tartuffe, even though she is in love with another, Valere. Meanwhile Tartuffe attempts to seduce Elmire, Orgon's wife. Elmire finally proves to her husband that Tartuffe has been trying to seduce her – but it is too late. Tartuffe has some incriminating letters belonging to Orgon and orders him and his family out of the house. However, all ends happily due to the intervention of the King; Tartuffe is put in prison and Orgon and his family return home.

In order that Tara's 'translation' of a classic European text was not simply perceived as superficial exoticism, Tartuffe simply becoming 'Tartuffe-ji', Jatinder Verma attempted to make 'connections' between European and Asian cultural traditions at the time the play was set. These were clearly identified in this extract of Jatinder Verma's production notebook for *Tartuffe*:

I am setting out to translate a seventeenth century French farce through an all-Asian company of performers. This entails a double translation: once from the French original to English; and secondly to English spoken by Asian actors, who have their own history of the acquisition of English speech. In other words, who are themselves 'translated' men and women – in that they (or their not-too distant forebears) have been 'borne across' from one language and culture to another. In order then to lay bare the full dimension of 'translation', I must take account of the specificity of my performers (their history): by conveying Molière's original play text into a form that allows the performers to make creative connections between their ancestral traditions and their English present [. . .]

(Verma 1998b: 131)

These 'creative connections' were realised historically, theatrically and geographically in the production. Jatinder Verma was able to make a case for the transposition of the setting of *Tartuffe* from France to India as a result of his historical research, which led to him framing Molière's *Tartuffe* as a play within a play being performed at the court of the seventeenth-century moghul emperor, Aurangzeb, to a French traveller,

François Bernier. Bernier appeared as a character to whom *Tartuffe* was performed in 'translation' by the court poet Pandit Ravi Varma.

The logic of this was underpinned by Jatinder Verma's research, detailed in *In Contact With the Gods* (1996a), during which he found a number of letters written by Bernier, a French traveller and compatriot of Moliére's, who wrote a letter while visiting the Moghul Court in India describing the nefarious activities of the fakirs who accept gifts and attempt to seduce the women of the house. There were also religious equivalents as 'Louis XIV was a religious monarch...[and] had perpetrated massacres against Protestants...[and] Arungzeb was doing the same against Hindus' (Verma quoted in Reade 1990). Indeed, these connections were also made structurally so that Ayub Khan-Din played both the emperor and Orgon in order to highlight the theme of religious hypocrisy as a critique of Arungzeb's well-documented intolerance for any faith other than Islam.

The play within a play ends with Orgon destitute and turned out of his own home. Ayub Khan-Din then uses a mask to change into the character of the emperor and tell the poet that even though 'we commend your play [...] the ending is not to our liking [...] inscribe another one' (Verma 1990a: 31). The poet dutifully relents by making the end of the play a eulogy to 'an Emperor who has declared war on falseness' (Verma 1990a: 3) and changes the story to save Orgon and his family from destitution.

Tara's all-Asian cast at the Royal National Theatre visually had the effect of foregrounding the company's cultural difference and challenging the audience's perceptions about the casting of a European play. However, the performance also drew on the particular hybrid cultural location of the Asian actor in Britain because 'had I used Indian actors in India we would not have been able to combine the elements of music hall tradition...[or] the slapstick of Groucho Marx [...] because that is not part of the imagination of the Indian actor [...] but it is [part of] the imagination of Asian actors in this country' (Verma 1990c).

In order to make a connection between the 'Binglished' *Tartuffe* and its original theatrical context Jatinder Verma drew on a form that was 'broadly derivative of Indian popular theatre conventions, most notably, *bhavai*, from Gujarat – a form that closely corresponds with *commedia dell' arte*, which influenced Molière' (Verma 1998b: 131). This comparison held because of the equivalence of stock characters in both genres as 'the commedia figure of the fool connects with both English tradition and the *vidushak* of Indian theatre' (Verma quoted in Hiley 1989a) as can be seen from his definition as a 'simpleton whose imbecility, real or assumed, is utilised for entertainment' (Varadpande 1979: 85).

Bhavai, a Gujarati folk theatre form, has been described as 'bawdy, raucous, obscene, satiric, poignant' (Brandon 1993: 81). The origins of *bhavai*, detailed in *The Cambridge Guide to Asian Theatre* (1993), are believed to date from the fourteenth century when Asiatar Thakar, a Brahmin, was expelled from his caste for eating with a woman from a lower caste. The Brahmin with no other means of income turned to writing and performing plays and in this respect carries the 'outsider' ethos now espoused by Tara Arts. *Bhavai* performances would normally be made up of several *vesas* (plays) performed through acting, dance and song. The *vesas* would only provide the basic storyline, with the actors having license to improvise dialogue and songs as well as addressing contemporary issues in the performance.

Jatinder Verma insisted he had 'taken elements of *bhavai* folk theatre [...] but there is no way this can be said to be a *bhavai* piece' (Verma quoted in Rea 1990), not least as it remained true to Molière's original in terms of plot, rather than being made up from a number of *vesas*. However a number of key theatrical elements have been combined into the 'Binglish' performance such as the use of song, bawdy jokes, actors playing stock characters and dance, which drew on *Kathak* and the folk *Garba* dance, as well as the ritual of bringing the elephant god Ganesha on stage prior to the performance. There was also the use of music as a means of differentiating characters, used to particular effect in *Miti Ki Gadi* through 'the rhythmic timing marked by drums and cymbals' (Zarilli et al. 1990: 244).

At the opening of *Tartuffe* a *rangapuja*, 'ritual of worshipping the stage, theatre' (Varadpande 1979: 73), took place at which the name of Ganesha was invoked.

> Gaao ganapati devhumrey
> 'Come Ganesha grace our play'.
>
> (Verma 1990a: 3)

The performance of *Tartuffe* began as one of the actors appeared in the mask of Ganesha. This was drawn from Asian performance tradition in which 'prayers are offered to Ganesha for the successful completion of the performance' (Varadpande 1979: 72). Verma admitted that the opening ritual was 'not strictly speaking from Indian theatre [...] it's my idea of a ritual [...] it may be a prayer or a salutation [...] but there has to be a gentle way to bring the audience in' (Verma quoted in Lustig 1990: 16). This concept was drawn from the *Natyasastra*, which listed 18 separate possible *purvaranga* (preliminaries) that may be taken prior to performance to 'provide a gradual bridging between the world of the audience and that of the play' (Brandon 1993: 68); these include a benediction and prologue that were performed in *Tartuffe*.

However, there was also another powerful and contradictory effect, created by the play opening with this 'tranquil ritual' (Lustig 1990: 16) that provocatively challenged the cultural assumptions of the audience.

'Whenever the play began I would never fail to hear people saying "This is Molière? I thought we had come to see Molière", and they would open their programmes and say, "No, they are all Indian names." The first sight that greeted them was this bunch of darkies, beautifully costumed, terribly lush, and coming out to the strains of some Eastern flute and speaking in Urdu, which of course devastated people: "What the hell are they saying? Indeed, are they saying anything?"' (Verma 1996b: 286).

'Binglish' language

A number of Asian language words in the text were not immediately translated but the sense was still largely apparent from the vocal or physical expression with which it was delivered or from a subsequent translation, as the following exchange between Tartuffe and Orgon demonstrates. In this scene Tartuffe shows mock humility in the face of Tameez's insults that he is a 'faking fakir' (Verma 1990a: 17) in order to deceive Orgon:

> TARTUFFE: [...] 'Call me Neech [Low Life], Traitor, Chor [Thief], Thief, Goonda [Thug], criminal, cover me with names more vile, I will deserve them all. I welcome, on my knees, this disgrace.'
> ORGON: No. Tartuffe-ji. No (*To Tartuffe*) Utho [Get up] – Please rise. Tartuffe-ji (*To Tameez*) Haraam-zade! [Bastard]
>
> (Verma 1990a: 18)

There were also intertextual references, in the following example drawing on the myth of Heer and Ranja, which holds an equivalent position to *Romeo and Juliet* in Western popular imagination. Munmauji, the daughter of Orgon, is the melodramatic 'Heer' of the play:

MUNMAUJI: I see. Since you of all people will not help me, there is no other way (*Picks up phial*)
ZHORBAI: Stop acting like a love-torn Heer!

(Verma 1990a: 12)

They then go on to quote passages from *Heer Ranja* in Urdu:

MUNMAUJI: He sent me poems from the legend of Heer Ranjha
TAMEEZ: Tell me
MUNMAUJI: 'Tujhko paana zindagi hai, tujhko khona maut hai [To have you is life] tujhko khona maut hai' [To lose you is death]
TAMMEZ: Wah! You are the sunshine of my life!
MUNMAUJI: There's another – 'Yeh aagh meyri nahi [This is not my passion] duan hai meyra! [It is my prayer!]

(Verma: 12)

The word 'wah' spoken by Tameez is a particular Asian exclamation pronounced with a 'v' rather than 'w' sound and signifies that someone is getting above themselves.

Jatinder Verma described how the performance would play with the convention of translation so that when:

the verse-exchange in Urdu finished, one of the storytellers strode forward to address the audience: 'Another translation!', she declared '[...] by this stage of the performance, the convention having been well established, a murmur of recognition would ripple through the audience [...] pausing a moment, 'Why bother!' she'd say and run back to her position on stage, the house having erupted in laughter.

(Verma 1994a: 60)

When Almirah, Orgon's wife, attempted to unmask Tartuffeji's hypocricy by seducing him she spoke to him in verse, which the storyteller then tells us is 'from the great Sanskrit love-poet Bhartrhari' (Verma 1990a: 23). This poetry was spoken in English and self-consciously cited as Verma attempted to make the audience aware that Molière's original was in 'play' with 'other' Asian texts.

The intellectual coherence of the connections were recognised by the critics and exemplified in the view that 'Mr Verma's all-Asian production has a perfect logic to it' (Billington 1990) giving credence to Jatinder Verma's belief that 'it works to take a French play and see it from an Asian point of view [...] and say [...] this is as much part of the national culture as a more conventional view of Molière' (Verma quoted in Rea 1990). Furthermore, the production's satiric attack on religious bigotry resonated with wider cultural concerns after a *fatwah*[4] was placed on Salman Rushdie in the wake of *The Satanic Verses*.

Rostand's original *Cyrano De Bergerac*

Cyrano, a gentleman soldier, is in love with Roxanne but dare not declare his love for her as he believes his extremely large nose means that she would not return his affection. Roxanne tells Cyrano that she is in love with Christian, who is a member of Cyrano's regiment. Cyrano composes letters for Christian with which he can win the love of Roxanne. As a result of Cyrano's help Christian successfully woos Roxanne and they are married. Cyrano and Christian are then sent to fight the Spanish and Christian is killed leaving a distraught Roxanne. Fifteen years later a mortally wounded Cyrano visits Roxanne in the convent where she has been mourning the death of Christian and delivers a last letter to her. His death leads Roxanne to realise that she has been in love with Cyrano all along.

Cyrano, first performed in the Cottesloe Theatre on 25 October 1995 was the next co-production with the National Theatre. The play was written by Jatinder Verma but directed by Anuradha Kapur, who had also directed Tara's adaptation of Gogol's *The Government Inspector, Ala Afsur* in 1990.

Cyrano was chosen by Jatinder Verma as part of his continuing engagement with European classics particularly because he felt that the play was 'a delicious fable about an outsider' (Verma quoted in Hoyle 1995), which dramatically keyed into the politics of the company. By now the critics were able to demonstrate their familiarity with the culturally hybrid nature of Tara's work in general and foregrounded this in reviews of *Cyrano* that had 'an Indian woman directing an ethnic Asian company in an English translation of a French play at the National [...]' (Wright 1995).

Rostand's grenadiers become a Parsi theatre company from Lucknow threatened with extinction, not by war, but by the newly developing Bombay film industry as the action is transposed from seventeenth-century France to India in the 1930s. Indian film star Naseeruddin

Shah, who played the title role, drew a parallel between the themes of Rostand's play and Bollywood cinema as with 'the sacrificing friend; the good looks versus the soul; the silent lover; these seem to touch an Indian sensibility' (Shah quoted in Wright 1995). Shah largely retained his film star looks as Cyrano with a 'proboscis that is prominent but far from grotesque' (Spencer 1995: 27) and which is likened among other things, to a *bindi*, in this 'Binglish' production.

Cyrano became Danmull Barchha, the company prompter, a job that appropriately reflected the character's role of putting words in the mouth of the lover, Kishan, whose looks exceeded his eloquence. The adaptation attempted to follow-through the theatrical parallels from Rostand's original as the object of Kishan's affection became Rukhsaan, a leading actress in a rival theatre company, and the villain, formerly the company commander, the Compte de Guiche, the theatre manager, Durgesh Prasad.

The parting of the lovers in this version was a result of Cyrano and Kishan being sent to make films in Bombay by the cinema-obsessed manager of the troupe, Prasad, while Rukhsaan confined herself to an ashram rather than a nunnery. When Kishan realised that Rukhsaan's love for him was based on Danmull poetry rather than his own virtues, he kills himself on the film set by deviating from his film script to enact the final scene from Othello in reality.

A number of critics perceived Kishan's demise as rather less heroic than the original Christian's doomed bravery in battle, and unlike *Tartuffe* and *Ala Afsur* (*The Government Inspector*), were unconvinced by Jatinder Verma's 'Binglish' relocation. Michael Billington titled his review 'cerebral brew's medium mix-up' (1995) while Martin Esslin worried that 'this kind of transportation of a classical text into a new mileau... [is] only justified if new insights can be derived from it [...] I fail to see that kind of gain' (1995). In this respect, the re-imagining of the action from a theatre of war, simply to the theatre, was widely criticised as 'a choice critically equivalent to a Dutch *Henry V* that involves the takeover of a tulip garden by British rose growers' (Nightingale 1995).

However, while Tara Arts' 'Binglish' productions of European and Asian classics gave Tara Arts 'a theatrical language for modulating with the centre' (Verma quoted in Cook 1991b: 6) and successfully carried them from the margins of British Theatre to the centre there was no doubt that the lukewarm critical response to *Cyrano* precipitated a change of direction. Indeed Tara were not to return to the National Theatre until 2009 with their adaptation of Hanif Kureishi's novel *The Black*

Album at the Cottesloe Theatre. This change of direction was further driven by a desire for Tara Arts to return to, and re-engage with, the constituent Asian community from which it had sprung, and had perhaps failed to carry with them. The result would be the creation of a postcolonial 'Binglish' epic trilogy of plays entitled *Journey to the West* (2002), which will be discussed in Chapter 7.

4
Tamasha Theatre Company 1989: Authenticity and Adaptation

Tamasha Theatre Company

Kristine Landon-Smith and Sudha Bhuchar founded Tamasha Theatre Company in 1989 and since that time have produced over 19 new productions of great diversity from adaptations of Asian novels, Bollywood musicals, verbatim theatre and intercultural performance as well as their critically acclaimed hit *East is East* (1996) that was subsequently made into a feature film. This chapter will focus on the company's genesis and three key aspects of their practice: the adaptation of novels set in India such as *Untouchable* (1989), *House of the Sun* (1991) and *A Fine Balance* (2006), the research-based methodology exemplified in *Balti Kings* (2000) and their experimentation with intercultural performance in *Women of the Dust* (1992).

The ambitious brief espoused in Tamasha's creative mission statement was to 'reflect through theatre the Asian experience' (Bhuchar and Landon-Smith 1998b). This 'Asian experience' did not limit itself geographically to Britain but ranged from 'British Asian life to authentic accounts of aspects of life in the Indian sub-continent' (ibid.). Although Kristine Landon-Smith and Sudha Bhuchar had met while working as actors with Tara Arts at Tamasha they adopted 'a British Western style of acting, naturalistic and realistic' (Bhuchar 1999d: 6). While the name of the company derives from the Hindi word 'Tamasha' meaning a show, spectacle or entertainment, it did not draw on the traditions of 'Tamasha' as a sixteenth-century Indian folk theatre form that utilised 'an amalgam of kathak classical dance techniques and indigenous folk dance' (Zarilli et al. 1990: 109) as well as song, music, improvised humour and stock characters. Indeed, their insistence that they were 'not trying to paint on a style and say this is the Tamasha style of acting' (Bhuchar 1999d: 6) could be read as a direct reference to the heightened vocal and physically stylised acting approach exemplified in Tara Arts' 'Binglish' productions.

The genesis of Tamasha Theatre Company in 1989 was the result of an intercultural exchange. Kristine Landon-Smith was invited to teach and direct the second-year students of the New Delhi National School of Drama under the auspices of the British Council. Rather ironically sponsored by the British Council as a *British* practitioner of theatre, she initially planned to mount a production of *The Seagull* by Anton Chekhov. Perhaps recognising that this choice was an implicit acceptance of an exclusively Eurocentric construction of British theatre, she decided on her journey to India to devise a performance piece based on the novel *Untouchable* by Mulk Raj Anand as she 'felt this would have many more reference points for the students' (Landon-Smith 1989). Furthermore, it allowed her to explore the possible intersections between herself as a British Asian director working with Asian performers in India.

Adapting the Asian novels: *Untouchable* (1989), *House of the Sun* (1991) and *A Fine Balance* (2006)

Untouchable (1989)

Untouchable follows a day in the life of 17-year-old Bakha, a *banghi* [sweeper] as he suffers the injustices that he and his family as members of the *dalit* caste endure. Bakha is not allowed to attend the school and his sister, Sohini, may not even draw water from the village well. Bakha is attacked by the whole village when he accidentally bumps into the *pandit* [priest] and when Sohini resists a sexual assault from the same *pandit* he accuses her of 'defiling' him. In order to be allowed to play in a hockey game Bakha has to pretend that he is 'Sahib's bearer' rather than a *bhangi*. The play closes with the visit of Gandhi to the village of Bulandshahar on his *Harijaans* [Children of God] tour. However, in spite of the visit, life for Bakha and his family goes on much as before.

Untouchable was a novel written and set in 1932 that highlighted the plight of the 'untouchable' caste in India. It should be recognised that the term 'untouchable' is now outmoded, insulting and discriminatory and has been replaced by *dalit* [oppressed]. The term *dalit* refers to someone who is not included in the four Hindu castes; *Brahmins* [Priests], *Kshatriyas* [Warriors], *Vaishayas* [Servants] and *Sudras* [Labourers] but are *panchjanahs* that became known as the 'untouchables'. Historically, Gandhi did indeed undertake a '*Harijaans* [Children of

God] tour' around India at that time that was aimed at discrediting the 'untouchable' status in conjunction with a fast against the practice of 'untouchability'. Kristine Landon-Smith used the novel as source material and devised a script through improvisation for a Hindi adaptation called *Achut [Sweeper]*. The reviews provide a sign of the importance Kristine Landon-Smith has attached since that time to achieving realism in acting and design, with *Achut* praised for its verisimilitude in 'capturing the environment and social background of the characters and their interaction' (Pandey 1988) and the set for its 'authenticity' (ibid.).

Kristine Landon-Smith and Sudha Bhuchar subsequently formed Tamasha Theatre Company in 1989 in order to reprise the play in Britain. *Untouchable* was first performed in Britain at the Riverside Studios, London, on the 4 December 1989 and heralded by the correspondent from *The Asian Times* as the arrival of 'an exciting new Asian theatre company' (1998). Their decision to stage the play in Hindi and English on alternate nights not only demonstrated the intercultural provenance of the play but also had the effect of attracting funding from the Greater London Arts and the Arts Council due to the bilingual nature of the project.

The subject of 'untouchability' was obviously culturally specific to India but Kristine Landon-Smith and Sudha Bhuchar were keen to make a political analogy between the position of the sweeper and that of the Asian migrant to Britain. While they stated in interview, 'Asians will recognise Bakha's situation as being similar to their own experiences as victims of racism' (Bhuchar and Landon-Smith 1989a), there was nothing in the text or performance to make that connection overt. However, it should also be noted that by addressing the subject of 'untouchability', Tamasha, like Tara Arts, demonstrated that they were not afraid to critique the Asian community and their culturally specific codes as well. Indeed, the production was very much from a subaltern perspective as Bakha, the child sweeper, was given centre stage so that the audience witnessed first hand the indignities of the 'sweeper' caste that may not draw water from the well, faced sexual harassment with no means of redress and were even ostracised from playing with other children. The play opened, appropriately enough, with a scene set in a toilet, representing the diverse views of different cultural groups in India to the subject of 'untouchability':

HINDU: The sahibs won't quit India and he's [Ghandi] fasting for the untouchables.
CHARAT SINGH: You don't understand what he's trying to do.

RAMANAND: They were born to serve us – and now Gandhi's upsetting the law of karma.

Chant – morning ritual

MUSLIM: If you people could, you'd get someone else to wash your hair for you – clean your teeth for you – nowhere in my religion does it say that someone is born to serve me. If our great prophet, peace be upon him, were here he wouldn't allow you to behave like this.

(Bhuchar and Landon-Smith 1999a: 9)

Untouchable (1989)
© Jenny Potter 1989.
Sudha Bhuchar playing Gulabo, a washerwoman, in *Untouchable*

The sympathies of the production were clear from the theatrical methodology that allowed Bakha to break with realist convention and breach the fourth wall after he has been beaten for accidentally touching and therefore 'defiling' a *pandit* (priest):

He receives the jalebis – wanders on – eats a jalebi – while he is looking around him, he collides with a Pandit

PANDIT: Haré Ram. Haré Ram. Are kutté. Are you blind? Couldn't you see me standing here? Why didn't you call, you swine, and announce your approach? Do you know you have touched me and defiles me, you cock-eyed son of a bow legged scorpion. Now I will have to go and take a bath to purify myself – on such an auspicious day with the Mahatma coming to town – this is a new dhoti and kurta I put on this morning.

(Bhuchar and Landon-Smith 1999a: 21)

This theatrical convention allowed Bakha's character to regain his position as the subject, rather than remaining a passive object of abuse, and explain his feelings to the audience unmediated. This he does powerfully with a series of rhetorical questions asking why he accepts such treatment and returning the stark answer 'Because we're sweepers – we touch shit, their shit' (Bhuchar and Landon-Smith 1999a: 22).

In order to create the sense of realism at the methodological heart of Tamasha's work the actors were already in place and in character as the audience entered the auditorium. The aim of the production to make the audience feel as if 'they are transported to an Indian village' (Correspondent 1989: 9) seemed to have been largely realised from the critical reaction that praised the 'authenticity clinging to both action and actors throughout the play' (Chaudhuri 1989). The specificity of this approach could be seen in the physicality of Bakha as he sat on his haunches and smoked a 'bidi', a crude form of cigarette rolled within a leaf; both the physicality of the actor and the 'bidi' that he was smoking culturally locating the South Asian site.

The critical reception in Britain to this Asian theatre company working in a recognisably Western acting approach was positive because 'the impression of people going about their daily affairs is remarkable' (Kingston 1989). The fact that *Untouchable* 'has a fine sense of detail which carries the audience willingly along an unfamiliar path' (Caplan 1998) suggested that Tamasha's realistic theatrical methodology made the Asian provenance of their work accessible to a non-Asian audience.

What particularly marked this production out as unique in terms of British Asian productions was the decision to perform the play in English and Hindi on alternate nights. Indeed, the Hindi production was a provocative performance of cultural difference as it was actively exclusionary to a non-Asian language speaking audience as opposed to Tara Arts' 'Binglish' approach discussed in Chapter 3. One critic who attended a Hindi performance felt that it is all 'very fine with one small proviso, if two languages are involved surely a synopsis would not be out of place in an otherwise well-documented programme' (Woddis 1989).

The 'English' version of *Untouchable* still aimed to represent the Indian locale as authentically as possible in the performance. Interestingly, the 'English' script was not simply a direct translation of the Hindi script but was linguistically hybrid as, 'in English we have tried to do the new language, streetwise without being Cockney, contemporary but with the regular Hindi phrases and rhythms' (Bhuchar 1990). This is exemplified in the very colloquial hybrid Hindi and English exchange between Lakha, the father, and his sleeping children:

> LAKHA: Bakha – are uth [get up] – come on, get up ma da chodh suer ke bache [mother-fucking son of a bitch]. Come on – you getting up or not? Get up you bastard or I'll give you a kick up the arse.
>
> (Buchar and Landon-Smith 1999a: 7)

The linguistic mixture of colloquial English phrases such as 'kick up the arse' playing off the Hindi colloquialism *'are uth'* [get up] effectively realised a hybrid form that mimicked the register in which these characters would speak Hindi.

Although Gandhi is heard appealing for an end to the oppression of the *dalits* in the play insisting that 'public wells, temples, roads, schools, sanatoriums must be declared open to the untouchables' (Bhuchar and Landon-Smith 1999a: 46), *Untouchable* closes on a pessimistic note with Bakha beaten by the community for daring, as an 'untouchable', to try and protect his sister from the *pandit*. This is underlined by the structural circularity of *Untouchable*, which is indicative of the repetitive oppression to be suffered by the protagonist, Bakha.

The reviews from the British press were very positive with *What's On* critic Khalid Javed praising 'an enlightening and arresting account of a life in the day of' (1989), *City Limits* highlighting it as a production 'presented in the round with great flair and immediacy' (Carole Woddis 1989) and Betty Caplan of the *Guardian* claiming that 'Tamasha deserve to be congratulated on its impressive debut' (1989). The Asian press were no less complimentary recognising 'an authenticity clinging to both action and actors throughout the play [...] attributed to the company's painstaking research for the set and prop design and its creative direction' (Chaudhuri 1989).

Tamasha's desire for 'authenticity' was developed further in their next production, another adaptation, *House of the Sun*, which premiered at Theatre Royal Stratford East on 12 April 1991. Kristine Landon-Smith and Sudha Bhuchar adapted *House of the Sun* from the novel by Meira Chand that took as its main theme cultural identity and diaspora and focused on the residents of the Sadhbela apartment block in Mumbai. The residents were primarily members of the Sindhi community who, as Hindus, were forced to flee their homeland around the Indus after partition when Sind became part of a predominantly Muslim Pakistan.

The director therefore believed the British Asian audience would make the connection not only with the Asian context but also with a play that was 'about a community of refugees coming into a host community' (Landon-Smith 1991: 21).

There was a notably large cast of 14 actors who played 28 characters, a rarity for a subsidised venue offering new work that was reflected in the comment of one critic who felt it 'a pleasure to see a stage crowded with actors for a change' (Caplan 1991). *House of the Sun* was episodic in structure with 30 short scenes constantly cutting between households in order to structurally interweave the stories of the inhabitants and accentuate the interconnectedness of their lives.

While the play was open to the complaint that, 'quality is lost by trying to interest us in so many characters' (Kingston 1991), this perhaps missed the point that although the story was a linear narrative it was the myriad relationships between the inhabitants and within the wider community that created the overall narrative tapestry of the piece. Perhaps the same reviewer's annoyance at the 'unwillingness of the characters to call each other by name' suggested an underlying insecurity of not being able to differentiate between this relatively large cast of Asian characters who were all on stage at once.

It was important to Sudha Bhuchar and Kristine Landon-Smith that the play would 'prove to be an authentic account' (Bhuchar and Landon-Smith 1991a) and this desire for 'authenticity' was evident from their working methodology. The process began with a three-week workshop in which they employed seven actors to improvise around the text to dramatise scenes from the novel. These improvisations were taped and transcribed as a basis for the final text. Sudha Bhuchar and Kristine Landon-Smith then arranged interviews with the Hindu Sindhi community in London and on the basis of these, and the actors' improvisations, produced a first draft of the play in October 1990. In order to address the geographical specificity of the work they then travelled to Mumbai to do further research with the Sindhi community.

Tamasha's naturalistic approach was underpinned by a remarkably realistic set that utilised the height as well as the width of the Theatre Royal Stratford East stage; it contained a working lift, stairs and screens that could slide up or down in order to cover or reveal the action. This allowed the audience to see into the block like an open dolls house and feel that they were eavesdropping on the lives of the inhabitants whose 'fourth wall' had, literally in this production, been removed.

Indeed, the company's performance methodology that used 'authentic' set design, in-depth research effectively combined with 'the improvisation afforded by Tamasha's semi-devised script lends each scene a sense of slice of life realism' (Feay 1991).

A Fine Balance (2006)

Dina Dalal is a widow trying to retain her independence from her financially supportive but overbearing, brother. She sets up a sowing business and employs itinerant tailors Ishvar and his nephew Om as well as taking in a student as a paying guest. The two tailors were forced to flee their village as a result of the persecution they had faced as 'untouchables'. The play was set in India in 1975 against the backdrop of the 'State of Internal Emergency' declared by the then prime minister, Mrs Gandhi. The Emergency has a direct impact on Ishvar and Om as they are left homeless as a result of 'slum' clearances, taken to a work camp and later rounded up and forcibly sterilised. In the meantime Dina is forced to take protection from the local gangster, the Beggarmaster, in order to stop her being evicted from her deceased husband's flat. However, this protection is short-lived as the Beggarmaster is murdered. Dina is forced to move back in with her brother and close her business leaving Ishvar and Om reduced to begging on the street.

Tamasha's adaptation of *A Fine Balance* (2006), Rohinton Mistry's Booker-shortlisted novel, followed previous adaptations, *Untouchable* (1989) and *House of the Sun* (1991), in dramatising life on the Indian subcontinent. *A Fine Balance* was first performed at Hampstead Theatre on 11 January 2006. Set in Bombay, India, between 1975 and 1977 during the turmoil of the 'State of Internal Emergency' presided over by Mrs Gandhi, the play follows the lives of Dina Dalal and her two itinerant tailors, Ishvar Darji and his nephew Omprakash, and her young boarder, Maneck.

A giant portrait of Mrs Gandhi dominated Sue Mayes' split-level set design that was linked by a ramp – Shankar, one of the beggars who had lost his legs, memorably skated up and down this ramp on his trolley. The programme listed the historical background to the 'Emergency' when from June 1975 to March 1977 India's president, Fakhruddin Ali Ahmed, declared a state of emergency and Article 352 of the Constitution was invoked for Mrs Gandhi to rule by decree. This resulted in a restriction of civil liberties and the suspension of judicial independence, allied to widespread illegal detentions and a programme of forced sterilisations as 'slum dwellers had to make way for bulldozers... [and] men and women were given transistor radios in return for their reproductive futures' (Khilnani 1997: 46); all of which was dramatised in the production. When Mrs Gandhi surprised commentators with the announcement of an election in March 1977 it did not deliver the democratic mandate she had expected; she and her son, Sanjay, were removed from office by the Janata Alliance and Moraji Desai became the new prime minister.

A Fine Balance
© Robert Day 2006.

Adapted by Sudha Bhuchar and Kristine Landon-Smith. Pictured in the foreground is Rehan Sheikh as Ishvar, behind him Amit Sharma as Omprakash and Sudha Bhuchar as Dina Dalal. Notice the 'working' sewing machines in Tamasha's determinedly realistic productions.

Tamasha's methodological decision to adapt the novel in the rehearsal room was criticised by Michael Billington of the *Guardian* in his review 'A history lesson, but where's the story' because, in his view, the production was 'a précis of a fine novel' but what was lacking was 'the organising skill of a master storyteller' (2006: 32). However, exercising her right to reply, in the same newspaper Kristine Landon-Smith gives some insight into the rationale for the company's process that privileged the actors' improvisations as much as the writers' skill:

> Sudha Bhuchar and I wrote this play in collaboration with our acting company, using a process that has been employed by many companies in Britain, Joint Stock and Complicité amongst them. I am only too aware of the pitfalls of bringing an epic novel to the stage: it is always a complex process, and one that demands the writer, in our case writers, to have a clear artistic vision of why the piece should be adapted in the first place.
>
> On first reading the novel, I knew it was the images, along with Rohinton Mistry's ability to juxtapose lyrically the personal stories with the political context of 1970s India, that I wanted to create for the theatre. I wanted to tell the story of an intimate relationship between four disparate characters trying to survive in troubling times, and life itself: a story of poorness of the rich and richness of the poor.
>
> Over the past year, Bhuchar and I were the 'mistress' storytellers examining how we could bring the images in the book to life. The actors improvised around the rehearsal text, bringing their cultural contexts to the work, and filling it with a detail, nuance and particular rhythm, as well as a unique perspective on India that could *only be found by employing this process.*
>
> (Landon-Smith 2006)

While Kristine Landon-Smith not only defends the process by placing Tamasha within the frame of established devising companies such as Shared Experience,[1] I would note her reference to the 'cultural context' of the actor.

She recently set out her approach to the issue of actor training and ethnicity in her speech 'Actor Training and Multiculturalism' at a conference on Asian theatre at Exeter University in which she recognised the imperative of locating the actor's cultural position, so that conceptually and practically she brings 'a given text to the performer [...] I don't ask the performer to reach out to the text' (2008). This practice was exemplified in the casting of Turkish actor Taylan Halici, who played the Beggarmaster in Tamasha's production of *A Fine Balance* (2007), in a part that had originally been played by an Asian actor in the 2006 production.

In this case, rather than Halici having to play the Asian character in the text Kristine Landon-Smith focused on 'bringing the given text to the actor' so that 'if I have a Turkish actor [Taylan Halici] in the rehearsal room and they are most comfortable in Turkish – we will probably spend the whole rehearsal period working in Turkish and capturing the spirit of the Turkish personality and then translate that back to the given text' (2008). In other words, the cultural context of the actor has a direct influence on the role.

The critical view expressed by the *Guardian* was shared by a number of commentators who found that the production was unable to find a theatrical register with which to capture the epic scale of the book so that 'incidents are crammed in and chronicled but not successfully moulded into dramatic shape nor brought to much of a climax' (Logan 2006). However the blame was largely pinned at the door of the devising methodology. It is clear that Tamasha's devising, research and rewriting process that had successfully been employed on *House of the Sun* to 'lend each scene a sense of slice of life realism' (Feay 1991) here struggled to realise a satisfactory dramatic structure. However, as with *House of the Sun*, the performances were praised, especially Sudha Bhuchar's 'stand out turn as Dina (Mountford 2006) as well as the company at large whose 'unforced performances and dialogue – from an uncredited script devised in the rehearsal room – create an evocative atmosphere' (Maxwell 2006).

Kristine Landon-Smith successfully realised some of the powerful images that had struck her so forcefully when reading the novel such as the 'positively sinister' (Mountford 2006) giant-sized portrait of Mrs Gandhi looking down as blindingly powerful headlights cut through the blackout and shine directly into the audience accompanied by a deafening soundtrack of heavy vehicles on the move. Perhaps most striking were the evocations of the sterilisation camp made up of huge white sheets hung as tents in which the brutal castration of Om was carried out in silhouette.

The production also utilised puppetry manipulated by Lindy Wright of a dog, a monkey and a little girl. In one memorable scene that exemplified the daily cruelties practiced in order to survive in the city the little puppet girl is put on top of a ten foot pole by her uncle, Monkeyman, who is a beggar, and swung round for 20 rupees:

MONKEYMAN: What's wrong she enjoys it. Like being on a merry go round. You call me *badmash*? [villain]

(Bhuchar and Landon-Smith 2007a: 34)

However, the end of the production leaves us in no doubt that Dina's belief that the Emergency was only something that affected the poor and dispossessed could not have been more misplaced. Indeed, characters such as Nusswan, Dina's brother, suggest that Mrs Gandhi's slum clearances and forced sterilisations had many supporters who believed that 'thanks to our visionary leader and her beautification programme this city will be restored to its former glory' (37). The production attempted to show us 'with a sense of painful but unhysterical reality' (Peter 2007) the personal cost of the belief that held that a large swathe of the population was expendable.

While Time Out felt that the production was 'a poor man's version of the original' Tim Walker in the Sunday Telegraph was very positive about 'an important and challenging piece of theatre' and the New Statesman's Rosie Millard praised the productions' storytelling ability, comparing it to 'the calm assurance of someone paying out the line of a kite' (2007).

The final scene of the play, set nine years after the assassination of Mrs Gandhi in 1984, is signified in the production by the lowering of her towering portrait. Her Sikh bodyguards killed Mrs Gandhi in retaliation for her ordering the storming of the holy Sikh shrine, The Golden Temple, in Amritsar. The Indian Government believed that the temple was a haven for Sikh extremists who had taken refuge in the temple and Mrs Gandhi launched 'Operation Blue Star' in order to remove them. The provocative operation, detailed in Mark Tully and Satish Jacob's book *Amritsar*, resulted in the death of 493 people according to official figures and inflamed the sensibilities of the Sikh community that led directly to the assassination of Mrs Gandhi.

While Dina has had to return to live in her brother's house and is treated like an unpaid servant she still remains in contact with Ishvar and Om who are now begging on the street. The play finishes on an optimistic note, even though they find themselves in straitened circumstances, as their friendship endures and their determination to survive remains undimmed.

Balti Kings (1999)

The play is set over one day in Shakeel's Restaurant as the owner, Yahsin, and his two sons, Shakeel and Shahab, prepare to beat their rivals in the Birmingham curry wars, Karachi Karahi. They have planned an innovative 'Curryoke' night complete with Bollywood stars in attendance and a 35-dish 'all you can eat' Balti banquet. However things do not go according to plan as Billa, the head chef, threatens to defect to a rival restaurant and the Bolly-wood stars promised to launch the event turn out to be lookalikes from the *Imposters* agency. However, all comes right in the end as the warring brothers make up, the lookalikes and food win over the diners and the evening is a great financial success.

Sudha Bhuchar explained that *Balti Kings* grew out of her recognition that 'in this country everyone likes Indian food, but nobody stops to think who makes it' (Bhuchar quoted in Arnot 2000), and was in line with Tamasha's aim to reveal the 'hidden stories' of the Asian community in Britain.

The source material for *Balti Kings* was the Ladypool Road in Birming-ham where it was alleged that the *balti*, rather unromantically meaning 'bucket' in Punjabi, was invented. In order to authentically dramatise these 'hidden lives' Kristine Landon-Smith, Sudha Bhuchar, co-writer Shaheen Khan and the designer Sue Mayes conducted interviews in a number of restaurants in the area with the chefs, waiters, owners and customers who worked and ate there. Their main research took place in one of the first *balti* houses in Sparkbrook, the Royal Al-Faisal, which opened in the mid 1970s.

We went in to these restaurants and asked these very personal ques-tions and we got these looks like who are the hell are you [...] and why should we answer these ask questions and they [...] thought we were from Inland revenue or the Home Office or had something to do with social security and we had to really try and win their confi-dence ... and say we are just two writers who are interested in their lives [...] where do you live, how do you live [...] are you married [...] are you single what are your wages [...] obviously as writers that is the material we want to get [...]
(Bhuchar, Khan and Landon-Smith 1999a)

Sudha Bhuchar described the process of moving from the research to creating the text:

> You also had to make that leap into it being a piece of fiction [...] one of the areas [...] we found quite painstaking [...] I mean we are both women and we were writing about a very traditional male patriarchal world and that was very difficult finding these voices [...] how these people speak [...] what their emotions were [...] how they relate to each other [...] but one of the devices that Shaheen and I use when we get stuck and also to fill in back stories because we were actresses [...] we would improvise.
>
> (Bhuchar, Khan and Landon-Smith 1999a)

The director Kristine Landon-Smith would then give these created characters to the actors and 'hot seat' them – i.e. ask them questions to which they would respond in character – as she believes it is methodologically both 'an imaginative way to begin the exploration of the character [...] and of drawing information from the actor' (1999).

The way in which the director developed the 'hot seat' exercise was evident from the rehearsal filmed by the company for the 'Making of the Balti Kings' promotional video. In the rehearsal were the two actors playing Shahab, the owner of the restaurant and Nadim, a waiter. The director first spoke to the actor playing Shahab and asked him how he deals with the staff to which he retorts that the staff are lazy. The actor playing Nadim then joined in the conversation and complained to the director of the low pay and poor working conditions he and the staff had to endure. The two characters then began to argue with each other, showing how, as Kristine Landon-Smith says, 'we can very easily move from a hot seat and suddenly turn it into a scene [...] you can begin to see how you relate to each other' (1999).

One of the exercises that the director employed to begin to integrate the movement of a working kitchen into the scene was to have the actors play their dialogue while carrying out their character's culinary tasks at the same time.

'I'm just going to give you numbers 1, 2, 3, 4, 5 and when I call out our number I want you do one cross in the kitchen, get something, bring it back [...] might be to check a saucepan [...] but give it a logic'.

(Landon-Smith 1999)

The first draft of *Balti Kings* was showcased in Edinburgh in August 1999 then opened at Birmingham Repertory Theatre on 15 September 1999, prior to a national tour. In order to make manifest the realistic performance methodology strived for by Tamasha, the actors were aided by a very realistic and 'working' – to the extent that the gas hobs worked – kitchen set by Sue Mayes.

Balti Kings (2000)

© Jenny Potter 2000.

Pictured above, chef Billa, played by Kriss Dosanjh, attempting to keep the peace. To his right Indira Joshi playing samosa-maker Khalida; to his left Ameet Channa playing dutiful son Shakeel; and in front Nabil Elouahabi playing 'entrepreneur' Shahab.

During the play, which is performed in the round, the actors actually chopped and peeled vegetables, made samosas and cooked on the stoves. Kristine Landon-Smith's production tried to get the audience as close as possible, literally, to the 'world' of a *balti* kitchen as 'spices fill the air ... [and] ... the tomatoes are slopped into vats on a stove almost splattering the audience on that side' (Walsh 2000).

> *Yacoub divides the spinach in the other karahi, keeps half aside in the second karahi that Nadim has brought and adds paneer to the one that's cooking, we have a short accelerated choreographed sequence where the cooking is done and three real dishes, chicken tikka massala, spinach lamb balti and Rogan josh get cooked and put into domes. At the end of the sequence dialogue resumes. (38)*

The reviews focused positively on the set and acting with Jane Edwardes in *Time Out* recognising 'the smells of Indian cooking are as winningly authentic as the humanity of the characterisations' and Charles Spencer in the *Telegraph* pointing out the 'acting has a superb understated naturalism' (2000). However, there were once more concerns about the script which is seen as, in general, being 'a bit aimless, as if it's enough just to present the people on stage' (Edwardes 2000).

While, as we have seen, a great deal of the research carried out by Shaheen Khan and Sudha Bhuchar was conducted in Punjabi, they were praised by one commentator, their 'skill as writers has been to turn this knockabout street language in to English that Asians can believe in yet can also be clearly understood by the whites in the audience' (Arnot 2000: 14).

> NADIM: Mujhe maaf kar do Billa bhai (I am sorry Billa, my brother)
> BILLA: Why are you asking me for forgiveness?
>
> (Bhuchar and Khan 1999: 59)

Apart from Muslim greetings such as *Walaikum Salaam* and *Salaam Alaikum* the text was predominantly in English. While the second generation sons of the owner, Shakeel and Shahab, spoke with slight Birmingham accents but 'good' English syntax, the language of the Pakistani waiter, Yacoub, was differentiated from this through his use of English colloquialisms such as 'ennet', a variation on the west London colloquialism 'innit':

YACOUB: Bet your leg don't stop you climbing over the goris [white women], ennet?

(Bhuchar and Khan 1999: 17)

and ungrammatical syntax:

YACOUB: When me mini cabbying, me taking Anil Kapoor to Aston university. Me get him there on time but he want me to take him round and round spaghetti junction. When I ask why, he say if people want you they waiting.

(Bhuchar and Khan 1999: 47)

Balti Kings was not a 'culture clash' comedy and the generational differences between the owner and his sons were more concerned with Shahab's attempt to restore the fortunes of the restaurant with Bollywood stars while his father extolled the virtues of 'Lloyd Grossman [...] who could be more famous than him?' (Bhuchar and Khan 1999: 21). The brothers at the centre of the drama were Shakeel, the dutiful son who respected the staff and his father, and Shahab, the 'entrepreneur' ne'er-do-well whose Bollywood lookalikes failed to show for the party. However, all family strife is resolved by the end of the play as the 'Curryoke' night is a success after all, the restaurant is saved and Shahab, rather sentimentally, gets his wish 'to make dad proud' (51).

There were some gently humorous cultural observations at the expense of English diners who order 'only individual small ones' [dishes] – as opposed to the Asian diners who share – and their desire for *Balti*:

KHALIDA: Balti, Balti these Whiteys are crazy after Balti. What is Balti huh? Bucketl In Jhelum where we come from horses eat out of Balti ennet? (3)

Balti Kings attempted to convey the economic reality for the low-paid workers such as Yacoub, whose boss tells him 'I could replace you (*clicking fingers*) like that [...] there's people coming every day begging for work' (29). A further interesting insight into *balti* kitchen life was explored through the characters of Miriam and Isaac, two Bosnian refugees. Perhaps surprisingly, the research revealed that there were a large number of Eastern Europeans working in Indian restaurants in Birmingham. While there is religious solidarity between the Bosnians and Asians, as the owner tells Miriam 'we're all fellow Muslims' (22) the play was prepared to look at the controversial topic of the exploitation of migrants by Asians as Miriam was made pregnant, and then disowned, by the cousin of the cook, Nadim.

While we subsequently find out that the mother of Isaac and Miriam, the Bosnian Muslim workers, was killed in the former Yugoslavia by Serb gunmen, this discussion is not developed. Miriam's situation is rather too conveniently resolved by Shakeel giving her the money from the karaoke evening and declaring his love for her. In this way *Balti Kings* matches its famous theatrical relative *The Kitchen*,[2] by Arnold Wesker for authenticity rather than its political imperative.

An intercultural experiment

Women of the Dust (1992)

Asha is expecting her first child and longs to return to her mother in the village in time for the birth. However, she is working as a labourer on a building site with her husband, Mohan, and does not have the money to buy her ticket. Two middle class sisters, Nisha and Mohini, arrive at the site to collect a donation from the owner of the yard for their charity aimed at helping the female labourers. The play ends as Mohini addresses a glamorous fundraising event and lectures the audience on the plight of the poor in India while Asha's mother waits in vain for her to arrive at her village.

Women of the Dust was first performed at the Bristol Old Vic Studio on 7 October 1992, then at the Riverside Studios in London. The subsequent tour to India in 1993 not only marked the first international tour for Tamasha but also an extraordinary intercultural event in which a British Asian theatre company from Britain were to perform a piece of theatre based on Asian women's experience in India for an Indian audience. This raised the methodological problem of performing a play about Asian women in India to a British/British Asian audience. Indeed, an examination of the 'tamasha' [commotion] created offstage, as well as on, by the production exposes the problems inherent in the methodological desire for 'authenticity' and the politics of representation on the hybrid site of British Asian performance.

The story of the women who leave their villages for half the year to work as migrant labour in the cities of India was well suited to the company's creative brief at that time to produce 'new writing based on factual research of a particular subject or community' (Bhuchar and Landon-Smith 1992a). The hybrid definition of Tamasha as a *British* Asian theatre company performing a play about women from the Indian subcontinent in India starts to become evident when we see that in Britain they were viewed as an Asian theatre company, however, in India, *Women of the Dust* was reviewed as 'A British Portrayal Of Indian Lives' (Staff Reporter 1994).

Sudha Bhuchar and Kristine Landon-Smith's third production, *Women of the Dust*, was commissioned and funded by Oxfam to commemorate their 50th anniversary. Although Tamasha were able to choose the subject matter, the proviso was that it should be related to the type of work that Oxfam were doing in India. The choice of subject for the play came about when Sudha Bhuchar met with photographer Sunil Gupta who had been working in India and saw the photographs he had taken 'of these women in their rural Rajastani breaking stones' (Bhuchar 1999d). For the first time, Sudha Bhuchar and Kristine Landon-Smith worked with another, non-Asian and non-Asian speaking, writer, Ruth Carter. While the fact that Ruth Carter was not Asian was not a problem of principle for the company, who unlike Tara, 'had never given [themselves] the boundary that we would only have an Asian writer' (Bhuchar 1999d) it did have methodological implications.

The research-based methodology focused on preparing a text for a British audience based on interviews conducted by Sudha Bhuchar, Kristine Landon-Smith and Ruth Carter in the village of Tilonia, Ajmar district in India. The interviewees told them that the land in Ajmar district was insufficiently productive to meet their needs, so for half the year villagers travelled as itinerant labour to building sites all over India; the play was set on one such building site in Delhi. Sudha Bhuchar interviewed the women in a mixture of Hindi and the local dialect and then she translated these conversations for the writer Ruth Carter. They used dictaphones to record the interviews verbatim and as a result of Ruth Carter not being a Hindi speaker, Sudha Bhuchar recounted how she 'would constantly say to me can you ask this, can you ask that' (Bhuchar 1999d).

After the interviews they would both go through the tapes listening not only to *what* the women said in terms of content and syntax but also crucially *how* they said it in terms of pitch, pace, intonation and musicality. From the following extract it can be seen that this detailed research methodology revealed both the 'what' and the 'how' in the speech of the women's Rajastani dialect that the production wanted to capture in order to attempt an 'authentic' portrayal:

> We recorded the women speaking a dialect of Rajistani, and we tried to do that not just in the writing but in the way we delivered it. It was nasal, it was higher [...] for instance they would all be talking over noise [...] it was kind of shouted [...] we tried to capture the speech and it's not always putting in odd Indian words [...] the women talked very different from urban speech [...] if you ask them are you hungry [...] they would say something like 'is the sky blue', 'does the camel carry water', it was littered with metaphors.
>
> (Bhuchar 1999d)

This research took four weeks in October 1991 and was followed on their return to Britain by a two-week workshop. On returning to London Kristine Landon-Smith faced the methodological problem of how 'you transpose the rhythms and cadences of an indigenous dialect into English without sacrificing a crucial degree of credibility' (Subramaniam 1994). The director's approach was to apply the research findings to a practical performance methodology by working on the vocal technicalities of voice projection, language structure, pitch and rhythm gleaned from the taped interviews with the Rajastani women. The actors were encouraged to attempt to imitate the sound of the speech for example by 'widening the lips and touching the soft palette lightly to the tongue to create a flatter strident tone' (Landon-Smith 1999d). While this hybrid English counterpart or version of the 'real' Rajastani speech was certainly viewed as 'authentic' to a non-Asian speaking British audience, that would not be the case when they performed in Delhi.

Designer Sue Mayes created an extremely realistically building site complete with a working cement mixer. The director exploited the set 'that leaves little to the imagination [...] cement mixer, trays of bricks' (Lawson 1992) by having the actors realistically perform tasks such as climbing ladders, carrying bricks and mixing cement.

The British critical reaction did not, perhaps unsurprisingly, focus on the 'authenticity' of the hybrid language painstakingly created by Tamasha for the building workers. Indeed, apart from remarking aesthetically on the 'sing song cadences of the women's speech' (Curtis

Women of the Dust (1992)
© Jenny Potter 1992.
Shobu Kapoor pictured mixing cement. (Note the 'working' cement mixer.)

1992), the production was largely praised for its documentary realism that created a 'credible slice of life' (Armitstead 1992). In terms of authenticity it was pointed out by an Indian critic that 'in the case of a British audience [...] their unfamiliarity with Rajasthani inflections [...] would serve to authenticate the cadences and characterisations as "real"' (Arora 1994). In Britain it was, wrongly, assumed that British Asian actors would provide an 'authentic' depiction of Indian women from the subcontinent

Women of the Dust was no polemic on behalf of the *mazdoors* [building workers] and was criticised for 'political timidity' (Armitstead 1992). Mohini, the middle class social worker, defended her fundraising activity on the grounds that when 'a starving child holds out its hand do you question the credentials of the benefactor' (Carter 1999a: 49). However, the fact that the 'benefactor' was the owner of the building site where the *mazdoors* work in such squalid conditions was clearly identified although not scrutinised. Indeed, while the women were sympathetically portrayed as they coped bravely and stoically with the hardships of their lives the play provided a platform for apologists of the women's situation.

The contractor's assertion that, 'the muzdoors are cheap labour [...] and they prefer to stay cheap' (Carter 1999a: 27) in order that they were not replaced by machines went unchallenged and was resolved by the politically apathetic rationale that 'India is a very poor country [...] for every solution you come up with two and a half more problems arise' (Carter 1999a: 27). The contractor may have been correct that 'India is polluted with saviours' (Carter 1999a: 26) but Tamasha were in danger of a 'romanticisation of the ethnic and the oppressed' (Pestonji 1994) as the play focused on the cultural exoticism of their intercultural subject.

Women of the Dust ended on a fatalistic note as the rains failed once more and Asha's mother, Charu, vainly waited by the roadside of her village for Asha to arrive to have the baby. The final refrain of 'Let the rains come' that peppered the villagers' final speeches suggested that the salvation to their situation was beyond their control and, indeed, the vision of the playwright.

In terms of taking *Women of the Dust* to India, Sudha Bhuchar recognised it 'would have been less controversial if [we] had gone with *East is East* as a British product' (Bhuchar 1999d) as politically a production dealing with British Asian concerns and set in Britain by a British Asian theatre company would have been less problematic. In order to mitigate charges of Western intercultural imperialism only four actors, Shobu Kapoor, Shiv Grewel, Rehan Sheikh and Sudha Bhuchar of the original nine cast members went to India; they were joined by four Indian actors Bhanu Rao, Paritosh Sand, Anita Lal and Saira Nair. Furthermore, the production team, including set and lighting designers as well as stage management, were Indian technicians from the locality of the tour, which visited Delhi, Bombay and Baroda.

The language used by the *mazdoors* in *Women of the Dust* was colloquial English with some Hindi words integrated into it.

> ASHA: Mohan, the Sikh in the *dukan* [shop] has a glass bowl for *dahi* [yoghurt].
>
> (Carter 1999a: 20)

Or, more colloquially, the *jamadar* addressing Mohan, Asha's husband, whose unfortunate business ventures included bulk buying 200 shoes, all right feet, and a television with no working parts inside, said:

> JAMADAR   [Foreman]: Your arse is where your head should be, you fool. Why don't you stick to what you can do? Accept your dharma [fate] instead of coming up with these wild ideas.
>
> (Carter 1999a: 23)

There was also a theatrically heightened choric approach to the writing of the *mazdoors*:

PARVATI: My head is splitting
KAMLA: My feet are swelling
PARVATI: A full month I am bleeding
ASHA: My back is breaking
DADI: The sun is killing.

(Carter 1999a: 1)

If the British critics received *Women of the Dust* as more documentary than drama, then for the Indian reviewers the production was judged more on its merits as a drama; the documentary element holding few surprises for that audience. This aspect of the production was roundly criticised for lacking 'the tension and energy needed to dramatise such a complex subject' (Vaish 1994) and the critics' interest lay 'in a more formalist direction' (Arora 1994). This focused particularly on the language and sound of the *mazdoors* both in relation to the production's attempted 'authenticity' and the cultural politics of this hybrid British Asian text. In terms of the sound of the *mazdoors*, the hybrid performance of English language with Rajasthani inflexion and cadence 'is so deceptive [...] that at first one is left a little confused [...] it sounds like Rajasthani Hindi but one can't get the words' (Vaish 1994).

While there may have been an 'authenticity' about the *sound* of the actors playing *mazdoors*, although even here 'in trying to simulate accent and lilt they often sounded ridiculous' (Nagpal 1994b), there was a further problem concerning the cultural politics of finding an English idiom for the *mazdoors*. The production did attempt to give a theatrical voice to the oppressed women workers, however, in creating this voice the writer was attacked for her decision to 'duplicate the syntax leading to nonsensical prose' (Nagpal 1994b) such as 'it's selling *to* them the same' (Carter 1999a: 45) or 'I will go to make *hard and fast* arrangements' (Carter 1999a: 19), which meant that, in effect, the *mazdoors* spoke 'bad' English.

This ran the risk of creating 'an orientalist stereotype of native incompetence [...] the Indian who uses English wrongly [...] the Rajastani who doesn't use even his own language properly' (Arora 1994) compounded by the fact that the two middle class women spoke grammatically correct received pronunciation English. The political implications of this were clear, especially when 'the fact that English in India is imbricated in a social and cultural problematic ensures that this formalist interest can never be pure and uncontaminated by the political' (Arora

1994), which suggested the *mazdoors* were less articulate and intelligent than the middle class contractor or social workers. So, while Tamasha's decision to create a hybrid sound, that was neither Rajastani nor recognisably 'English' in order to achieve an authentic representation of their situation to a British, largely non-Asian speaking audience may have been methodologically defensible it became theatrically and politically flawed when the play was performed in India.

5
Tamasha Theatre Company 1989 – *East is East*: From Kitchen Sink to Bollywood

Introduction

Tamasha's further experiments in form will be examined in this chapter, including the staging of a Bollywood film in *Fourteen Songs, Two Weddings and A Funeral* (1998, 2001), the *West Side Story*-inspired dance-led drama *Strictly Dandia* (2004), the exploration of verbatim theatre in relation to the Asian experience in *The Trouble with Asian Men* (2005) and a methodology for cultural inclusion and representation in *Lyrical MC* (2007). By contrast the Tamasha production that was a 'cross-over' critical success, popular with both Asian and non-Asian audiences alike, and the first new British Asian play to transfer to, and have a successful run, in the West End, was a very traditional piece of 'kitchen sink' drama, *East is East*.

East is East (1996)

Set in the early 1970s, *East is East*'s central characters are the Khans, an Anglo-Pakistani family who run a local fish and chip shop in Salford. While mum, Ella, tries to keep the peace her husband, George, is secretly arranging a marriage for two of his sons, Tariq and Abdul. When the secret comes out the children confront their father but he will not listen to any arguments. The long-awaited meeting with the prospective in-laws, the Shahs, arrives at which the two sons are introduced their brides. However, the

---

95

suggestion that the two Khan boys move in with their in-laws when married proves too much for Ella and leads not only to an end of the marriage plans but also an end of the autocratic regime of Mr Khan over his family.

East is East (1996)

© Robert Day.

Imran Ali playing Sanjit, a character based on the author Ayub Khan-Din, wearing his trademark parka in *East is East* (1996).

Tamasha found critical and public acclaim in 1996 with Ayub Khan-Din's *East is East*, a semi-autobiographical account of growing up in a working class 'mixed race' family in Salford in the 1970s. The play was developed in a writers' workshop held by Tamasha in collaboration with the Royal Court Theatre and the Birmingham Repertory Theatre Company. It was first performed at the Royal Court Theatre Upstairs, at The Ambassadors Theatre on 19 November 1996 and then played at Theatre Royal Stratford East before transferring to the Royal Court Theatre Downstairs, which was temporarily housed in the Duke of York's Theatre in the West End from 26 March 1997. *East is East* was subsequently made into a feature film directed by Damien O'Donnell and produced by Film Four.

The play was very much in the vein of Tamasha's 'slice of life' realism, or indeed Royal Court 'kitchen sink'[1] drama and focused on questions of cultural identity for British Asian children growing up in a northern working class family to an English mother and Pakistani father. The play was universally well received by the critics with John Peter in *The Sunday Times* setting the tone with his view that 'first plays don't come much better than this' (Peter 1996), Charles Spencer in the *Telegraph* claiming it as 'one of the best pieces of modern Asian drama I've ever seen' (1996) and Michael Billington's emphatic 'don't miss it' (1996).

The play opens as George discovers, much to his chagrin, that his youngest son Sanjit, pictured above in his ever present parka coat, has not been circumcised and he 'can't look the mullah in bloody face now!' (Khan-Din 1996: 3) because everyone at the mosque knows. This provides much amusement for the other children as Maneer, Saleem and Meena, who are in the habit of eating bacon sandwiches when their father is out, tell Sanjit that 'foreskins are dirty' (18); removal 'lessens the feeling on your nob' (18) and 'me dad's having your nob cut off' (18). While this religious faux pas is remedied by a trip to the hospital, the other staple of Asian theatre, the arranged marriage, is utilised by Khan-Din as a vehicle of both drama and high farce.

George has secretly arranged Tariq and Abdul's wedding to Mr Shah's daughters without telling his wife, Ella. Although Abdul is resigned to his marriage, wanting to avoid the fate of his brother Nazir who has been ostracised from the family, Tariq insists 'I'm not gonna marry a Paki' (27). However, when Saleem tries to intervene on their behalf telling George that they have a right to choose their own wives his father physically attacks him. The play manages, with some skill, to balance the drama and comedy so the violence of that scene is counterpointed by an 'eruption of family anarchy into a teatime meeting with a prospective father-in-law [which]... has a touch of Marx brothers madness' (Billington 1996).

At the beginning of this final scene we see the whole household in preparation for the visit of the upwardly mobile Shahs. Meenah is wearing a sari, Ella is getting her jewellery out of the safe and Abdul and Tariq are, unusually, dressed in shirts and ties. The Shahs' arrival is heralded by Sajit's warning, amusingly devoid of irony, 'Mam, quick, the Paki's here!' (51) and the prospective in-laws are shown into the front room or 'parlour' as Ella now describes it in her newly adopted 'posh' voice. However, the strained decorum between the two families finally reaches breaking point when Saleem returns home with a sculpture he has been making at college. Saleem maintains his artwork symbolises 'female exploitation in art' (60) or as Sajit more prosaically describes it to his mother, 'a woman's fanny in a box mam!' (60). As Ella tries to take the offending article from Saleem, the hair comes off in her hand and the vagina ends up on Mr Shah's lap:

> MR SHAH: This is an insult to me, and to my family [...] I will never let my daughters marry into this jungly family of half-breeds!
> ELLA: They may be half bred, but at least they're not bleeding in-bred like these two monstrosities. (INDICATING THE PICTURES) (61)

This precipitates the Shahs' exit and George's assault on Ella for her perceived disrespect to the visitors and for bringing shame on the family. This time Abdul intervenes and restrains his father insisting 'he's got no right to tell us what our culture should be, he lost that when he settled here and married me mam' (64).

While on the face of it the critics read *East is East* as a straightforward 'culture clash'. It was Khan-Din's portrayal of the Asian father, George, or 'Genghis' as the children referred to him, which might be read as problematic. While an unsympathetic Asian character would not necessarily be automatically problematic, it became so because George was the *only* 'Asian' central character. Theatrically marked out as such by his strong Asian accent, the character could be read as emblematic for Asian values per se so that 'the "traditional" Muslim father is framed as restrictive and abusive in regard to his liberal and progressive children and wife' (Desai 2004: 67). The reaction to the character of George was, indeed, unforgiving so that 'what stays in the mind is his readiness to knock his wife down' (Kingston 1997). Indeed, a story of an Asian man who had married a white woman, beat her, had another wife back in Pakistan and arranged marriages for his children without consulting them might fit comfortably into any racist discourse.

Ayub Khan-Din did little to defend himself from accusations that he was 'betraying the Asian community' (Khan-Din quoted in Hattenstone 1997) in his portrayal of George Khan. He was unrepentant about his depiction of the father on the grounds that 'my Dad was like that... [I] am not interested in what people want me to say' (ibid.). While that defence was of course, a writer's prerogative, it suggested that Khan-Din had little concern for the cultural politics of the marginalised Asian subject. However, if we look at how *East is East* dealt with the children who are neither 'English nor Pakistani' (Spencer 1996) we see that the play is a much more nuanced and sympathetic examination of hybrid or hyphenated cultural identities than the 'knockabout comedy' (ibid.) might suggest.

This complexity can be read in Khan-Din's portrayal of George who we see not only the bully who has secretly arranged his children's marriage but also his alienation and frustration in the chip shop as he '*goes over to the counter, leans against it and sobs into his hands*' (27). While there was no doubt the children unequivocally abhorred the father's violence towards their mother, finally physically intervening in order to prevent it, in many ways they embraced many of his cultural values. One of the most lyrical moments in the play occurred in the second act as we see George, alone, practicing his Muslim prayers. His movements are described as 'poetic and gentle' in the stage directions and this 'gentleness' carried over into the comforting embrace he gave to his son immediately after his prayers were finished. Abdul, the eldest son appreciates this and describes how 'when I got home my dad was here praying [...] and it was right to be here [...] to belong to something' (Khan-Din 1996: 49).

East is East does dramatise some robust arguments between the children over cultural identity and brooks no preciousness as Maneer, the most committed Muslim among the children, is caustically referred to as Ghandi by his siblings. Even the devout Maneer has a liberal view of religion, which he believes, in contrast to his father, should be a matter of personal choice. Although Tariq, in his desire to assimilate, rebels against his Asian heritage claiming, 'we speak English not Urdu' (Khan-Din 1996: 40), it is Abdul who recognises that identity is not only constructed from within but also without as 'no one round here thinks we're English, we're the Paki family who run the chippy' (Khan-Din 1996: 39). The play pointed out that the cost of assimilation for Abdul was having to laugh at racist jokes and deny his own culture, a price he found too high as he realised, 'I don't want that out there [...] it's as alien to me as me dad's world is to you' (Khan-Din, 1996: 49). In this way the play refused to accept the narrow and exclusive definition of 'Britishness' that cannot also encompass British Muslim cultural difference. Indeed, the author's explicit directions for the set design, which calls for 'contrast' rather than 'clash', symbolises the possibilities of coexistence and fusion in the play:

> THE CONTRAST OF CULTURES SHOULD COME OUT IN THE SET DRESS-ING, WALLPAPER, OIL CLOTH, ISLAMIC PRAYER STICKERS, A COFFEE TABLE WITH A PICTURE OF THE TAJ MAHAL ... (3)

Indeed the signs of the children's hybrid identity could be read in *East is East* as they spoke in English and Urdu with northern accents, mimed and danced to Bollywood film songs, dressed in both traditional Asian clothes and Western ones, attended mosque but were also prepared to help out when the Catholic parade was short-handed.

That British Asian provenance was evident in Khan-Din's assertion that *East is East*, both the play and subsequent film, were 'as much Northern pieces as they are Asian pieces' (Khan-Din 1999: 6). *East is East* recognised the Khan children's insistence on asserting their hybrid identity in spite of their father's warning, born of bitter experience, that 'English people no accepting you' (Khan-Din 1996: 47), and asserting their right to be British *and* Asian. Finally, perhaps one of the key reasons *East is East* was so successful was Khan-Din's readiness to deflate cultural and religious dogmas with extremely well-crafted comedy, which is clearly evident in the following exchange.

George has ostracised his oldest son, Nazir, for refusing to have an arranged marriage and becoming a hairdresser:

> ELLA: (UNDER HER BREATH, BUT AUDIBLE ENOUGH FOR GEORGE TO HEAR) Yeah, just like you fixed our Nazir.
> GEORGE: I bloody hear what you saying Mrs, I no bloody daft. Why you always mention this pucker baster name to me, how many times I tell you he dead.
> ELLA: No, he's not, he's living in Eccles [...] (26)

Fourteen Songs, Two Weddings and A Funeral and Strictly Dandia

---

Fourteen Songs, Two Weddings and A Funeral (1998 and 2001)

Rajesh and Prem are two brothers whose parents have been killed in a car accident. Rajesh falls in love with Pooja and they marry and have a son while Prem falls in love with Nisha, Pooja's sister. Prem and Nisha plan to marry but disaster strikes when Pooja is killed in an accident. Nisha must forsake her love for Prem and step in to marry his brother, Rajesh, as is the duty of the younger sister. However, all turns out well as Rajesh realises Prem is in love with Nisha and heroically steps aside so they can be together.

Fourteen Songs, Two Weddings and A Funeral was a radical departure for the company as they eschewed their usual research-based approach and aesthetic of realism and attempted to adapt the 1990s Bollywood 'hit' film *Hum Aapke Hain Koun [Who Am I to You]* for the stage. The play was first performed at the Lyric Studio, Hammersmith, on Wednesday 11 November 1998 and then returned to the Lyric Theatre main house, in 2001 before touring nationally.

Jen Harvie has pointed out in *Staging the UK* (2005) that the title mimicked Mike Newell's quintessentially 'English' film *Four Weddings and A Funeral* that starred Hugh Grant. Drawing on Homi K. Bhabha's notion of mimicry[2] she recognised that *Fourteen Songs* operated ' "almost the same" as *Four Weddings* in its title, its narrative organisation around weddings and a death, and numerous features arising from the fact it was a romantic comedy' (Harvie 2005: 175), which had the effect of destabilising a 'whitewashed' construction of Britain by being peopled by Asian characters.

Indeed, the production can be read as a celebration of Asian culture as it 'did not try to play down what some see as the embarrassing conventions of Bollywood' (Harvie 2005: 172). Kristine Landon-Smith initially adapted *Hum Aapke Hain Koun [Who am I to You]* for a radio production. Her aim with the radio adaptation was to 'achieve a Bollywood feel and playing style' (Landon-Smith 1998a) but the hybrid provenance of the project soon emerged, exemplified in her treatment of the songs.

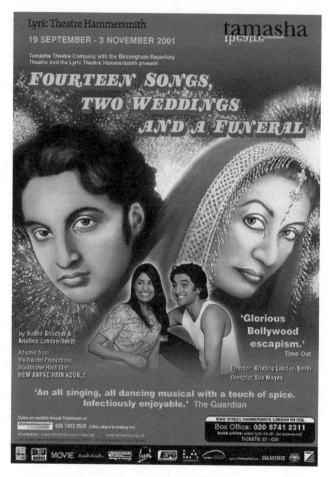

Fourteen Songs, Two Weddings and A Funeral (2000)
© Tamasha Theatre Company.
The flyer for *Fourteen Songs, Two Weddings and A Funeral* (2000), featuring the two leading actors Pushpinder Chani and Mala Ghedia.
The poster mirrored the style of 'authentic' Bollywood film publicity posters.

Although the original soundtrack was retained, the actors also spoke a simultaneous English translation alongside the Hindi songs. This was taken a step further in the stage version as the songs were recorded by the actors and done in 'playback' in performance as the actors mimed over their own vocal. This was, of course, very much in line with the methodology of the Bollywood film genre, except in Bollywood stars would have their own playback singer to which they would mime.

While the songs remained faithful to the values and melodies of the original, what was notable about them, as well as about the text, was that they were translated into English. Interestingly, the decision to 'anglicise' the songs was criticised by Jatinder Verma, artistic director of Tara Arts, because it denied the possible use of 'language as a medium of cultural exchange' (Verma 2001a). He suggested that the songs should be performed in Hindi with English surtitles. However, the hybrid form that Tamasha created in their adaptation, or cultural translation, of the Bollywood film to the stage, and its British location, could be said to operate in the creative hybrid space 'in-between' British and Asian espoused by the 'Binglish' methodology.

Kristine Landon-Smith also wanted to find an acting style that would celebrate the Bollywood genre, rather than lead to a parody or 'send up' of it, and, indeed, the production was praised for playing with 'straight faced sincerity' (Billington 2001). The British Asian actors in the production, who were mainly trained in a Western naturalistic style of acting found it difficult to adapt to a style of acting that they perceived as melodramatic. Kristine Landon-Smith set the actors exercises in rehearsal such as finding their character's most Bollywood 'moment' in the play in order to find a vocabulary to be able to move quickly between heightened emotional states. This was deemed successful as critics noted that the 'acting has a lovely freshness [...] turning on a sixpence between tragedy and comedy' (Spencer 2001), thus realising the director's aim for the cast to be 'good actors in a Bollywood film' (Landon-Smith 1998b).

The Bollywood genre has often been characterised as melodramatic by Western critics, which as Vijay Mishra explained in *Bollywood Cinema – Temples of Desire*, was due to the historical fact that Bombay cinema began as a colonial form that borrowed from the literary form of melodrama. Indeed, Jen Harvie has pointed out the way in which Bollywood cinema was a hybrid form in India and Mishra draws on Peter Brook's discussion of French melodrama in order to characterise its form so that 'within an apparent context of "realism" and the ordinary, they seemed in fact to be staging a heightened and hyperbolic drama' (Brook quoted in Mishra 2002: 37).

The difficulties of negotiating the form of melodrama for actors more used to acting in a realistic style was evident in the director's advice that they should 'never lose the fun to be had with a stock character but [...] don't push them too far so as not to believe or empathise with them' (Landon-Smith 1998a). So while determinedly reaching towards a new form the basis remained anchored to a level of Stanislavski-based psychological realism. This hybrid balance of styles seemed to have been successfully achieved as the production was praised for 'the way it combines the gentle poking of fun at that genre's unusual conventions with sensitivity and conviction when it matters most' (Logan 1998).

The success of the original film was based on its 'return to romance and song' (Mishra 2002: 146) with 'narratives built around the idyllic extended family order' (Mishra 2002: 218), in contrast to the trend for more violent and sexually adventurous Bollywood films. However, this return to 'traditional values' epitomised by *Hum Aapke Hain Koun* was problematic in respect of the gender politics of the film, particularly when played in Britain. That extended family 'order' was 'within a dominant patriarchal Hindu order where a woman's sexuality/sensuality is circumscribed by respectable social norms and where the model is [...] as the devotee of her husband-lord' (Mishra 2002: 218). While Prem's compliment to Nisha that 'I am already a fan of your singing and dancing. Now I am a fan of your cooking' (Bhuchar and Landon-Smith 2001: 40) certainly underlined the traditional values of the text, to much amusement from the contemporary audience, there were more problematic instances.

When Bhagwanti, the stock character of the interfering social climbing auntie goes 'too far' in suggesting that recently widowed Rajesh should remarry and have his son brought up by an 'ayah' (nanny), her husband slaps her across the face.

(ARUN *slaps her*)
ARUN: It is this sour nature of yours that has kept us childless all these years.

(Bhuchar and Landon-Smith 2001: 52)

As Jen Harvie has pointed out the Bollywood film industry was 'sexist in its representations of women, both visually, in imagery replete with bare bellies and deep cleavages, and in narrative, where women are often the objects of exchange between men' (Harvie 2005: 160). The performance of *Fourteen Songs*, perhaps unwittingly, engendered these politics. Indeed, on the night I saw the performance, the audience clapped at this point. This audience reaction was of course precipitated both by the dramatic structure and unsympathetic portrayal of the dominant wife finally given her comeuppance by the eternally put-upon husband. While this may have been in line with the politics of the original film, it is doubtful that the introduction of domestic violence, albeit in a Bollywood form, was something that Tamasha would want to endorse. There was perhaps an opportunity for Tamasha to re-inflect the production and the form itself with a more progressive approach to gender in the British context within the confines of the 'Bollywood' form.

Traditional or not, the non-Western form of the musical was indeed provocative to one critic who was nonplussed by the evident enjoyment of the British Asian audience 'laughing both at and with the actors' (Myerson 2001). His admonishment that Tamasha needs to 'befriend those of us with Western theatrical expectations' surely missed the point that this was now a *British* form; if proof were needed Andrew Lloyd Webber produced his own Bollywood musical *Bombay Dreams*, which opened on 19 June 2002 at the Apollo Victoria Theatre. Tamasha's new theatrical form was also critically vindicated as Tamasha won the Barclay's New Musical Award in 1998 and the BBC Asia Award for Achievement in the Arts in 1999 for *Fourteen Songs*.

Strictly Dandia (2003)

It is the *Navratri* dance festival and Preethi is competing for the title of *Diwaali* queen with her dance partner and prospective *Diwaali* king, Raj. However Raj is actually Raza, a Muslim, who must pretend he is a Punjabi Hindu so he can take part in the competition. When the secret becomes known Raza is forced to leave the competition and Preethi is forbidden to see him anymore. However, when the father of the competition's choreographer is beaten up in his newsagent's kiosk, Raza is on hand to save the day. Although Preethi has been given a new partner to dance with, at the last minute Raza arrives and he and Preethi win the competition and are crowned *Diwaali* king and queen.

After the success of *A Tainted Dawn*, a play marking the 50th anniversary of partition at the official Edinburgh Festival in 1997, Tamasha were invited by Brian McMasters to return in 2003. The publicity for *Strictly Dandia* promised 'smart moves and Gujarati grooves' and drew comparisons with *West Side Story* as well as Baz Luhrmann's film, set in the world of ballroom dancing, *Strictly Ballroom*.

The action in *Strictly Dandia* is centred on the amateur dancing competitions that take place during the nine nights leading up to *Diwaali* (Festival of Lights) in the Hindu festival of *Navratri*. The *garba* dance originated in the Indian state of Gujarat and is usually performed at the time of *Navratri* festival, a celebration of harvest time. The word *garba* is derived from the Sanskrit word '*garbadeep*', literally meaning 'a lamp inside a pot' that symbolised knowledge and creativity and around which the dance would take place.

The dance is technically straightforward and 'is done by a group of dancers going round and round in circles, bending to the right and left and forwards, stamping the feet in a rhythm of four counts and clapping the hands in sweeping gestures' (Bhavnani 1979: 190). *Dandia* has as its basis the *garba* but the dancers also have *dandia* sticks that are polished and decorated sticks approximately a foot long and struck together in time to the music. In *Strictly Dandia* other dance styles such as disco, salsa and hip hop were fused with the *dandia* in order to add choreographic variety.

While the original idea was based on the rivalry between the Australian Gujarati communities in Sydney and Woolagong, Sudha Bhuchar relocated the action to one of the community centres dotted along the North Circular Road in London not least because Kristine Landon-Smith 'was fascinated by the idea of people going into leisure centres wearing their glitziest clothes at seven o'clock on winter evenings when it was freezing cold and the British were all going home after their games of squash' (Landon-Smith quoted in Batten 2003). Utilising the Tamasha research methodology, the writer, director and actors spent a number of months in observation, gathering first-person testimonies and improvising with the material gathered back in the rehearsal room.

At the centre of the drama was the forbidden romance between Preethi, the Hindu, and Raza, the Muslim. The animosity between Hindus and Muslims – or 'slims' as they are derogatively referred to – in London is contrasted with the idyllic picture of religious tolerance painted of East Africa, where most British Gujaratis hail from, in which 'your people celebrated our Diwaali and only because I am a vegetarian I couldn't eat your biryanis on the Festival of Idd' (Bhuchar & Landon-Smith 2004a: 8). Raza and his Muslim friend are forced to pretend they are 'saucy [...] HP's [...] Hindu Punjabi's.' (Bhuchar & Landon-Smith 2004a: 14) because if 'anyone finds out you're "slims", literally hell is gonna come on earth' (ibid.). The writers then added further fuel to the dramatic fire by making the dancing competition 'inter-caste', something that would not traditionally occur, as a critique of the apparent insularity of the Gujarati community. Sudha Bhuchar felt that even though the 'Gujaratis are very open there is still this underlying thing that the partner should be from the same caste. Or, if not, at least from another Gujarati caste. If not that, maybe a Hindu boy will do.

There are degrees of acceptability, but a Muslim boy is something you would not contemplate' (Bhuchar quoted in Brown, 2003). However, Tamasha's plea for tolerance is articulated in the plot as Raza and Prethi are crowned *Diwaali* king and queen and the chair of the committee reminds the gathered community of 'how often we Gujaratis have been the outsiders and have asked to be accepted in?' (54).

If the script was rather harshly critiqued for its predictable structure – 'the fight in the car park, the separation, the external event which forces them back together, the final dance off, the happy ending' (Scott 2004) along with the 'stilted dialogue' (Parry 2003) – there were also reservations about the production. This was most pointed in the *Independent's* 'This thin offering is strictly amateur fare' (Walker 2003). Reservations remained concerning the production and there was disappointment that the 'show was a great opportunity missed, full of good intention which it dismally fails to deliver' (Spencer 2004).

This bruising encounter with the critics left Kristine Landon-Smith discussing the wider difficulties of being labelled as an 'Asian' company and being viewed 'as part of a collective, of a movement labelled Asian Theatre [. . .] whereas Complicité [. . .] Trestle [. . .]. Out of Joint [. . .] are categorised by their art form [. . .] Tamasha is categorised by its ethnicity' (Landon-Smith 2004), which she felt has the effect of marginalising the company from mainstream British theatre. However, it was noted by one critic that one of the important functions of companies such as Tamasha is representation and with productions such as *Strictly Dandia* they were recognised for creating 'theatre that we as Asians growing up in the UK can cherish as part of our unique British Asian culture without having to constantly refer to the subcontinent for entertainment' (Hundal 2004).

Verbatim theatre: *The Trouble with Asian Men* and *Lyrical MC*

Tamasha's verbatim piece *The Trouble with Asian Men* initially came about as a collaboration with Louise Wallinger, co-founder of the Non-Fiction Theatre Company. The methodology of the Non-Fiction Theatre Company that Tamasha adopted for this production was to 'gather and record actual speech/conversation, shape it, and perform it live using headphones' (Non-Fiction Theatre Company 2002). *The Trouble with Asian Men* was first performed at the Arts Depot on Tuesday 15 November 2005 and subsequently toured nationally until 2007.

The Trouble with Asian Men (2007)
© Robert Day.
Amit Sharma with earpiece in *The Trouble with Asian Men* (2007).

The company interviewed a variety of mainly 'second-generation' British Asian men and women from a number of different Asian communities around the country. In all they interviewed 191 people and recorded them onto MiniDisc, producing over 150 hours of taped material. This was then edited down to a 60-minute aural text of monologues and dialogues that were then relayed to the actors during the performance, What is noteworthy about this particular verbatim praxis is the fact that the actors do not learn the text but hear it for the first time in the performance and attempt to replicate, as *exactly* as possible, the rhythms, inflexions, pauses, idiosyncrasies and hesitations of the speaker so 'the result is surprisingly naturalistic and genuinely theatrical' (Evans 2006).

Of course, while verbatim is defined as using exactly the same words, which is what gives the verbatim theatre form its *appearance* of authenticity, it should also be remembered that the material has been structured and edited, while performatively 'there's a skill to delivering it this "real" and the company of four [...] performs the material with artfully casual confidence' (Halliburton 2006). So although the critics recognised that the form of *The Trouble with Asian Men* was 'certainly artful [...] its truth comes through loud and clear' (Woddis 2006).

The publicity material focused on the light-hearted aspect of the show featuring the personal relationships between Asian men and their mothers, gender relations, and negotiating between cultures rather than the political as:

Macho men or metrosexual guys?

Mummy's boys or fellas under their missus' thumbs? These successful, soulful and spirited Asian men have come along way from their origins, but they've all got roots!

(Tamasha 2005)

In this respect the content and aims of *The Trouble with Asian Men* were far removed from political verbatim works such as David Hare's *The Permanent Way* (2003), Robin Soans's *Talking to Terrorists* (2005) or the Tricycle Theatre's groundbreaking series of plays: *The Colour of Justice* (1999), *Guantanamo* (2004) and *Called to Account: The Indictment of Anthony Charles Lynton Blair for the Crime of Aggression Against Iraq – A Hearing* (2007). Indeed, any discussions of such topics as the radicalisation of young Asian Muslim men or wider geopolitics were kept purposefully light-hearted and oblique in *The Trouble with Asian Men*, with the result that it 'never gets past a self-consciously jokey level of debate' (Gardner 2006):

Man 7 'we were called the 'Arabian Nights' and we were very proud to say we were the number two [...] we were the second best break dancing crew in Peterborough; cos you used to have challenges against all these crews. And then suddenly about three of them grew beards and started wearing gowns (*laughs*) [...] what the fuck? (*laughs*) And kept saying 'in-shala ma-shala brother' (*laughs*).

(Bhuchar et al. 2006: 10)

Perhaps the rationale that 'there is far too little theatre addressing Asian issues and portraying this generation sympathetically' (Fisher 2006) resulted in the choice of content:

Man 6 (2 mins 35 sec): It was when I got rid of it that I really noticed that people did see you differently if you had a turban on. Realised it was a hassle, realised that it was a bit of a waste of time. I booked an appointment at Vidal Sassoon, I said 'I want your best hairdresser, this is a big job.' Dad was like 'if you do that then uh you're gonna leave, you've gotta leave the house.' I said 'look ok uh I'm not leaving the house but I'm getting it done. (*laughs*) Uh and mum was like 'ok, why you want to do that?' I was like this is why because it's a hassle, uh it's very uncomfortable, my head hurts, I can't you know [...] you can't do anything, you can't go swimming, you can't think. So she said ok well then you know at least then do Bart everyday. Like fuck yeah penance. But the guy um the guy came out, his name was Rex or something, so I let my hair down and all the other hairdressers they all looked round thinking 'my God what have we got here?' [...] (*laughs*) [...] 'this is incredible what is this like some sort of test [...]. ' (*laughs*) [...]. when was the last time you got your hair cut? I said 'oh it's never been cut' and he said 'so what you know what caused you to neglect your hair for so long? (*laughs*) and I said 'well, it's religion you know it's a religious thing.' And he said 'oh yeah it [...] so is the is the purpose that when your buried that you leave some of the hair poking through the grave?' (*laughs*) I said [...] I said 'No actually no I'm not sure [...] (*laughs*) [...] I'm not sure what you're getting at an interesting concept but that's not the idea. Um I'm not actually sure what the idea is and that's why I'm getting it cut.' So anyway he pulls it up, he's like you know 'are you sure?' gives it [...] you know I give him the nod, he gives it a snip. I was worried that he wasn't gonna be able to pull it off, I was thinking no [...] this is no way how's this gonna work. It was [...] I I.. it felt uh it felt liberating but at the same time it felt quite worrying cos [...] more that anything what was on my mind what's gonna be the reaction of mum and dad. I mean I turned up mum came out of the kitchen and she was like 'oh, oh you've done it.' And she I mean she was quite together I think she had got rid of all her emotional stuff the day before. I mean dad walks in and he was like 'oh very nice, you look very nice now.' (*laughs*) like you know playing the sarcastic card.

The speech above gives a humorous insight the cultural themes of the production, cultural identity, intergenerational relationships and, of course, hairdressing. It should of course be said that the reason Sikhs do not cut their hair, unbeknown to the interviewee, is that it is one of the five articles of faith set down for adherents of the religion to wear.[3]

The transcript contains all the hesitations, ums and ahs of the recorded speech and replicates the authentic flow and rhythm of the interviewee's speech, which are then reproduced by the actor. Notice also the timing at the top of the speech that reminds us that this is a crafted and structured piece of theatre. While Sudha Bhuchar was clear that the personal stories are at the heart of this piece and they do build up a bigger picture of the experience of second generation Asian men, the critics felt that the problem with the form was that 'it might articulate the heterogeneity of being Asian and male but it can't put it into the dramatic context that would allow the debate to be taken a step further' (Alfree 2006). Indeed, because of the cross-section and range of voices in the production we are never allowed to follow any story for long and therefore the character narratives do not develop.

One key theme that did constantly reoccur, however, was that of the relationship between Asian men and their mothers, complete with Freudian slips:

Man 5 (2 mins 38 secs)

Man 5: [...] I think love and romance that's fine but uh outside of marriage. It's what I mean is you know [...] as long as you're not married to each other love and romance survive.

Marriage is like the kiss of death, the minute you get married [...] you know the love just

dies in a relationship; well it certainly did in mine. Marriage was the sort of last um

sort of pit-stop, there's obviously kids [...] um but kids don't um necessarily add to the

bond that you have with your partner [...] um kids can be quite disruptive in a

relationship um and obviously a a woman's body goes through lots of changes,

before and after a birth. And um you know unless you know what to expect [...] it can

be a pretty daunting experience and I just wasn't able to accommodate the changes.

And my father died in 1995 um so what uh what started as a temporary move back to

my mother's to look after her, to make sure that she didn't feel the void [...] um has

turned out [...] turned into turned into a more long-term arrangement, I'm still here um

ten years on.

Oh I I have no problems about that because we have um um my wife, my wife, my

mother is very understanding woman. She's not uh she's not like uh [...] you know your

usual [...] your normal controlling mother. Um she realises I have needs, she realises

that I need my freedom [...] um you know we we both live together but we have a very

sort of separate life. You just saw me make my own tea. Uh you know it's it's

something that raises eyebrows when people learn that I'm still living with my mother

at 43. No it hasn't it hasn't interfered with with anything at all in my life uh to be

honest. Um it's given my mother a lease of life. Um I've tried to meet the right

person but I don't think the right person actually exists. I'm hoping that [...] you know if

there is somebody out there with uh with a perhaps deeper understanding of a

mother-son relationship um then things will work better.

My mother has never ever ever raised the subject of marriage to me. Never once

has she said that I should get married, not even hinted. Uh it's almost like [...] you

know perhaps she doesn't want me to get married.

(Bhuchar et al. 2005: 9)

The performance was staged with the actors sitting on sofas and chairs throughout and while some reviewers complained this made the 'production [...] somewhat static' (Marlowe 2006) the benefit was that it allowed the audience to focus on the voices and subtleties of the performances of the actors 'who respond eagerly to the unusual mechanism of the piece' (Hepple 2005). Overall, the critical response was positive, finding *The Trouble with Asian Men* 'highly entertaining, enough to make you snort with laughter' (Gardner 2006a) but with a plea for the company 'to get out there and bring back stronger material that would more vividly illuminate the present crisis' (Spencer 2006).

Lyrical MC

The genesis of *Lyrical MC* (2007) was the TIME (Tamasha Intercultural Millennium Education) 2001 Conference, which showcased the results of Tamasha's two-year professional development partnership with drama teachers to practically address, and engage with, cultural diversity in the classroom. The conference was convened to address the demonstrable need for a methodology that could provide teachers with the practical tools they clearly needed:

> in my class I have a girl of Turkish origin, a bi-lingual speaker and others of Asian and African origin who have never revealed anything about their cultures [...] I now see it is up to me to create a culture in the drama classroom where they are invited to make contributions, because the cultures they are from and the languages they speak are key [...]
> (Maric quoted in Brahmachari & Landon-Smith 2001)

Kristine Landon-Smith responded with a practical demonstration for the attending teachers using actors who had been asked to research, through observation, a close family member or someone known to them in their particular 'cultural context'. They were then asked to play this character in a 'hot seat' exercise that had been innovatively developed by Kristine Landon-Smith as means of 'drawing information from the actor' (2008a). In her approach the director adopts two key functions in the 'hot seat' improvisation: Firstly, she will maintain her position as director and speak directly to the actor commenting on their body language, voice, and responses and also draw other characters into the improvisation, as she deems appropriate.

Secondly, and uniquely to Kristine Landon-Smith's methodology, the director may also take a provocative role in the exercise, sometimes adopting a role in order to engage with the actor in the 'hot seat' functioned as described above. If that character spoke in a language other than English, or a mixture of English and another language, the actor should do so, even though the director participating *may not* have knowledge of that language. The example below may be instructive:

A student of Bengali origin (A) was attempting to play her own grand-mother. Her friend, a young girl of Irish origin (B) informed her that she was getting it wrong. B had spent a lot of time with A's grandmother. The teacher/director asked student B to sit next to student A and help her capture her grandmother's gestures and way of moving. While student A conducted the whole hot seat in Bengali, student B jolted A's memory about the physicality and gestural qualities of her grandmother.

(Brahmachari & Landon-Smith 2001: 17)

As Kristine Landon-Smith pointed out, the director must try and 'glean what the student is saying from the gesture and tone of voice [...] where a complicated or specific idea is being articulated [...] he/she will very naturally slip in some English words' (2001: 17). This mediation between English and other languages is, of course, key to cultural representation, in particular the Tamasha's intracultural[4] approach, which aimed to explore 'the dynamics between and across specific communities and regions within the boundaries of the nation state' (2000: 6).

Sita Brahmachari realised that the delegates at the TIME conference had been sceptical about Tamasha's intracultural theory but were convinced when the 'hot seat' methodology was utilised to create a scene between characters:

[...] there were two girls of African origin from a Birmingham school and two African girls from a London School [...] and they all had characters that they had excavated [...] aunties [...] mothers [...] who were from different areas of Africa, so suddenly [...] they met across the room in character [...] and they were quickly able to realise that so and so was Yoruba [...] and there was this whole tribal thing going on and [disre-specting] each other and there was this amazing theatre text and that's what people recognised [...].

(Brahmachari 2008)

It is the ability of the 'hot seat' to engage with the ethnicity of the performer that leads to the creation of an 'amazing theatre text' peopled by characters that are largely absent from the British stage. This methodology was then applied in order to create a play text for *Lyrical MC* with pupils from two schools, Featherstone School in Southall and Islington Arts and Media School.

I would immediately say 'choose someone, you can do your mum' [...] this is great and then I'd start working [...] all I'd do is keep leading them on to do more and more in that voice, in that character [...] and then I might find out if there is anyone else from a Caribbean background [...] come on [...] you want to do your mum as well [...] anyone else who can do a Caribbean mum? [...] and then I'd put them together [...]

(Kristine Landon-Smith 2008a)

This material was then recorded, edited and shaped by Sita Brahmachari into a performance text. The production of *Lyrical MC* was a collaboration between Tamasha and Southwark-based community arts group, Rewrite, whose particular aim was to 'include in our work, young people from different cultural, social, international and economic backgrounds' (Rewrite 2008).

Lyrical MC asked the audience to 'tune into the lyrical chat of students in our inner-city schools and colleges' and used 15 young actors drawn from the REACT youth theatre, incorporating Latvian, Somali, Mandarin, Spanish and Dari [the Afghan dialect of Farsi – Persian] languages.

The piece was approximately the running time of a school lesson and was first performed at the Oval House Theatre on 6 February 2007.

Lyrical MC (2008)

© Robert Workman (2008).

The actors in *Lyrical MC* were: Emmanuel Abubakar, Busola Aderemi, Sarah Akinsanmi, Andre Bromfield, Roxanne Brown, Stefon Fenelon, Joshua Hayles, Amari Shakir Hassan, AliKhawari Shuang, Liu Aldo Maffei, Katrina Naumova, Nana Owusu-Agyare, Funmi Taiwo.

The list of characters demonstrates the range of 'cultural contexts' that were engaged in the piece:

All actors play young people of about 14-15 years old
Emmanuel: of mixed race African-English origin
Roxanne: of Basian origin with strong Basian accent, except when acting as Jasmine
Ali: Boy of Afghanistani origin
Dragon Stefan (physicalisation of Dragon): boy of Afro-Caribbean origin
Shuang Liu: Girl of Chinese origin
Sarah: Girl of African/Caribbean origin
Busola: Girl of African origin
Nana: Girl of African origin
Shakir: Boy of Somali origin
Katrina: Girl of Latvian origin who speaks Latvian
Funmi: Girl of Afro-Caribbean origin
Dragon Amari: Boy of Afro-Caribbean origin
Josh: Boy of Afro-Caribbean origin
Josh: Boy of Afro-Caribbean origin
Aldo: Boy of Columbian origin

As we can see from an example of the text below the performers would switch between English and 'other' languages, syntaxes and accents.

ALI: Begins speaking in his language, explaining how alone he has felt. After a few lines switches to English

I was alone, I cannot speak never English, so difficult. So many different, different people living to this country. I just quiet and sadly. I just try to learn English. Looking for someone to speaking with him in my country. If I need to help someone my country he helps me.

Ali speaks in Dari

So difficult because not my first language so hard for me to understand. Then I find my brother. So I can speak something in my heart to him, because before all the time I alone. Slowly, slowly I understand something about how I can take a bus, how can I move from one area to other area.

SARAH AS CARIBBEAN MOTHER:

You lucky cos I is a Christian

And you is over dere.

You better tank di lord, sister

You is over dere

Me na know

My boy gonna tell me some ting about you

My son, is my son

It tek two fe Tango, ya know

Da young people Dem na know

What dey listening to today

From what I did hear from Michael and Patrice. She already had a half

di man

in a town centre. She been a playing around wid man herself.

When you go to Church what you hear about fornication?

Matthew 3: 16

Tell me now?

What he say

What he say

My son is my son.

Me teach him di manners.

(Brahmachari 2007: 5)

While the desire for cultural authenticity and the political imperative of representation underpins the project it is, of course, a performance; something the writer, Sita Brahmachari, was very aware, as she described:

I used the recordings and we had them transcribed [...] I always went back to audio [...] I was very keen that the original voices of the young people would be in the production [...] for me that was very important as it had to do with authenticity [...] it was very important that the interface between whoever performed it, and the work, and the piece of writing [...] so in a way it was transparent where it was coming from because that can be problematic with verbatim.

(Brahmachari 2008)

The themes that emerged, perhaps not unexpectedly being set in an inner city environment, were the negotiation of cultural identities, the attendant dangers of violence and drugs, and marginalisation.

Although Kristine Landon-Smith attempted to cast the actors so they matched the characters as closely as possible, some of the material was reworked with the new actors' 'cultural context' in mind. A Bangladeshi boy, Amar Bartnan Ali, who had researched and brought his uncle into the 'hot seat', originally spoke the text below, however, in *Lyrical MC* the character was changed to Shuang Lui and was spoken by a Chinese girl in English and Mandarin who redrew the character based on someone from her 'cultural context' and took that to the text. Very little of the original text was changed for the performance except for removing the specific cultural references to religion so that 'to Allah' after 'I just pray' was taken out.

SHUANG LIU

Story. Story, OK, I tell. I only work in restaurant. Restaurant name E5. Boss always tell me off. I say I need job. Boss say Ok you don't understand English, I give you job. Police office come with guns puts hands behind my back. Police Office talks to me badly. Can't say my name properly. They don't know I illegal immigrant. I think that is why. But no they want to know about sugar packet. Boss always swapping sugar packet with people for money – lots of money.

Shuang Liu Talks in Mandarin

I just wash plates I make blue plates white, I clean hard. I from Shanghai. When I think about my wife and my son, I feel like crying but man don't cry. I just pray. I need help. English, no so good. I only be here 5 months – how much English can I speak. Once I go from this place I'm not coming back.

(Brahmachari 2007: 4)

In this way *Lyrical MC* was a performance text predicated and responsive to an engagement with the ethnicity of both the participants and the performers. The 'hot seat' methodology utilised to facilitate this process in *Lyrical MC* was also a key tool in the 'Individual Actor' workshop offered by Tamasha as one part of their Developing Artist Programme.[5]

6
Kali Theatre Company 1990–2007: Producing British Asian Women Playwrights

Kali Theatre Company (1990–present)

New theatre writing by South Asian women

The influence of the Kali Theatre Company, since its inception in 1990, is clear from its verifiable claim that of 'all the new plays by British Asian woman playwrights presented since 1988 in the UK, nearly a third have been presented by Kali and of the plays by new writers, over 75% were presented by Kali' (Kali 2009). The catalyst for the creation of the Kali Theatre Company was the murder of Balwant Kaur – who was killed at the Asian Women's refuge in Brent, west London, on 22 October 1985 – which led to Rukhsana Ahmad writing *Song for a Sanctuary*. In this way the politics behind the foundation of Kali by Rukhsana Ahmad and Rita Wolf shared parallels with Jatinder Verma beginning Tara Arts in response to the racist murder of Gurdeep Singh Chaggar.

Prior to writing *Song for a Sanctuary* Rukhsana Ahmad had written two theatre-in-education pieces for Tara Arts, *Sepoy's Salt, Captain's Malt* (1985) about the British Raj and *New Constitution* (1987). She was also a member of the Asian Women's Writing Collective, formed in 1984, whose aim was to 'promote creative writing by Asian women through a supportive environment' (Randhawa). Rukhsana Ahmad's experience of AWWC's workshop/work-sharing methodology, and the feminist politics it espoused, was applied to Kali within a theatre context so that women theatre writers of South Asian descent could not only meet and share their work but also access the dramaturgical and production knowledge that might equip them for the theatre.

Rukhasana Ahmad described how 'the Balwant Kaur murder had played a big role in politicising my own work. I was so shocked it was the first time I went on any marches with the Asian Women's Writers Collective' (Ahmad 2008) However, as the programme specifically pointed out, *Song for a Sanctuary* was 'not a documentary drama but *an artistic response* to the horrific murder of an Asian woman' (Kali 1992). Indeed, Rukhsana Ahmad was keen to point out that 'it is not however, a documentary or a biographical play [...] it is a fiction, concerned as much with conflicts which arise between women who are under siege and are at crisis point in their lives, as it is with domestic violence' (Ahmad 1993: 159). In this way, the unique aspect of *Song for a Sanctuary* was the way in which it addressed the political, cultural and class differences between the women, both Asian and white, that meant the play 'bypasses the predictable clash between right-wing apathy and right-on sympathy to explore more intriguing rifts within the friendly camp itself' (Denford 1991: 91).

> I felt like I wanted to write something but I wasn't sure what, until there was an incident at a refuge where the residents had actually locked out the Asian women who were running the refuge [...] there was a row between the women [...] that was the starting point for the play [...] why did it happen? I went to research and investigate and there was a culture clash [...] with the women being quite political, left-of-centre, the women coming in were right wing, traditional [...] they had been forced out of their homes but they are not ready to lead a revolution. Essentially the story I wanted to tell was about women coming to understand what it is that divides them [...] I was less interested in why male violence happens.
>
> (Ahmad 2008)

The play was originally commissioned by Monstrous Regiment, a feminist theatre company whose name derives from a speech by Scottish Protestant reformer John Knox 'The First Blast of the Trumpet Against the Monstrous Regiment of Women' attacking women, which was published in 1558. Unfortunately, they were unable to produce the play, in part due to some concerns over the play's development, but primarily due to financial constraints.

It was at this stage that Rita Wolf became involved in the project even though she 'didn't know Rukhsana Ahmad [...] I'd heard that a play had been written based on a true incident at a woman's refuge in London. I felt the subject was so important that I sought out Rukhsana, and became very involved in the play's development' (Wolf quoted in Zahno 1991). Wolf was as good as her word and contacted Rukhsana

Ahmad and organised a number of rehearsed readings at Soho Poly
Theatre, Common Stock and the Riverside Studios throughout 1990,
utilising her contacts at ATC (Asian Theatre Co-operative) of which
she was a founder member. Rita Wolf was a well-known actress, having performed at the Royal Court Theatre in Hanif Kureishi's *Borderline*
(discussed in Chapter 8) and having played a major role in his film *My
Beautiful Launderette* as well as being known for her role as Flick Khan,
one of the first Asian characters on the northern 'soap opera' *Coronation
Street*.

Rita Wolf and Rukhsana Ahmad then applied for, and received, Arts
Council funding in order to develop the play and set up the company
that would become Kali in September and October of 1990. The aims of
the company were clear:

1. To create opportunities for Asian Women in the field of theatre and
   especially to give them a voice in the field of new writing
2. To show a commitment to the work of new women writers in Britain
   as well as to showcase work of existing South Asian writers who may
   not be known in this country
3. To train Asian women as theatre practitioners as well as writers in
   Britain

(Kali Archive 1990).

The name Kali, derived from the Hindu goddess Kali, known for her
colour and power, was chosen as it exemplified the feminist position
of the company. Over its 19-year history, Kali have produced a tremendously diverse range of new writing within its expansive brief to 'present
the distinct perspective and experience of Asian women' (Kali 2009),
albeit usually in a realist form. Kali's key strategy since its inception has
been to 'support encourage and promote' (Kali 2009) new and emer-
gent South Asian women writers alongside producing and touring new
work. This is currently done through a range of tailored development
programmes: 'Kali Futures', 'Kali Shorts' and 'Kali Labs'.

Kali Shorts is a grassroots programme that seeks out Asian women
who want to write for the first time. From a wider-ranging callout for
scripts, each chosen writer receives support and advice from an experienced writer and the opportunity to see their writing workshopped and
then presented by professional actors to an invited audience who are
encouraged to give constructive feedback.

Kali Futures aims to support and encourage the development of Asian
women writers discovered through Kali Shorts with a programme of

1-1 dramaturgical advice and workshops with professional actors and a director, culminating in a public reading' at Soho Theatre and Writers Centre. Futures graduates have received commissions from the BBC, Channel 4, other theatre companies and have been taken on by agents. Our 2005 full productions, *Bells* by Yasmin Whittaker Khan and *Chaos* by Azma Dar, were plays developed through Kali Futures.

Kali Labs is a week-long in-depth development period on a new text involving detailed dramaturgical input and workshops with actors and a director focused on assisting a writer to refine or explore experimental aspects of her writing. These are held as required to develop new work for Kali's full productions (Kali 2009).

Song for Sanctuary (1990)

Rajinder has left her violent husband and taken her three children to the women's refuge. However, she finds herself at odds with the values of her Asian caseworker Kamla at the refuge, as well as the other residents. Rajinder's daughter, Savita, is befriended by Sonia, another resident at the refuge, and confides in her that her father has been abusing her. When Rajinder finds that men have been invited into the refuge by one of the residents she decides to return home. While at home Savita finally confides in her mother about her father's sexual abuse and they return to the refuge. However, Rajinder's husband, Pradeep, tracks her down to the refuge and stabs her to death in front of her daughter.

Song for a Sanctuary achieved project funding the following year and was directed by Rita Wolf and first performed at the Worcester Arts Workshop on 8 May 1991. It then toured to the Lyric Studio, Hammersmith; Unity Theatre, Liverpool; Hoxton Hall, Hackney; Rotherham Arts Centre; Norwich Arts Centre and finally Birmingham Repertory Theatre. The play was subsequently broadcast on BBC Radio 4 on 18 February 1993.

As the play opens, Rajinder, who has recently arrived at the refuge, is cleaning out her store cupboard in the kitchen when she meets her fellow resident Sonia for the first time. We learn that Rajinder has carefully planned her departure, even making an 'inspection visit' the week before she arrived with the children, as the previous time in a refuge she 'went in an emergency situation, and it was a mistake' (161). Although the two women share a common need for the refuge their experiences and backgrounds are radically different and well-differentiated, exemplifying Rukhsana Ahmad's refusal to stereotype because, as the experienced social worker Eileen points out, 'the situation is the same but women are so different' (166). So while Rajinder is a well-spoken, highly educated Punjabi married mother-of-three who has only been to a refuge once before, Sonia is a white, childless, and much to Rajinder's horror, unmarried with a physically abusive boyfriend to whom she constantly returns.

In the same way, while Rajinder and her caseworker Kamla may both be Asian 'the cautious sometimes hostile encounters between [them] ... provide the most interesting aspects of the play' (Hoyle 1991). Kamla, as Rajinder points out, may have an 'Indian name but she didn't look very Indian' (161) as she's dressed in jeans and a t-shirt in contrast to Rajinder's sari. As Sarah Dadswell has pointed out, Rukhsana Ahmad, like many of the women at AWWC, 'were first generation migrants to the UK and therefore had at least one South Asian language, which informed their sense of cultural identity and is frequently expressed in their writing' (2010).

As a consequence Kali, like Tara Arts and Tamasha, recognised that encouraging writers to use their 'other' languages, alongside English, was a powerful exemplar of the ways in which it might be possible to dramatise the heterogeneous cultural differences and diasporic identities of Asian women and assert difference. This use of 'other' languages literally articulates the cultural differences between Rajinder and Kamla (despite the fact they are both black women) as she asks her:

RAJINDER: [...] Where do you come from Kamla?
KAMLA: South London
RAJINDER: 'Tusi Punjabi boalday o?' (163) [Do you speak Punjabi?]
KAMLA: I'm sorry I don't.
(160)

Although Kamla's family diaspora was from the Caribbean, as a second generation British Asian her understanding of home is the UK, or more precisely, 'South London'. Kamla has actively attempted to shed any signs of her Asian cultural identity and assimilate because 'who cares for all that crap anyway?' (164). Rajinder clearly does 'care' and confronts Kamla:

RAJINDER: Call yourself an Asian, do you?
KAMLA: I am one.

RAJINDER: I wouldn't go that far! Black you may be, Asian you certainly are not.

KAMLA: You can't deny me my identity, I won't let you. You people with your saris and your bloody lingo and all your certainties about the universe, you don't have a monopoly on being Asian. You can't box it and contain it and exclude others. I'll define myself as I bloody well want to (183)

However, the play tries to unpick some of the complexities of 'belonging' to a cultural community. On the one hand the Asian community

Song for a Sanctuary (1991)

© Kali Theatre Company.

In the foreground is Rajinder played by Kusum Haider, with her abusive husband, Pradeep, played by Simon Nagra, standing in silhouette behind.

is seen as colluding in the oppression of women such as Rajinder and on the other it provides a place where 'children can grow up with some sense of who they are' (171). There is also a generational split, so that for the second generation British Asians such as Kamla, and indeed Savita, there are questions as to the place of cultural traditions in their lives as 'language classes, music lessons, dance lessons, they tried it all [...] it was no use to me' (164).

The class concerns are clearly articulated in the play as Kamla feels that Rajinder is 'quite well off' and is sceptical that she really needs to have a room in spite of her colleague, Eileen, protesting that she 'doesn't think anyone comes here out of choice' (163). Indeed, Rukhsana Ahmad was praised for the complexity of characterisations such as Kamla, which showed 'her courage in allowing the women running the refuge to expose the ambivalence of motives of anyone involved in caring for others' (P.L. 1991).

Rajinder is not afraid to articulate her class-consciousness in order to defend herself, so that when Kamla insists she go to the housing officer she feels able to refuse as 'I'm not one of your illiterate working class women to be managed by you' (174). While the play is sympathetic to Rajinder's understandable abhorrence of 'washing my dirty linen in public' (175) it also powerfully supports Kamla's seemingly academic case that 'it's the privatisation of women's lives which keeps us from seeing domestic violence in a socio-political context' (175). Rajinder's circumstances are ignored by the police as a 'domestic', resulting in the sexual abuse of her daughter and Rajinder's murder.

Kamla is unable to understand Rajinder's reluctance to seek help from the housing authorities and social services because she does not appreciate what it like to live within the Asian community. While Kamla may try on Rajnder's shawl or try and recall Indian songs and dances she learnt as a child she does not appreciate or understand the possible repercussions for Rajinder of creating a 'scandal' when she has a daughter who must marry within that community.

As Gabrielle Griffin has recognised, Rajinder has 'fully internalised her communities' prescriptions of honour and shame' (2003: 153), so when Rajinder confides in her older sister Amrit about the abuse she is suffering she is accused of selfishness. Amrit emotionally blackmails Rajinder into keeping quiet so that she does not upset her mother with the allegations.

Rajinder's family have known for some time that she has been suffering domestic violence from her husband but have refused to believe her, even when she told them that Pradeep tried to push her out of a window when she was pregnant. Amrit's insistence that 'honour is always prefer-able to disgrace' (171) is an unambiguous instruction for Rajinder to acquiesce to the treatment she is receiving at the hands of her husband. This point was theatrically driven home with the 'doubling of Simon Nagra as both Rajinder's crazy husband and mealy mouthed sister-in-law [...] an inspired stroke' (Denford) with the scene being played behind gauze, symbolic of a veil being drawn over this issue by the Asian community.

Savita has not only witnessed her father's physical violence towards her mother, describing how he threw plates at her mother for answering him back and an incident when they returned home late to find him polishing his kirpan [dagger], but also sexual abuse. While Savita tells her mother 'she knows about the porno films, in the house [...] he forced you to drink and [...] and [...] he made you do things you didn't want to do' (177), Rajinder does not realise that Pradeep has also been sexually abusing Savita. When Rajinder does find out that Sonia has brought a man into the refuge and insists on returning home, Savita reveals her terrible secret:

> (PRADEEP *stands still behind her. Pause. Enter Savita wearing a short frilly black 'naughty' nightie. [...]. Rajinder moves into the spotlight with* Savita)
> SAVITA: Here I am Mummy
> RAJINDER: Where did you get that?
> SAVITA: It was a secret present from Papaji
> RAVINDER: What are you saying, Savits?
> SAVITA: Here's the card, I've still got it. Read it, if you don't believe me.
>   (RAJINDER *takes the card.* PRADEEP *reads out*)
> PRADEEP: To Savita, for being so lovely, Papa. (Pause. SAVITA holds out two porn magazines to RAJINDER)
> SAVITA: He gave me these too.
> (181)

This scene is played out to dramatic effect as Rajinder and Savita are spotlit with Pradeep literally haunting the action before he interpolates himself into the scene.

The structuring of the play in which 'the three act play has fewer and fewer scenes in each act as Rajinder's time runs out' (Griffin 2003: 150) builds to a dramatic crescendo that ends with the murder of Rajinder. As Rukhsana Ahmad has stated, she had no interest in writing a play about the psychology of male violence in *Song for a Sanctuary*. So while

Pradeep's physical presence looms large over the action, he is effectively silenced, as the stage is given over to the female characters and the only rationale for his violent actions are 'her punishment for taking away what was mine' (186) as he stabs Rajinder to death. Indeed, the final line of the play from Sonia that 'someone will be here to help us soon, I'm sure' (186) rings chillingly hollow in Rukhsana Ahmad's 'perceptive and moving play' (Vaughan 1991).

In 1992, Rita Wolf moved to New York and eventually had to relinquish her role as artistic director on logistical grounds. However, she remained a key supporter on the board of Kali. Rukhsana Ahmad took on the position of artistic director until 2002.

Critic Alex Sierz recognised the ambition and clarity of the text in Kali's next production, *River on Fire*, written by Rukhsana Ahmad in which 'the debates about belief and faith are clear and compelling and the play also bravely grapples with big spiritual ideas' (Sierz 2000).

River on Fire (2000)

Set against the background of the Hindu–Muslim riots in Bombay, precipitated by the destruction of the Babri mosque, the writer Seema Siddique is dying. On Seema's death, her Hindu daughter from her first marriage, Zara, and her British Muslim children from her second marriage, Kiran and Bobby, are divided over her funeral rites. Kiran is starring in a Bollywood film written by her mother, based on Sophocles' *Antigone* and set in the court of Mogul ruler Akbar. The story of her fictional character, Shola, increasingly starts to resemble her family situation. The family confrontation on communal lines eventually leads to tragedy, as Zara is killed when she becomes caught up in the wider conflict. An omnipresent Seema watches helplessly and asks 'why should birth determine your fate?'

River on Fire, directed by Helena Uren, was praised for being a 'high paced provocative and absorbing piece of drama' (Clews 2001) was first performed at the Lyric Theatre, Hammersmith, on 31 October 2000 and developed from a radio drama *An Urnful of Ashes*, first broadcast on BBC Radio 4.

River on Fire was a contemporary reworking of Sophocles' *Antigone*, set against the backdrop of the communal riots that erupted as a result of the demolition of the Babri mosque in Ayodhya on 6 December 1992 by Hindu militants. The site on which the mosque had been built was believed by Hindus to be the birthplace of Ram, a Hindu god. These riots in turn sparked unrest in Muslim Pakistan and Bangladesh that resulted in Hindus being attacked, which precipitated counter-demonstrations in Bombay that resulted in further deaths and curfews. The riots resumed in January 1993 with an escalation in the number of attacks on Muslims and on 12 March ten bombs exploded in the city. The *River on Fire* programme details these events and that an estimated 784 people were killed overall.

Seema was born a Hindu and remained so when she married her husband of the same faith, however when Seema went to university she became an atheist. After her marriage floundered she married a Muslim and she herself became a Buddhist before returning to atheism. The character of Seema was based on Ismat Chughtai, a radical feminist writer championed by Muslims, who died in 1992 in the wake of the riots caused by the destruction of the Babri mosque. In contravention of her desire to be buried at sea her grandson cremated her, thus angering her Muslim supporters. In this way, Rukhsana Ahmad used the conflict within the family to explore the wider context of religious unrest in India which contrasts to Seema's liberal belief that 'If I were God I'd rather have my worshippers *choose* me. Pick your moment, I'd say to them – confirmation, bar mitzvah, initiation, *bismillah*, navjot [...]' (11). Indeed, Ahmad deliberately complicates the religious lineage of the mother in order to make any claim to co-opt her death for one particular side patently absurd as, for her, the play was 'my attempt to understand our need for religion and ritual' (Ahmad quoted in Clews 2001).

River on Fire breaks from realistic convention so that Seema is omnipresent throughout the play as she *throws off the covers and rises from the dead with a lithe quick grace, scans the audience* (11) and directly addresses the audience in order to give her thoughts on the unfolding conflict in the family. Seema's first line is an indication of the key preoccupation of the play, the interplay between faiths – 'I might even be able to tell you soon who waits across the river: God or Raam or Allah' (11). She even at times offers some light relief, as she tells the audience that if she had bought a £6.99 will at WH Smith stating her wishes all this trouble might have been avoided.

Kiran and her brother Bobby are Seema's daughter and son from her second marriage and are nominally Muslim while their half-sister Zara, from their mother's first marriage, is Hindu. Kiran and Bobby have been brought up in London and the cultural difference between them is exemplified in the first meeting between the half siblings: as Bobby attempts to shake hands with Zara, she puts her hands together in a formal greeting, *namaste*, and he then attempts to imitate her.

In the play-within-a-play, Kiran is starring in a Bollywood film set in the court of the religiously liberal Moghul ruler Akbar. She is playing the role of Shola, an equivalent to Antigone, whose brother is to be buried in accordance with Muslim custom by the command of Emperor Akbar. However, in a parallel of the confrontation she will have with her own family she insists that the brother be cremated in accordance with Hindu rituals as her character is forced to 'think how you'd feel if you weren't allowed the ritual you wanted' (23) by the director.

The theme of religious dogmatism and corruption are explored through the Bollywood story line. Seema's script is not in safe hands as the director, Waheed, is more interested in 'sex appeal' (14) than historical accuracy. The film is backed by Hindu fundamentalists so that Akbar is portrayed as an intolerant Muslim ruler in opposition to the religiously principled Hindu character played by Kiran. This was not at all what Seema intended as 'Shola was my Antigone – not Joan of Arc' (43). In other words, Shola, like Antigone, should be read as standing up to the power of politicians, not as a religious crusader, like Joan of Arc. Kiran quits the film as it becomes increasingly biased to the Hindu heroine's religious defiance and anti-Muslim sentiment.

Kiran's work and private life intersect as the play progresses. She realises that Zara's husband, Ashok, a politician, is not only one of the backers of the film but is also trying to exploit Seema's death for political advantage. Ashok has put great pressure on his wife to insist on Seema being cremated, even sending out press releases to publicise the funeral. He aims to exacerbate the situation for his own propaganda claiming 'she was born a Hindu – that was her original faith. That's who she was' (30) while conveniently ignoring the other religious aspects of her life and her Muslim children's wishes. In this respect Ahmad succumbs to making Ashok a convenient target as he becomes an increasingly unsympathetic, violent and corrupt character linked to slum clearances.

The escalation of conflict within the family also mirrors the wider communal violence as relations between the half siblings deteriorate further at the cremation that opens Act Two. As the *pundit* recites the Hindu prayers, Kiran and Bobby compete with their own Muslim prayers 'La – I laaha, ill – Allah' (57). Their opposition leads to a violent confrontation as Ashok strikes Kiran to stop her chanting her prayers and the bigotry at the heart of the conflict is exposed as Zara claims that 'the Muslims are not blameless [...] they're insular, suspicious, full of self pity' (62).

The reality of the communal violence is brought home to the insulated Kiran when she goes to Shantinagar to address a rally by Aawaaz, an extreme Muslim organisation, and sees it has been razed to the ground. She realises that her mother would not have agreed with her militant tendencies:

KIRAN: All I wanted was to declare that Amma [mother] hadn't gone over to the other side. She wasn't one of *them* –
BOBBY: *Us, them*! There you go again
KIRAN: Sorry –
BOBBY: You know, don't you, that's not how *Amma* [mother] thought or felt?

The play ends on a pessimistic note as Zara goes to find Kiran and Bobby in order to apologise and is set upon by Muslim militants and killed with the only comfort being 'she did not die for some chauvinistic drum beating god – but in search of peace. [...] surely this *is* a cause worth dying for [...] ?' (86).

In 2002, Rukhsana Ahmad stepped down as artistic director and was replaced by Janet Steel at a time when the company moved from project funding to revenue-funded status by the Arts Council. Janet Steel originally worked as an actor, including for Tara Arts, and had directed at Battersea Arts Centre, Northampton, and Coventry Belgrade prior to joining Kali. The first play she directed for Kali was *Sock 'em With Honey* by Bapsi Sidhwa about a Parsee girl in love with a Jewish boy. This was followed by Shelley Silas's *Calcutta Kosher*, which was first performed at the Southwark Playhouse on 4 February 2004.

Calcutta Kosher (2004)

Set in the Jewish community of Calcutta, the action unfolds over one *shabbat* evening dinner. Mozelle has called her two daughters, Esther and Silvie, back home to Calcutta so they can be at their mother's side as she recovers from a heart attack. It is many years since Esther, who has been living in England, and Silvie, in California, have visited their mother. As the evening progresses and their mother's health deteriorates it is revealed that Maki, the house servant the daughters have always looked down on, is actually their half-sister.

Shelley Silas's previous play, *Falling* (2002), about a couple facing up to the fact they will never have the child they long for, was produced at the Bush Theatre where she was the Pearson Writer-in-Residence. In *Calcutta Kosher* she explores themes of religion, belonging, cultural identity and mother-daughter relationships as she asks 'what keeps our identity and our culture going when we are physically removed from it?' (Silas 2004a). The programme goes out of its way to explain for a British audience the little-known presence and origin of the Jewish communities in India. It describes how the Jews of India are distinct from Eastern European Jews [Ashkenazii] with the Calcutta Jewish community established by Shalom Aaron Hakohen, a Baghdadi Jew, in the late 1700s. Indeed, the play has some gentle fun at the expense of the food that Ashkenazii eat:

> MOZELLE: Fish balls?
> ESTHER: Of course.
> MOZELLE: I didn't know fish had them. (17)

Food, of course, is a key part of any cultural heritage and in the back of the script a number of the particular hybrid Indian-Jewish recipes such as *Chukla Bukla*, *Aloomakallas* and *Granny Lily's Mahmoosa* mentioned in the play are set out. The publishing of the recipes functions as a means of trying to preserve the Jewish Indian culture by the author and Mozelle admonishes the two daughters in the play for not cooking Indian-Jewish food for their families because their non-Indian husbands won't eat it. *Calcutta Kosher* not only makes visible this little-known marginal community in India, and its difference from the wider Jewish community, but also functions as a 'voice speaking of India's traditional religious tolerance' (Ahmed 2004) towards Jews, in stark contrast to the experience of Jews in Europe.

Although Shelley Silas came to live in England aged two, having been born in Calcutta to Jewish parents, she 'wouldn't call myself English [...] I do call myself "other" [...] I have a very strong connection to India and Calcutta' (2004b). Her own biography clearly informs her exploration of hybrid cultural identities in *Calcutta Kosher*. Interestingly, she points out that this 'otherness' is not predicated solely on 'race' or its synonym, skin colour, but on more complex articulations of ethnicity and hybrid identities as 'my skin is white but I definitely wouldn't call myself English. I don't think your cultural identity is related only to colour of your skin' (Silas 2004a). This is dramatised to comic effect in the play as the daughter Silvie describes how people are confused by her not adhering to the stereotype of a Jewish person.

MOZELLE: And who did you sit next to?
SILVIE: An incredibly unattractive short fat man. He couldn't believe that I was born in Calcutta and a Jew. So I gave him a brief history, the usual when, where and how our ancestors left Baghdad hundreds of years ago. He said I didn't look like a Jew.
MOZELLE: And what did you say?
SILVIE: Oh, and why is that?
MOZELLE: And what did you say?
SILVIE: Because you have a small nose.
MOZELLE: And what did you say?
SILVIE: You don't look like a man.
MOZELLE: And what did he say?
SILVIE: Oh and why is that?
MOZELLE: And what did you say?
SILVIE: Because you have a small *dunda*. [penis] (Silas 33)

The dialogue, praised by critics for being 'sharp and witty' (Parker 2004) cleverly mixes background information on the history of Jews in Calcutta for the audience written in the form of an entertaining American-style comedic *stichk*. This, allied with the use of the Hindi slang '*dunda*' on the tagline, allows the hybrid identity of Sylvie's Indian Jewish diasporic cultural identity to be performed with great dramatic economy. Indeed, the fluidity of hybrid cultural identity is articulated by Sylvie in the play:

SYLVIE: You know, I think my identity keeps changing. When we were sent to school in England I wanted to fit in, but I never did. I looked different, I sounded different. Then I went to America and it started all over again. When people ask me where I'm from, I say I was born in Calcutta to a Jewish family. 'So you're Indian?' Well not 100%. 'But you were born in India?' Yeah. 'And you're Jewish?' Yes. 'But you're American as well?'(89)

The play takes place over one Sabbath supper and opens as Mozelle is preparing for the return of her two daughters, Esther and Sylvie. The first shock the daughters will receive when they arrive is to find that their mother, who 'symbolises the dying community' (Silas 2004b) has

Calcutta Kosher (2004)

© Robert Day.

From left to right, Jamilla Massey as Mozelle, Harvey Virdi as Esther, Shelley King as Silvie and Seema Bowri as Maki.

just suffered a heart attack and discharged herself from hospital. Like Mozelle, the Jewish Indian community is on the brink of collapse, with prayers now held at only one of the few synagogues due to a dwindling number of worshippers.

Esther, who is living in London with her husband Peter and two children Amy and Alice, has not seen her mother for 10 years. Esther has become very anglicised, as a result of being sent away to boarding school in London, so she no longer cooks Indian food and has forgotten all but a few words of the Hindi that she used to speak fluently. Similarly, her sister Silvie has become assimilated into American culture and eschews her Jewish Indian heritage, rarely going to synagogue. Neither daughter follows their mother's wish to 'keep our tradition, keep our food, keep our culture and our identity' (89).

In contrast to the rather staid Esther, with her sensible hat and low-heeled open-toed shoes, the stage directions tell us that Sylvie 'bursts through the doors Hollywood style' (28) as befits a rather stereotypical resident of Los Angeles. Sylvie's claim that she is the 'bad' sister is supported by the fact that she has inadvertently smuggled cocaine into the country and then cajoles Esther into trying some.

(ESTHER hesitates is about to try some when Saddique appears between the women)
SIDDIQUE: (loudly) Bath Karega? (Ready for your bath?)
(Esther jerks backwards, spills all the cocaine as Sylvie watches.) (45)

The critics were very complimentary of Silas's use of humour in *Calcutta Kosher* recognising that she 'has a way with a comic set piece and she writes wicked one liners' (Curtis 2004).

Sylvie, like Esther, has not visited her mother recently but also wants her to come back and live with her. However, Mozelle wants to die in her own home and is not enamoured with the prospect of returning with either daughter as 'Esther is more English than the English and Silvie has turned into an American nightmare' (Silas 2004: 55). What the daughters do have in common is their surprise in finding that Maki, a servant in their eyes, is still in their old home and is looking after their mother. What they do not realise is that she is in fact their half-sister – even when Mozelle tells Esther that Maki is her daughter she does not believe her:

ESTHER: I know she's been living in this house since she was a child, but she can't be your daughter. It's ridiculous.
MOZELLE: It's true.
ESTHER: And I'm Ghandi
MOZELLE: Indira or Mahatma? (18)

The play performs a number of Jewish rituals for the audience, doing *Kiddush*, saying the *Shema*, with care being taken in the production that these were accurately performed in order to fulfil the self reflexive didactic aims of the play. The author combines plot and ritual to dramatic effect when the *Kiddush* is to be done, a blessing of the wine before the *Shabbat* meal:

Maki continues to lay the table, taking out two silver candlesticks from the cupboard. She also takes out a silver goblet, a bottle of wine and a prayer book and a Kippah, from Iraq. She places these on the table.
MOZELLE: The youngest daughter will make Kiddush tonight.
SYLVIE: Oh, you know I can't read Hebrew.
MOZELLE: Maki will read.
Maki picks up the prayer book.
(60)

Mozelle reveals she is not *like* a mother to Maki but *is* her mother before literally choking on her *Shabbat* bread as Act One closes. In Act Two the details of Mozelle's affair with a Hindu man, Ravi, are revealed, together with the fact that Maki was born in Darjeeling where her mother used to stay for the summer without her husband. When Maki was born she went to live with her father but he died when she was four and so she returned to her mother's house, but as a servant.

Silas mobilises 'other' languages in the play to demonstrate the importance of cultural identity that would resonate for a British Asian audience. When Mozelle attempts to make amends and allay Maki's fears for the future she speaks to her in Hindi, a language her other daughters no longer use;

> MAKI: Hum kea kuraga? Koi nai hai hamara waste. [What will I do? I don't have anyone.]
> MOZELLE: You have two sisters.
> MAKI: Wo lok parwa nei kurta hamara waste. Khalipaisa mankta. [They won't care about me. Just about the money]
> MOZELLE: Hamara paisa jaiga teen hissa. [My money will be split three ways.] (56)

Maki, like Esther and Sylvie, is indeed Jewish, but in contrast to them, she is determined to carry on the Jewish traditions, insisting that they do not abandon the synagogues even though, rather like Mozelle, they are crumbling. Interestingly, Silas makes the point that although both Mozelle and Maki conducted relationships with non-Jewish men, Mozelle with the Hindu Ravi and Maki with Mohammad, the Muslim caretaker of the synagogue, they are both the most committed to preserving their faith. In this respect *Calcutta Kosher* is not only a eulogy to a dying community but also celebrates 'the idea of the precious irreducibility of complex cultural identities' (Shore 2004).

Deadeye (2006) by Amber Lone

Life in the Chaudhry household is difficult for Deema as she tries to keep up her studies, apply for jobs and keep her family together. Her father, Rafique, spends his time dreaming of living a millionaire lifestyle in the Cotswolds, rather than inner city Birmingham, and refuses to get a job even though the phone has been cut off and the house is about to be repossessed. Rafique's long-suffering wife, Zainab, spends her time tending her Kashmiri plants in the garden and trying to convince Deema to settle down and get married. Tariq, Deema's brother, is a drug addict who brings trouble into the house when he is accused of stealing a large amount of money from his drug dealing cousin, Jamil. Deema's choice is stark, either stay at home and sacrifice herself for her family or leave and make a new life for herself in London.

Deadeye was first performed on 12 October 2006 at The Door, Birmingham Repertory Theatre, and then toured to Nottingham and Manchester before opening at Soho Theatre, London, as part of the 'Asian Women Talk Back' festival in which 20 pieces of new work by Asian women writers in various stages of development were showcased. Amber Lone's first full-length play, *Paradise* (2003), also produced by Birmingham Repertory examined the radicalisation of Muslim youth in Britain. She was then selected as one of the six writers for Soho Theatre's Writers Attachment Programme in 2004/5 and subsequently given a second commission by Birmingham Repertory in order to write *Deadeye*.

Through the main protagonist, Deema, Amber Lone set out to explore how and 'why certain male relatives felt able to judge and control the girls and women around them' (Lone 2006a: 3) in the Asian community. In congruence with the Kali ethos, as Lyn Gardner pointed out in her review for the *Guardian* 'there have been plenty of plays that explored the second- or third-generation Asian immigrant [*sic*] experience, but this is the first I have seen with such a distinctly female perspective (And with barely a mention of arranged marriage)' (Gardner 2006b).

While the play is specific to a Kashmiri family from east Birmingham and dramatises the tensions of specific intergenerational cultural attitudes, Amber Lone was at pains to stress that *Deadeye* was a 'discussion of issues rather than race [...] themes which are universal such as loss and love, displacement, hopes, fears, faith and how people try and communicate but can't' (Lone quoted in Parkes 2006). This plea to reach out to an audience beyond the Asian constituency and contest her classification as an *Asian* writer exemplifies a recurring complaint that Asian writers feel that their ethnicity is privileged over their profession in an attempt to proscribe them from writing beyond their own constituency.

Deema is studying at college, helping her mother run the house and contributing financially to the house but her father, Rafique, is only interested in his son Tariq. In contrast to Tariq, Deema does have the chance of a good job and is down to the last 100 applicants to become an air steward; a job that offers a literal, as well as symbolic, escape from the family. However, Rafique's plans for his daughter extend only as far as trying to arrange a financially expedient marriage for her to his nephew Jimmy.

Amber Lone uses Zainab, Deema's mother, to model a very traditional approach to marriage in which Deema 'used to watch dad when he came in after a day out cruising the Peak District or touring with friends [. . .] Soon as he was through the door, you'd be there with tea, roti. I'd watch him lie down on the sofa, put his legs up onto your lap and you would press them for hours' (78). Zainab expects Deema to show the same level of self sacrifice to all the male members of the household, not just her husband, and 'be sensible [. . .] settle down [. . .] there is Tariq to think of' (79). However, this subservience is shown to yield little reward and Zainab's own experience of marriage has proved less than salutary 'do you think they asked me if I liked him? [. . .] We did what we had to do. We would never hurt our parents' (54).

A clear irony is exposed by the writer that, while Zainab and Rafique came to Britain as it afforded them the very opportunity to work and become self sufficient, they now wish to deny Deema on account of her gender. A picture is painted of a community in which appearance is more important than fulfillment:

> RAFIQUE: Cabin crew. (*Clears his throat*) You must think carefully. We will talk later. I have to get ready.
> RAFIQUE EXITS
> ZAINAB: Kooriyeh [girl] . . . clear the dishes.
> DEEMA DOESN'T MOVE
> DEEMA: It's well paid and I get loads of time off. (*beat*) Why can't you be pleased for me?
> ZAINAB: And what do I explain the friends, the neighbours, your family [. . .] why my children run from me.

Amber Lone shows that living in the tight-knit Asian community can be a double-edged sword, on the one hand its a supportive network that lends Rafique money, on the other, its judgemental and at times petty as the neighbours taunt them for their financial plight 'Zainab jee [. . .] your phone is out of order again . . . you have bad luck naa? My phone is tip top' (37). The fact that the phone has been cut off is not only indicative of the poor state of the family finances but is also symbolic of the family being increasingly ostracised by the community, and is indicative of the breakdown of communication within the family.

The male characters in *Deadeye* are all seriously flawed, either addicts, extortionists or ineffectual. Rafique has purchased 500 cookbooks at a cost of five pounds each, on credit, which he plans to resell at ten pounds in order to address the household's near bankruptcy. The only drawback, as his wife, Zainab, points out to comic effect, is finding someone 'who will buy bacon photos in this area' (36) and the small matter that none of their neighbours read English.

While Rafique aspires to the quintessence of English respectability symbolised by the Cotswolds properties he dreams of owning, Amber Lone is clear that for many migrants the 'dream' of success and belonging are just that. Deema reminds us that these seemingly harmless aspirations have had real consequences on his family so that while he claimed 'tomorrow we'll be rich [. . .] too rich. Today we have no school clothes, bus fare, food' (92).

The inauspicious first impression of Tariq trying to steal from his sister's purse while she is asleep is borne out as the play progresses. When he is later accused of stealing £9,000 from his cousin Jimmy and is forced to go on the run, the burden of responsibility again falls to Deema; who is forced to sacrifice her own ambitions, symbolised by her letter of acceptance from the airline. Tariq, like all the male members of the family, is more concerned with getting assistance from his sister:

DEEMA: You're always desperate. Meanwhile, I go to college, apply for jobs, get the shopping mum needs, help pay the bills, wash the dishes, make the roti [. . .] tell dad lies about where you are [. . .]. (58)

While the unbending traditions of the parents will cause a rift with their British-born daughter, Asian culture is portrayed in the *Deadeye* as something that can also unite generations and transcend ethnicities. One of the rare moments of harmony between the mother and father is when Rafique and Zainab recite a *ghazal* together:

ZAINAB: This will not grow on your English farm. (*She presents a pot containing a small leafy plant*) You didn't recognise the leaves?
RAFIQUE: Raath Kee Rani.
Rafique recites the fourth line of Nasir Kaazmi's ghazal beginning 'Zabaan sakhun ko, sakhun baankpan ko tarsega [. . .]' Zainab joins him and together they recite the fifth line. (35)

However, the plant that reminds them of their life in Kashmir, which only thrives in full sun, will struggle to put down roots in England.

Amber Lone portrays the parents' beliefs as heartfelt but misguided but is less sparing of the religious hypocrisy of her own generation:

JIMMY   Don't say nothing in the Qur'an about hash!
TARIQ: It's nushaa ... still gets you high
JIMMY: I read Jum'aa every Friday [...] while you're burning the gear
TARIQ: So you're a hypocrite? (28)

One of the few moments of warmth in *Deadeye* is mediated through the cultural exchange as Kerry and Tariq sing the Nazia Hussan song together, in an echo of Rafique and Zainab and the *ghazal*.[1]

KERRY: Sing me that song [...] you know [...] the one we used to hear when we were at school.
TARIQ: Fuck off! [...]
TARIQ: Alright Alright. 'Aap Jaisa koi mairee zindagi naa ayee, Baath bun jaye [...] '
KERRY: Uhuh Uhuh.
TARIQ: Baath bunjayee [...]. '
KERRY: 'Bot ban jai! Bot ban jai!' Once more go on [...]
(51)

If, as Amber Lone states, 'theatre should be about crossing barriers and introducing people to other cultures' (Lone quoted in Parkes 2006) then the character of Kerry functions as means of examining and explaining cultural differences, as well as the similarities where gender intersects 'race'. Kerry mistakenly believes that Jimmy is going to take her to Kashmir to meet his relatives so they can get married. However, her romanticised view of Asian family life is sharply at odds with her own experience in which 'Pakis are the worst [...] they like turn up, sardine packed in the car and call 'em honkie bitches if they won't gang bang' (43).

Deadeye utilises all the elements of the thriller genre, suspense, plot twists and blackmail, to drive the drama. Act One culminates in an offstage struggle at the Chaudhry's house as Tariq's parents hold off Jimmy's thugs who have come to retrieve his stolen money. As Tariq tries to escape out the back door we hear '*a thud and a scream*' (71) and then blackout; leaving the audience with a classic 'cling hanger' until they return after the interval.

When Jimmy catches up with the badly beaten Tariq after the interval he gives him an ultimatum; to return his money to him at the mosque by Friday prayers – or else. In a second act plot-twist we find out it is actually Kerry, Jimmy's girlfriend, who has stolen the money. *Deadeye* deploys a classic trope of the thriller genre, blackmail, in order to reveal this.

JIMMY: Don't say you haven't thought about it.
Jimmy picks up the envelope and throws it at Deema.
Open it [. . .] Just have a look.
Deema opens up the envelope and finds two tickets in it.
Two tickets to Islamabad. Rafique is up for it, believe me.
DEEMA: You seriously think I'm gonna catch a plane . . .
JIMMY: He told my dad it'd be the happiest day for him [. . .] his daughter married to a boy with such good prospects and a family union.
(83)

In response to Jimmy's suggestion, Deema plunges a screwdriver into his leg, adding an element of 'In Yer Face' theatre to the proceedings. As Jimmy writhes in agony Kerry enters from the bedroom, tears up the plane tickets and walks out with his money.

At the close of the play, Zainab's Raath Kee Rani plant is dying, despite her best endeavours, and the family are making a pyre of all Rafique's unsold cookery books – and his hopes of financial salvation – in the tandoor. The Kashmiri plant's failure to flourish is symbolic of the parents' inability to adapt to this harsh and alien environment, and the family's fragile roots. However, there is hope as Deema's valedictory 'I am ready to breathe again' (95) indicates her acceptance of an autonomous future and partial reconciliation with her parents. Nevertheless, Amber Lone makes clears the intolerable pressures on Deema as an Asian woman:

DEEMA: D'you know what it feels like. I can't watch it any more. Every time I look at you, it's like someone's stuck a knife in my guts, they're twistin' it all round and they just won't stop. Every time dad an' mum [. . .] that knife digs in a bit more and it's like the blood is filling up in my lungs until it's in my throat and I'm suffocating [. . .] I'm suffocating. (95)

Deadeye (2006)

© Robert Day.

Shane Zaza as Tariq unearthing his mother's Raath Kee Rani plant to get to his heroin

Deema's insistence that she has no plans to return home suggest the playwright's view is an unsentimental one: 'if you can't save everyone at least you should save yourself' (Grimley 2006a). Her decision to leave is vindicated as the play ends with Tariq digging up the heroin he has been hiding under the Raath Kee Rani plant. Reviewers offered uniformly high praise for the performances and Lyn Gardener of the *Guardian* rightly insisted that 'whatever the inexperience of Amber Lone as a writer she draws on her own experience of Asian life to good effect and writes about it with an unaffected directness' (Gardner 2006c).

7
Tara Arts 1997–2007: Mapping a 'Binglish' Diaspora

Introduction

The roots, or as Jatinder Verma prefers 'routes' (Verma 2006b: 385) of Tara Arts' 25th Anniversary Trilogy *Journey to the West* (2002) could be said to lie in his journey from Kenya to England, aged 14, on Valentine's Day 1968. The rising level of Kenyan Asian immigration to Britain at that time had been triggered by the increasingly restrictive 'Africanisation' policies, which came into force against those Asians unwilling to take up Kenyan citizenship after Kenya gained independence from British rule on 12 December 1963. In Britain, the dire warnings of Conservative front bench politician Enoch Powell, of 'a nation busily engaged in heaping up its own funeral pyre' (Powell 1968), symbolised the apocalyptic tone of the 'non-white' immigration debate. Indeed, contrary to Powell's predicted figure of 50,000 Kenyan Asians entering Britain every year the 'Government data showed that the number of Kenyan Asians entering was 6,149 in 1965, 6,489 in 1966 and 13,000 in 1967' (Jones and Gnanapala 2000: 13).

The Labour Government's 'Commonwealth Immigrants Act' of 1968 was passed in just three days and 'had the effect of treating Kenyan Asians with valid British passports as "aliens" allowing only those who had ancestral connections with the UK to enter freely' (Jones and Gnanapala 2000: 15). In the light of this, it was fittingly ironic that the work of Tara Arts in its previous 25-year history had been purposefully incendiary in its desire to contest and indeed recast notions of 'Britishness' as well as British theatre practice.

In *Journey to the West* (from here, *JTW*) trilogy Tara mapped an Indian diaspora to Kenya and Britain over the course of the last century in a self-conscious act of postcolonial historical recovery from a subaltern perspective that was theatrically realised through the application of their

'Binglish' methodology. *Part I* followed the 32,000 Indian workers who were transported to Kenya at the turn of the nineteenth century to work as indentured labour for the British and build the East African Railway. *Part II* is focused around the experience, shared by Jatinder Verma, of the Kenyan Asian 'exodus' to Britain in 1968, while *Part III* interrogated a hybrid British Asian identity in contemporary Britain in the light of this diaspora. While the postcolonial provenance of the *JTW* trilogy was in part a straightforward attempt to recover and make visible an Asian history overwritten by and inextricably linked with colonial power, it also attempted to give agency to a subaltern Asian voice through methodology that underpinned the theatrical realisation of the work.

The *JTW* trilogy signalled a change of emphasis for Tara Arts as they focused on reconnecting with the Asian community from which they had sprung in 1977. Perhaps it was a tacit admission that, while Tara Arts had found critical acclaim and a mainstream profile at the Royal National Theatre in the early 1990s with shows such as *Tartuffe* (1992), *The Little Clay Cart* (1994) and *Cyrano* (1995), they had lost touch with and, indeed, failed to carry with them their constituent Asian audience. For Jatinder Verma 'the project was about artistically rebuilding a bridge with the Asian community' (Hussein 1999: 1). This was to be achieved methodologically by going out and interviewing members of the Asian community and documenting the stories of their experiences of living in and then leaving Kenya in the 1960s as source material for the performance.

Jatinder Verma has commented himself that the death of his father in 1995 crystallised the realisation that the chance to document those personal histories was receding. His belief that a 'people without a history are a people without a future' (Verma 1998c) further underpinned his personal and professional desire to document and dramatise these histories with Tara Arts. The *JTW* trilogy articulated the particular diasporic journey that led to a Kenyan Asian presence in Britain from which their postcolonial, as well as anti-colonial, position can be read, as 'anti-colonial positions are embedded in specific histories and cannot be collapsed into some pure oppositional essence' (Loomba 1998: 15).

In 1997 Tara Arts received a stabilisation grant from the Arts Council, the purpose of which was described as to help 'arts organisations to develop and refocus their work' (Arts Council 2006), thus addressing the financial as well as artistic implications of this project. Tara were then in a position to embark on 'this grand plan' (Hussein 2001: 3) as their then dramaturge, Iqbal Hussein, described the protean *JTW* trilogy project. While the final production was to showcase three plays under the banner of the *JTW* trilogy it should be remembered at this beginning of the project that there was only one strand decided. The aim was solely to mark the 30th anniversary of the Kenyan Asian 'exodus' to Britain by staging *Exodus* in 1998. In fact, the *JTW* trilogy 'had initially been conceived as a set of projects which would include a number of groupings within the South Asian diaspora – East African, Caribbean, subcontinent' (Hussein 1999: 5), but this was to change through the stages of *Exodus* in 1998 as Jatinder Verma decided to focus the remaining two parts of the *JTW* trilogy on the East African Asian diaspora.

The rationale for this decision was to maintain and build on the relationship with the interviewees contacted for *Exodus*. Furthermore, this established pool of contacts could provide further material for use in other sections of the *JTW* trilogy and therefore, pragmatically, this decision also minimised the methodological and financial aspects of further research. Subsequently, in 1999, *Genesis*, which dramatised the transportation of 32,000 Indian workers to Kenya at the turn of the nineteenth century to work as indentured labour for the British and build the East African Railway and would become *Part II*, was developed and toured to community venues. Then, in 2000, the final strand, *Revelations*, which would become *Part III*, interrogating a hybrid British Asian identity in contemporary Britain in the light of this diasporic history, was produced.

'Binglishing' the text

The 'Binglish' text of the *JTW* trilogy was made up of an array of languages, including Punjabi, Hindi, Gujarati, Swahili and English, in what may be termed colloquial and 'correct' usage. In this way the language followed the politics of introducing the audience 'to a greater auditory experience and, by implication, challenging them' (Verma 1996: 198) as well as addressing the fact that Tara 'have to think in terms of multiple languages, simply to do with the kind of community that I am faced with: Asian and non-Asian and the sense of the fractured' (Verma quoted in Majumdar 1998: 10).

As with Tara's 'trandaptions' of the European classics discussed in Chapter 3 this hybrid linguistic confection was purposely 'provocative' for the non-Asian language speaker. The political rationale that underpinned this theatrical convention was that the languages employed in the productions 'form part of the linguistic map of modern Britain [...]. and cannot be expected to be absent from modern British theatre' (Verma 1996: 198). In this way, the use of Asian and African languages in the 'Binglish' text of the *JTW* trilogy 'abrogates the privileged central-ity of "English" by using language to signify difference while employing a sameness which allows it to be understood' (Ashcroft et al. 2002: 50). Indeed, the effect of 'delivering most of the punch lines in languages that leave the Asian spectators laughing like drains, but the Anglo-phones feeling a bit left out' (Rubin 2002) directly demonstrates the ramifications of what is 'understood' and by whom.

Dramaturg Iqbal Hussein's comments below, written after a work-in-progress production of *Genesis*, the basis for *Part I* of the trilogy, illustrate how the inclusion of languages other than English in the 'Binglish' text was obviously a way of marking cultural difference:

> Here was an audience who understood the 'in jokes' – for whom *gora khuta* [white dog] meant something, *haramzade* [bastard], observing the non-Asian children at times I felt that they were left out, but then I thought how regularly Asians are left out of the 'mainstream'. Without going down the poisonous road of revenge the presentation stood as a defiant statement, an assertion, a determination not to apologise for speaking out.
>
> (Hussein 1999: 24)

This difference, as we have said, de-centred the privileged position of English speakers so that the non-Asian speaker experiences moments of marginalisation in relation to the meaning of the 'Binglish' perfor-mance. This was not, as Hussein insisted, out of 'revenge' but as a means of marking and simultaneously transgressing the concept of discrete cul-tural borders. 'Binglish' allowed the audience an opportunity for 'an active engagement with the horizons of the culture in which these terms have meaning' (Ashcroft et al. 2002: 64) and, at the same time, this gap of understanding between the 'British' and the 'Asian' marked its difference.

Reconnecting with the Asian community

Work began on *Exodus* in 1997 when Tara Arts circulated invitations in Urdu, Hindi and Gujarati to a range of British Asian societies and meeting places in London, Leicester, Birmingham and beyond, asking those with a memory of the Kenyan 'exodus' to come forward. Those who replied were interviewed and recorded on digital video and then transcripts were made, with the emphasis on getting as much source material on the detail of life in Kenya as possible: schooling, housing, entertainment and marriage as well as the relations between 'whites' and Africans. The actors conducted the interviews and, as one of them,

Ravin Ganatra, recalls, this facilitated their artistic process, as they were able to build characters 'based on real evidence, real research, first hand experience' (Ganatra 2001: 3).

One problem for Tara Arts in collecting such an embarrassing wealth of documentary material was evident in a criticism of the *Exodus* production at Battersea Arts Centre that 'it feels as if the story of every single one of the 150 people interviewed is being recounted' (Curtis 1998: 53). Jatinder Verma addressed this criticism in the final trilogy by deciding to eschew an attempt at documentary in favour of the creation of an epic narrative, by linking all three parts of the trilogy with an invented genealogy between the main protagonists and thereby shifting the focus away from the particular.

Exodus (1998)
© Tara Arts, 1998.
The cast of the *Exodus* production with some of the interviewees at Battersea Arts Centre

However, this decision was questioned by critics who believed that the 'content has a tendency to float away from the specific to rhapsodies of mythical experience' (Kingston 2002) because 'a distrust of documentary [...] turns original first hand accounts into an epic...[so that]...what should be invigorating is merely admirable' (Clapp 2002). However, lines drawn from the actual reminiscences of interviewees – such as when an immigrant is told by a fellow refugee in *Part II* that 'an underground train from Heathrow [...] will take you straight to Manchester' (Verma 2002b: 21) – meant that 'you hear the ring of individual voices in some flinty exact moments' (Clapp 2002) and demonstrated how this research material could have been productively incorporated further into the text.

In accordance with the recognised aims of a 'community theatre', which were 'to perform to different, non-theatre-going audiences, and to engage them in a different relationship' (Khan 1980: 61), *Genesis* and *Revelations* did not play at mainstream venues in stark contrast to Tara's work at the National in the 1990s. However, a major shift in Tara's policy occurred in May 2000 with the arrival of a new administrator, Nirjay Mahindru, who subsequently programmed the tour for *Revelations*, the work-in-progress for the *Part III* of the trilogy and a new production, *The Odyssey/Ramayan*. While the *Revelations* work-in-progress production went ahead still focused on community venues, the *Odyssey/Ramayan* was to play larger more established venues such as the Everyman Theatre, Liverpool, and Riverside Studios in London.

Tara's new marketing strategy was to work in tandem with established theatres that had their own systems already in place, in stark contrast to many of the community venues that did not. The move to mainstream venues was not only an indication of a shift in marketing strategy but also of an artistic recognition that in order to realise this epic piece of 'Binglish' postcolonial theatre, and find an audience for it, it would be necessary to play in better equipped traditional theatre venues.

In line with this new policy, the *JTW* trilogy tour was to go to higher profile, middle scale venues. The tour began on Wednesday, 13 March 2002 at Contact Theatre, Manchester, then to Haymarket Theatre, Leicester, the Repertory Theatre, Birmingham, and West Yorkshire Playhouse, Leeds. It then went on to Darlington, Cardiff and Westcliffe-on-Sea and finished at Hexagon Theatre, Reading, on 1 June 2002. In this new approach to middle-scale touring the community venues were abandoned.

Journey to the West: Part I
Dhows, Desserts and Dirty Tricks 1896–1901

In desperation, Fateh, a Sikh from the Punjab, leaves his famine-struck home and accepts an offer of work from the British colonial power. He is employed as an indentured labourer and transported to East Africa to build a railway covering the 581 miles from Mombassa to Lake Victoria. In return for this labour, he and the other 32,000 workers are each promised five acres of the land.

Almost 2,500 workers were killed during the construction of the railway and *Part I* makes visible the colonial exploitation of the British who callously refused to honour their land promise after the work was completed. *Part I* also celebrates the pioneering spirit of these Asian workers, exemplified in Fateh, who 'wants to climb mountains', and their tenacity in the face of disease, man-eating lions and attacks from the indigenous population. In contrast to a more rigidly stratified and differentiated former life in India, *Part I* marks a more socially inclusive approach to caste and religion as a result of the diaspora. Fateh, although still married, has a relationship with Majisa, a Masai tribeswoman. Tragedy strikes as Majisa is murdered but *Part I* ends on an optimistic note as Fateh finds a baby abandoned at the end of the railway tracks. He adopts the baby and names it Kala Singha (Black Lion), who 'born on the waters between India and Africa' symbolises the racial ambivalence and irreducible hybridity of the Asian identity as a result of diaspora.

Journey To The West Part I (2002)
© Stephen Vaughan 2002.
The workers' journey from India to Africa on the dhow

Journey to the West: Part II
Rifts, Refugees and Rivers of Blood – 1968

Part II opens in post-independence Kenya and is centred on the friendship of three teenagers: Ranjit, Sita and Liaquat, who are descendants of the workers of *Part I*. Their romantic entanglements in *Part II* mirror those of Dilip Kumar, Raj Kapoor and Nargis in the popular Bollywood films of the 1960s. The religious plurality and almost idyllic cohesion of the Asian community in Kenya epitomised in *Part I* is continued and symbolised in *Part II* through the close friendship between Sikh, Hindu and Muslim. However, *Part II* also depicts the rising animosity of the African people to the insularity of the Asian community who 'live in Muindi [Asian] areas, love within Muindi homes [...] watch their films in Muindi cinemas'. The play then shifts to Britain as Ranjit, Liaquat and Sita arrive as part of the Asian 'Exodus' in order to beat the impending legislative deadline restricting Kenyan Asian immigration. Continuing the journey motif, Ranjit takes a job on London Underground where he encounters racism from his white colleagues. As Ranjit's mother, Daljeet, forms a Union we also see the increasing politicisation of the Asian community in the face of oppression; the play draws on the actual Grunwick dispute of 1976. As the old ties between the three friends and those of the Kenyan Asian community start to fragment, Ranjit strikes up a friendship with a white girl called Helen. This relationship meets resistance from Ranjit's own community as well as outright hostility from her family who warn him to 'get his wog hands off her'. This warning goes unheeded and results in Ranjit being stabbed to death in a racist attack at the end of the play. This echoes the killing of Gurdeep Singh Chaggar in Southall in 1976 by white youths; this murder was the catalyst that led to the formation of Tara Arts.

Journey To The West Part II (2002)
© Stephen Vaughan 2002.
The chorus of Asian women washing saris in Kenya

Journey to the West: Part III
Bhangra, Bollywood and British Bulldog – 2002

The genealogical narrative link continues in *Part III* as the protagonist, Kamaal, is the son of a Hindu mother, Sita, and Muslim
father, Liaquat, whom we met in *Part II*. We follow Kamaal on
his journey, by road this time, to scatter his grandfather's ashes
at Hadrian's Wall on the border of Scotland and England. This
is a metaphorical as well as literal journey on which Kamaal
attempts to reconcile his desire to 'belong [...] in a team, a group,
a gang, a tribe' with his hybrid Asian identity that makes him
'part Hindu, part Muslim, part Indian, part Pakistani, part African,
part English.' This contemporary strand of the trilogy addresses
the fragmentation of the Asian community in which 'our own
radio stations have banned the word Asian from the airwaves so
you're either Hindu Muslim or Sikh', which in *Part I* and *Part II*
had signified cohesion.

The journey takes Kamaal through three fictional places. The
first, Caxton Gibbet, symbolises the notion of a disavowed Asian

identity. Kamaal's guide there, Athar, advocates a path of cultural assimilation that Kamaal rejects in the light of his own Muslim heritage. His next stop is ColeyBingham, 'the free Islamic state of Coventry, Leicester and Birmingham', which advocates a separatist stance justified by the racism encountered by the Asian community. Kamaal again moves on, as this would mean denying his Hindu identity. A mystical encounter with a roadside cook reminds Kamaal that the identity that unites us all is that of a shared diasporic origin from Africa that will 'allow us to rise over the closet of nations'. Kamaal finally reaches Hadrian's Wall, a tangible reminder of England as a once-colonised nation as well as a coloniser. As Kamaal scatters his grandfather's ashes he determines to accept and celebrate his hybrid identity and 'make this England, our England, full of all your long journeys West'.

Signs of the 'Binglish' performance – The *JTW* trilogy

'Binglish' design

The three plays that made up the *JTW* trilogy ran consecutively from Wednesday to Friday, and then on the Saturday all three parts were played over the course of the day. On the days on which the full trilogy was performed, the Front of House was taken over by a *chaandi* [silver] bazaar that included fashion, crafts, an historical exhibition and perhaps most importantly, food – since people watching all three parts of the trilogy would be spending over nine hours in the theatre. Caterers provided *pakora* (crisp potato fries), *patra* (fried spinach rolls), mango juice, *choley* (curried white peas) and Asian sweets such as *barfi* (coconut) and *jalebi*. There was live African and Asian music, as well as demonstrations by *henna*[1] and *rangoli*[2] artists, Indian head massages and stalls selling DVDs of Hindi films and costume jewellery such as *bindis*.

The key elements of the set for the *JTW* trilogy, that remained through all three parts, were the five ropes that hung down from above and were evenly spaced across the mid stage with five narrow drapes behind these in front of the cyclorama. The design was integrated into the action so the ropes were 'plaited, sat on, knotted and swarmed up with great dexterity' (Clapp 2002). In order to achieve this, part of the performers' preparation involved learning climbing techniques from a circus trainer, which they found 'was very tough...[we] couldn't get out of bed or get dressed for the first week because we were so badly bruised, and we used muscles we didn't know existed' (Mousawi 2002). However, this hard work made for some effective stage images such as the use of the ropes to make a *dhow* [sailing ship]. The *dhow* in which they travelled from India to East Africa was made by stringing the five ropes together so that they formed one large knot suspended two feet above centre stage with the four free ends of the ropes falling onto the stage floor. One of the actors stood on the knot that was suspended above the stage that now represented the sea as if on the prow of the *dhow*. The four remaining actors picked up the free ends of the ropes and formed a semi-circle around the 'prow' and in unison gently rocked from side to side, creating the effect of a wave motion on the *dhow*.

To then create the storm that strikes the dhow on the crossing, the actors who held the ropes simply increased the range and rhythm of their movement. They stamped out an increasingly high tempo rhythm while traversing the stage from side to side so that it now appeared the *dhow* was being rocked by 'a wall of water' (Verma 2002a: 8). The lighting then bathed the stage in dark blue as sporadic flashes illuminated the scene in a strobe-like effect, the performers raising their voices as if shouting over the increasing noise of the storm, exemplifying the way in which Claudia Meyer's set was 'entwined and climbed to great effect throughout the plays' (Kingston 2002).

The use of the ropes was developed in *Part II* as Sita arrived at British immigration. The immigration desk at which she was informed by the customs official that the 'deadline for automatic right of entry was midnight last night' (Verma 2002b: 22) and was told to return to the last port of embarkation, which was of course Nairobi, was set downstage right. Sita's return to Nairobi was realised theatrically as she swung through the air on a rope to the other side of the stage where the African immigration officer caught her. The officer refused her entry, as she had a British passport and so belonged to Britain and then pushed Sita on the rope so she swung back across the stage to the 'British' side. This was then repeated a number of times as Sita was followed by a spotlight to the sound of a ticking clock. This scene was based on a historical reality. A number of Kenyan Asians with British passports became effectively stateless, having missed the deadline introduced by the legislation in the Commonwealth Immigrants Act of 1968. They were referred to in the press as 'shuttlecock Asians', 'Asians who have left Kenya, and will not be allowed either to return or to stay in India' (Deschampsneufs 1968: 1) or be allowed into Britain; a fact that Jatinder Verma incorporated with sly irony into his script by making the character of Sita a badminton champion.

'Binglish' music

The discrete border that traditionally functions in Western performance between musician and actor was purposefully unsettled in the trilogy. At the opening of the *Part I* the *sutradhar* shooed Najma Akhtar, who provided the live music and singing in the trilogy off the stage 'to practice your singing' (Verma 2002a: 1) when she attempted to take over his telling of the story about the Nagar king. She then went and took her position cross-legged on the floor with the harmonium and *dhol* drum downstage right just off the acting area; as discussed in Chapter 3, an Asian musician sitting on the floor is a sign of cultural difference on the British stage.

Indeed, this theatrical flexibility of function was exploited in the scene dramatising the journey to Africa in which the dhow was becalmed and water strictly rationed. The *sayyad* [holy man], played by Akhtar, who is on board 'wakes in the dead of the night and pours *lota* [pot] after lota of fresh water over his face' (Verma 2002a: 11). When he is discovered, the captain threatens to throw the *sayyad* overboard as a punishment. The *sayyad* only manages to avoid this fate by promising that when they reached land he will 'build for my fellows a mosque, a gurudwara, a temple, whatever people want' (Verma 2002a: 11). Rather than go into the acting area where the *dhow* was set, she played the scene from where she was downstage right of the acting area; hence extending the audience's understanding of the spatial borders of the performance. When the captain threatened to throw the character overboard, he did through the dramatic convention of gesturing that he would throw the harmonium she was playing into the water.

The chorus of Asian women also utilised song in the trilogy, such as when they were washing their saris down by the river in *Part II*. As they were soaking, slapping and drying the saris a rhythm developed in which the chorus put new words to the 60s Bollywood hit, 'Eena Meena Dika' 'that was associated with the twist' (Verma 2002b: 1). In this hybrid 'Binglish' version of the song the chorus were dancing the 'twist', dressed in saris, performing lyrics with newly incorporated Swahili words such as *falooda* (a kind of knickerbocker glory), *machunga* (Swahili for an orange), *jaamun* (a purple fruit indigenous to East Africa) and *ghanna* (Swahili for sugar cane).

When the Kenyan Asians made their journey to England by aeroplane in *Part II*, realised by the actors climbing the ropes at ascending heights across the stage, the chorus reprised the song that the *sutradhar* sang in *JTW: Part I* as the *dhow* set sail from India to Africa:

> Ohre taal miley nadhi kay jhul meyn
> Nadhi miley saagur meyn
> Saagur miley kaun say jhull meyen
> Koi jaaney na'
> [Oh the beat is mixing with the river's sound
> The river meets the ocean
> What sounds does the ocean mix with
> Nobody knows]

(Verma 2002b: 22)

This lyrical link theatrically connected the historical fissures of the Asian diaspora and also suggested the magnitude of the displacement was in no way lessened or mitigated on this more contemporary journey.

The 'Subaltern' speaks

Dramatically, *Part I* was unrepentantly partisan in its representation of history from the perspective of the Asian and African subject suffering the effects of white colonial oppression. This was exemplified in the unsympathetic portrait drawn of the historical character Colonel Patterson, the white colonial overseer of the building of the railway. The Asian actor who played Patterson donned a pith helmet and stick with his Asian costume and adopted a stereotypical upper class English accent to portray the character. Patterson's claim that he was part of an altruistic 'civilising' mission in 'turning the blazing light of England on this dark continent' (Verma 2002a: 6) was clearly dispelled in the play as he talked excitedly of Africa as a source of 'coffee, tea, beef and milk to satisfy the stomachs of folks back home' (Verma 2002a: 42). Patterson's insistence on referring to the Asians working on the railway by number rather than name and his use of one of them as 'bait' to trap a man-eating lion dramatically illustrated the point in *JTW: Part I* that 'colonialism not only exploits but dehumanises and objectifies the colonised subject' (Loomba 1998: 22).

Part II continued its exploration of racism experienced by Kenyan Asians when they left Africa for Britain. Continuing the railway theme from *Part I*, Ranjit takes a job on the Underground, on his arrival in England in *Part II*, where he encounters racist 'jokes' from his supervisor;

REG: What's wiv the towel on the 'ead, Gunga Din?
RANJIT: Towel?
REG: On yer 'ead!
RANJIT: That's a turban. I'm a Sikh –
REG: Whatchu doin' here then, if you're sick?

(Verma 2002b: 23)

Ranjit's Asian colleague on the underground, Bob, advises him that the best way to survive as an immigrant in Britain is to 'bend into the wind and don't walk against it' (Verma 2002b: 26) and assimilate. Bob, whose real name was Bhupinder Singh, told Ranjit that he had a 'big bright green turban when I landed here from India [...] one week at work and on the first day off, I went straight to the barber and cut it off' (Verma 2002b: 26). For Sikhs, the wearing of a turban and not cutting their hair is a crucial aspect of religious observance so we can see there was a very high cultural price for Bob's 'fitting in'. A 'fitting in' which means when a 'chiti chumldi [white flesh] makes a joke at your expense laugh with him' (Verma 2002b: 26).

The politicisation of the Asian community can be read through the character of Daljeet, Ranjit's mother, and a first generation migrant. When she comes to England she finds a job but is told that for reasons of 'health and safety [...] no saris in the work place' (Verma 2002b: 27). The realisation of this scene in which an official removes her sari on stage developed an intertextual connection.

As the official slowly gathers in the seemingly neverending sari, this echoes the episode in the *Mahabharata* in which Dussashan, younger brother of Duryodhana, attempted to disrobe Draupadi. In the legend, Draupadi appealed to Krishna for protection and he made sure her sari did not unravel before Dussashan fell exhausted at her feet. However, with no Krishna to intervene this time, Daljeet was stripped of her sari and left standing centre stage metaphorically naked in slacks and a blouse. The 'Binglish' performance utilised the epic intertext to high-light the personal cost of the cultural sacrifice made by Asian women in order to work, which left Daljeet wondering 'Hai rubba! [Oh God] How am I to look my man in the eye?' (Verma 2002b: 27).

However, the chorus of Asian women also provide a parodic inversion of the stereotyping that was more normally aimed at Asian immigrants to facilitate some humorous introspection. As the women do their washing they complain about the British food and accent as they 'can't understand what they say, behn-ji [...] they eat their words because they have no proper food. Beer and chips, what kind of food is that?' (Verma 2002b: 27).

Part II also highlighted the differences between the newly arrived Kenyan Asian immigrants to Britain 'looking more Indian than Indians. In your saris and turbans, carrying your blankets [...] and their Punjabi, Gujarati, Urdu, Swahili' (Verma 2002b: 26) and those from the Indian subcontinent. As Helen, Ranjit's girlfriend, tells him the Kenyan Asians were not only more 'Indian than Indian', but in speech more English than the English because 'you speak English but more correct somehow [...] like I can see the comma and the full stop [...] you cross your t's and dot your i's you do' (Verma 2002b: 28). While the fact that Ranjit's colonial education 'only brought us boring Queen's English' (Verma 2002b: 46) this in no way mitigated the racial animosity towards him as 'to be Anglicised is *emphatically* not to be English' (Bhabha 1994: 87). The 'Binglish' performance that modelled all five of the different languages that Ranjit can speak dramatically contests the colonial construction of 'Englishness' for a postcolonial world. In this way Liaquat's complaint that he 'sat the senior Cambridge exams in Kenya and still they think I can't speak English' (Verma 2002b: 45), suggested the fruitless task of trying to find acceptance through assimilation as Asians can only always be 'almost the same but not white' (Bhabha 1994: 89).

Constructing an Asian identity

When the *sayyad* was killed in an accident in *Part I*, his promise to build a mosque, a gurudwara and a temple was reiterated by the chorus as 'a dream we must honour' (Verma 2002a: 26), symbolising the religious plurality and tolerance that the *JTW* trilogy presented as a cornerstone of the Asian identity.

In *Part I*, the role of diaspora in forming the migrant Asian identity was not only examined in the changing relations between different religious groups but also in terms of caste and region. Life on the subcontinent was portrayed as fragmented and antagonistic because 'in our old life the butcher couldn't get on with the merchant, the builder hated the farmer, the Sikh thought all the Gujuraits were all banias' (Verma 2002a: 17). In Africa a heterogeneous and inclusive Asian identity was dramatised as a sign of solidarity exemplified on the stage as the characters' 'pranaam [worship] this red earth we stand on and eat together' (Verma 2002a: 17).

While the African character, Majiza, pointed out the oppression of her people under colonial rule, her relationship with Fateh offered a vision of a united interracial subaltern future. When Majiza became pregnant with Fateh's child she not only carried his 'dreams' (Verma 2002a: 45) but also those of a pluralistic future. The provenance of the unborn child also underlined the hyphenated hybridic possibilities that would make up Asian identity as a result of diaspora. However, the realisation of this hybridic vision is shattered at the end of *Part I* by the murder of Majiza at the hands of Fateh's friend, Ishwar, before she gave birth, once again in *Part II* with the murder of Ranjit, and only realised in *Part III* at the destination of Kamaal's journey.

The social cohesion of the heterogeneous Asian community portrayed in *Part I* was mirrored in the strong bonds portrayed in the extended families across caste, religion and region in *Part II*. The value of this extended family was exemplified in *Part II* when Sita was the only one from her family to obtain a ticket for England so Daljeet, Rangit's mother, who was also going agreed to look after her 'like my own daughter' (Verma 2002b: 19). The romantic idyll for the Asian community begins to unravel in *Part II* after Kenyan independence from the British, when it detailed how Kenyatta became the first president on 12 December 1964. Indeed, the dearth of African-Asian relationships in *Part II* was part of the critique of the separatism of the Asian community. Asha's admonishment to her daughter Sita, 'you want to go out looking like a jungli Masai?' (Verma 2002b: 8) implied the casual racism inherent within the Asian community. Indeed, it was not until Sita actually had to work in England and was viewed as 'black' that she is politically awakened and recognises 'how the African servants we had must have felt' (Verma 2002b: 42).

The cultural insularity of the Asian community was also critiqued through the relationship between Ranjit and his white girlfriend, Helen. When Ranjit invited Helen to the cinema to see the Hindi movie *Junglee*, his mother pointedly told her the film was about 'a boy who comes to London from India to study and loses his culture' (Verma 2002b: 40). In spite of this, Helen's recognition that the star of the Hindi movie was like 'Elvis', as she shared Ranjit's *chulli* (corn), suggested that this cultural gap was not unbridgeable even if Ranjit's mother insisted that 'she can't cook English' (Verma 2002b: 40).

If the friendship between Ranjit and Helen, in which she taught him English slang and he translated Hindi film songs for her, was a symbol of a culturally hybrid future, then the final scene of *Part II* struck a deeply pessimistic note. After an evening out together, Helen and Ranjit were stopped by Pete, her brother, who ordered Ranjit to 'get his wog hands off her' (Verma 2002b: 48). When Ranjit tried to leave, Pete stabs him with a knife. The final tableau of *Part II* shows Ranjit slowly collapsing to the ground on a red carpet that is unfurled from the back of the stage. As he lies dying, snow begins to fall. This racist murder echoed the actual killing of Gurdeep Singh Chaggar in Southall in 1976 by white youths; this murder was of course the catalyst that led to the formation of Tara Arts.

Part III, set in contemporary Britain, presents a fragmented Asian community and focuses on Kamaal's metaphorical journey, which offers the paths of assimilation, separatism or acceptance of his hybrid cultural location. He rejects the cultural assimilation symbolised by Caxton Gibbet when he remembers listening as a child to stories about his ancestors while sitting on his grandfather's knee. This flashback scene also self reflexively modelled the didactic mission of the 'Binglish' performance that privileges the importance of recovering and disseminating the Asian diasporic history.

The notion of cultural separatism was epitomised by his next stop in ColeyBingham, whose description as 'the free Islamic state of Coventry, Leicester and Birmingham' provoked a great deal of laughter of recognition from the largely Asian audience. As a rationale for the creation of ColeyBingham, his guide, Shiraz, cited contemporary racist attacks done by 'footballers who kick our heads in for a laugh' (Verma 2002c: 20), invoking the names of real victims such as Gurdeep Chaggar, Ricky Reel and Altab Ali, thus interpolatating a welcome and powerful immediacy into the theoretical debate about cultural identity being staged in *Part III*

Kamaal continues his journey and encounters an enigmatic character who appears in a puff of smoke, leading Kamaal to take him for a *djinn* [spirit]. As the *djinn* prepares a kebab for Kamaal he tells him whether you are 'Pakistani, Indian, English, we're all from the same land which rises in the mountains of the Moon' (Verma 2002c: 26), in other words Africa. This vision of Africa as a cradle of civilisation that unites all people in a shared diasporic origin resonates throughout the trilogy. The final destination of *Part III*, Hadrian's Wall, was chosen as it literally marked the constructed border of England and Scotland and was also a tangible reminder that England, as well as being a coloniser was itself colonised by the Romans.

It was here that there was no simple resolution of Kamaal's hyphen-ated identity as he is no closer to answering 'who do I play football with?' (Verma 2002c: 22). The *djinn* tells Kamaal that the Asians are *roho tabu* [wandering souls] who 'lifted their feet out of their homes and now always roam' (Verma 2002c: 30). This espouses a vision of an overarching concept of a diasporic identity, signified by the footprints on the *JTW* programme.

This diasporic construction of identity allows Kamaal to literally 'rise over the closet of nations and the prison of belonging' (Verma 2002c: 31) as he sits high above the stage, after climbing to the top of the centre rope, picking stars from the firmament. Each star Kamaal picks repre-sented a *roho tabu*, reprising the Masai legend of *Part I*, that 'when a child is born it receives the spirit of that star' (Verma 2002a: 37). As Kamaal plucks the star he reprises the lines of Fateh from *Part I*, modelling the postcolonial mission of the trilogy to recover those histories for future generations. His final statement exemplifies Tara's intent with the five-year *JTW* project to 'make this England our England, full of all your long journeys West' (Verma 2002c: 31) and thereby attempt to contest 'those ideological manoeuvres through which "imagined communities" are given essentialist identities' (Bhabha 1994: 149).

While the critical responses were less positive to the script in general and the 'aimless wanderings' (Rubin 2002) of *Part III* in particular there was a general recognition of the scale and theatrical ambition of the trilogy. While the cavils with the realisation of the documentary mate-rial gathered have been discussed, Tara was rightly praised for bringing 'an important story with beautiful effects' (Clapp 2002) to the stage and creating a 'work of rare visual beauty and historical insight' (Grimley 2002c).

After the trilogy

After the trilogy, Tara explored a diverse range of artistic departures such as the high art aesthetics of *A Taste for Mangoes* (2003) at Wilton's Music Hall, productions for children, and the site-responsive *Tara in the Sky* (2007) in Trafalgar Square. However, this period can largely be char-acterised by a return to the 'Binglishing' of European classics, which concluded with a drastic and unexpected cut in funding by the Arts Council in 2008.

A Taste for Mangoes (2002) took as its inspiration a painting of Sir David Ochterlony by an unknown artist held at the British Library: the painting depicts Sir David smoking a hookah while watching a *naatch* (dance presentation) by a group of Indian women.

The production opened on 18 November 2003 at Wilton's Music Hall, and explored the motivations and repercussions of Sir David, the first East Indian company representative 'resident' at the court of the Mughal emperor, Shah Alam, going 'native' in pre-Raj India. As Ochterlony, Gerard Murphy, an associate member of the Royal Shakespeare Company, captured the ambivalence of a figure who enthusiastically adopted the dress and customs of his new home, including 12 wives, and yet recognised he had attained a position and life in Indian society that would have been beyond him in England.

Artistically this was a lavish production, which played against the backdrop of the faded grandeur of Wilton's Victorian Music Hall to create what Michael Billington called a 'richly beguiling spectacle' (2003: 22). However, critic Rhoda Koenig raised doubts that the dramaturgy matched the mise-en-scène and the mixture of dance, art and music, and suggested that the immediacy of the drama had been overtaken by Jatinder Verma's aesthetic concerns:

> though *A Taste for Mangoes* has plenty of physical movement, with actresses in Claudia Mayer's lovely red, white and green gauzy costumes performing classical Indian dance, dramatic movement is sparse and halting.
>
> (2003)

The high dance-theatre aesthetics of *A Taste for Mangoes* were evident again in the summer of 2007 when Tara was invited by Greater London Arts to take part in their *India Now* season. *India Now* was a three-month programme from July to September, 'centring on an exploration of India's culture and London's interaction with India's rapidly growing economy' (Livingstone 2007) with events such as a seven-stage *mela* in Gunnersbury Park, Regent Street turned into a Goan beach, and Nitin Sawhney creating a film score with the London Symphony Orchestra for the classic Indian silent film *A Throw of the Dice*.

In responding to the invitation, Tara presented *Juggernaut: Tara-in-the-Sky!* over three days, 9–12 August 2007, in an open-air performance for the Trafalgar Square Festival, which ran from 2–19 August 2007. The performance took place beneath Nelson's Column and employed dance and music to explore the relationship between London and Delhi, drawing on the *chakra* (wheel) design of the Indian national flag for the motif of the twirling umbrellas and bowler hats used by the performers.

Tara-in-the-Sky! (2007) **Trafalgar Square**
© Claudia Mayer.

The piece was directed by Verma, with choreography by Dr Vena Ramphal drawing on the classical dance-form *bharatanatyam*, and the cast was made up of professional dancers and young people aged between 13 and 21, including those from hard-to-reach groups of young carers and young refugees. The performance was seen by an estimated 8,000 people and featured three main movements.

The first section divided the performance-space between the 'English' side in bowler hats and carrying black umbrellas, who approached the lushly coloured, costumed 'Indian' side to shake hands; the latter then give the *namaste* greeting in return. The second movement saw the 'English' side 'colonising' the Indian space, and the third culminated with the Indian dancers rising over 50 feet into the air and 'repulsing' the 'English' back to their borders. The piece closed in a spirit of detente and co-operative interaction as both sides meet in the middle and join in one circle, throwing their hats into the air as hundreds of balloons are released into the sky.

A return to 'Binglish'

While *A Taste for Mangoes* and *Tara-in-the-Sky!* were interesting developments, the singularity of these projects suggested an eclecticism in the artistic vision of the company of which Verma was only too aware when he admitted in 2006 that 'the years since the *JTW* trilogy have been characterised by an acute sense of restlessness' (Verma 2006b:

388). That restlessness in fact saw Tara return to the pre-trilogy approach of 'Binglishing' European classic texts, with productions of *The Merchant of Venice* (2005), *An Enemy of the People* (2006), *The Marriage of Figaro* (2007) and *The Tempest* (2007/8).

Verma's production of *The Merchant of Venice* opened on 21 September 2005 at Waterman's Arts Centre in west London, and in contrast to other 'Binglish' productions largely left Shakespeare's text intact. The setting was relocated to Cochin in the southern Indian state of Kerala in the sixteenth century and a new frame given to the play in which a troupe of Indian actors, who have been converted to Christianity by the Portuguese settlers, perform the play. The intellectual rationale for this 'trandaption' was the connection between the anti-Jewish feeling in the Venetian setting of the original, and that precipitated by the Catholic Portuguese traders in Cochin in the new location.

Verma was particularly drawn to the play by the marginal position of the character of Shylock, because 'as an Asian living in Britain I sympathise with his outsider status' (Verma 2005: 33). The small cast, led by Anthony Bunsee who, played Shylock, worked with anti-realist 'Binglish' performance methodology, so that 'the five actors change from character to character indicating the change by an item of clothing (a scarf or coat usually) and [...] a change of voice and of body language' (Lathan 2005). There were also the usual signs of the 'Binglish' approach: a non-naturalistic set, which had a large black picture frame hung centre stage used as a distancing device, a movement vocabulary informed by Kathakali and live music integrated into the performance provided by the onstage musician, V. Chandran. However, what is clear in the productions of this time is a marked diminution in the production values and epic staging of the *JTW* trilogy or, indeed, of earlier work at the National Theatre.

The suggestion that Tara were revisiting 'Binglish' rather than developing it was compounded in *The Marriage of Figaro*, which opened at the New Players Theatre in London on Tuesday 17 October 2006, and signalled the return of Ranjit Bolt's collaboration with Tara. In Bolt's adaptation of Beaumarchais' play, the action was transposed to eighteenth-century India: so the Count of the original became the Nawab, 'an old-fashioned potentate who expects women to put up with whatever is dished out and not fight back' (Bolt quoted in Billington 2006a).

Verma once again drew on the Indian folk form of *bhavai* for an equivalent to the French traditional form of commedia dell'arte, as he did successfully for Tara's production of Bolt's adaptation of *Tartuffe* at the National Theatre in 1990. While the markers of the 'Binglish' performance were very much present in the form of masque integrated live music and stylised movement, there was still an underlying criticism that the formality of the 'Binglish' production was 'undermining the play's power to move when the characters suddenly stumble on their true feelings at the close' (Shore 2006) and 'winking and eye rolling replace, rather than represent, real emotion' (Logan 2006).

There was a growing critical concern about the ability of the 'Binglish' form to engage with the seriousness of the material as Tara programmed *An Enemy of the People* (2006) to coincide with the centenary of Ibsen's death:

> compulsively playful tone [...] partly necessitated by the frantic doubling ... [and the] comic lightness of touch creates confusion about the show's attitude to Ibsen's hero, whose shift from idealism to radical elitism can only be described as proto-fascist.
>
> (McMillan 2006)

While the intellectual connections made in the 'tradaptions' were still coherent and critically admired, the form was accused of giving 'an airy weightlessness to proceedings that looks old fashioned' (Cooper 2006). The action was relocated to late nineteenth-century British India: so Ibsen's Dr Stockman became Dr Tushal Somnath, the medical officer of the local baths. The play's themes of the right of the individual over the majority and the 'cost' of morality were played out as Dr Somnath discovered that the town's holy water shrine and economic generator, was polluted: this led to a conflict between safeguarding the townspeople's health and the cost of closing it down. The rationale for this 'tradaption' given in the programme notes drew parallels between Norway and India as colonised countries, by Sweden and Britain respectively, and the endeavours of Gandhi in India and Krohn in Norway on issues of public health.

This pared-down approach continued as Tara returned to Shakespeare with a production of *The Tempest* that transferred from the Tara Studio to the Arts Theatre in the West End of London in January 2008. The play was set, according to the programme notes, in 'Moorish world – Mediterranean Muslim', with Robert Mountford playing Prospero as a 'learned Muslim plagued by his desire for vengeance' (Powell 2007) and Jessica Manley, a veiled Miranda. The cast of only six doubled a number of roles and the text was cut back to a playing time of just 105 minutes.

The set was characterised by six ropes hanging down, which functioned not only as a symbol of the characters' imprisonment, both psychological and physical, but as practical props climbed by the actors and used as the sails of a ship, as swords, or Prospero's staff. It was reminiscent of the *JTW* design. Critics were willing to see weaknesses instead of invention so for Sam Marlowe, the physical strengths of the 'Binglish' form were losing their powers; 'the shipwreck, in which the actors clutch the ropes and wing from side to side, suggests that the tempest is a remarkably gentle one' (Marlowe 2008); and while there was, as ever, praise for the conceptual ambition of Prospero being played as a Muslim scholar, the execution was seen to be 'vague overall' (ibid.), and the 'interpretation feels increasingly unanchored in text design and on-stage relationships' (McGinn 2008).

While the new directions explored post-trilogy have been artistically interesting and real developments of Tara's aesthetic, these departures have not heralded a coherent artistic vision for the company, and the return to 'Binglishing' European classics has seen diminishing artistic and critical returns.

In 2008 Tara Arts were dealt a 50 per cent cut to their Art Council grant. This resulted in their three-year funding being slashed from £341,266; at the start of April 2008 the amount was reduced to £170,000. This was their most serious funding crisis since 1987. This cut reflected the Arts Council's belief that Tara Arts should focus on educational and small-scale work and was interpreted by Jatinder Verma as a 'kick in the teeth for any Black or Asian company which chooses to focus its work on the classics [...]. Shakespeare, as far as the Arts Council are concerned, is not for Black or Asian-led companies' (Verma quoted in Paddock 2008).

The Arts Council's insinuation that Tara as an Asian theatre company should confine themselves to 'social work' is not only politically unpalatable but also completely at odds with the reason the company have excelled in the past. It was the theatrical scale of Jatinder Verma's artistic and intellectual engagement with classic texts that led to the success of *Tartuffe*, *The Little Clay Cart* and the development of *JTW*. It should not be forgotten that it has been Tara's insistence on the recognition of the Asian presence in Britain that led to the creation of their innovative theatrical form of the hybrid 'not quite English' (Verma 1996: 200) 'Binglish' and irrevocably broadened the cultural parameters of British theatre.

8
New Writers from 1977: Kureishi, Bancil, Bhatti and Khan-Din

This chapter will look at some of the key works by British Asian playwrights since 1977. The prefix 'Asian' before the term 'writer' is problematic and often resisted by these playwrights because, as Tanika Gupta has pointed out, 'nobody goes round describing Harold Pinter as a Jewish white playwright, so why does everyone go round calling me an Asian woman playwright? If you get labelled you get boxed in' (Gardner 2006b: 22). However, while their writing often explores the particularities of the British Asian experience, these reflections necessarily also include an engagement with the wider British community of which they are a part.

This chapter will explore the pioneering main stage British Asian work of Hanif Kureishi in the 1980s, the underground/underclass world of gangs and petty criminality in the work of Parv Bancil in the 1990s, the extraordinary reaction to the work of Gurpreet Bhatti in 2000 and the continued mainstream success of Ayub Khan-Din with *Rafta Rafta* (2007).

Hanif Kureishi

While it has been Hanif Kureishi's film and novel writing that has brought him to wider public and critical attention he began his career as a theatre writer in the early 1980s. In films such as *My Beautiful Launderette* (1985) Kureishi successfully showed the ways in which Asian cultural identity is constituted by more than just 'race' and is intersected by 'class, gender, sexuality and ethnicity' (Hall 1995: 226), in opposition to conceptions of the essentialised 'other', as he 'complexly rendered the heterogeneous and hybrid subjects of postcolonial Britain' (Desai 2004: 60).

However, Hanif Kureishi's early theatre work was also critically acclaimed, as is evident in his being given the Most Promising Playwright of the Year Award in 1981 by the London Theatre Critics for *Borderline* (1981) and *Outskirts* (1981). Hanif Kureishi was born in Bromley, the child of an English mother and Pakistani father, but his own cultural biography is remarkable for the absence of Asian characters and themes in much of his early work. *The King and Me* (1980), produced at the Soho Poly Theatre, was a piece of realistic theatre set in a rundown suburb of London and perhaps most remarkable for having no Asian characters. Kureishi's main target, which was to resurface in *Outskirts* and *Borderline* was the social environment of his characters, as themes of wasted lives and unrealistic dreams of escape are played out against a backdrop of urban decay and social disintegration.

Outskirts (1981) was produced by the Royal Shakespeare Company at the Warehouse Theatre in London and won the George Divine Award. It was a problem play that attempted to explore the motivations behind the 'racism' of the white working class community towards the incoming Asian and black communities. It was, again, remarkable that the only Asian presence was a symbolic one, represented by the Indian passport of the victim of a racist attack. While Kurieshi suggested that social disadvantage and political neglect contributed to racism, the playwright's cynicism as to its cure troubled critic Michael Billington because 'there seems little to choose between illiberal brutality and liberal education: a conclusion that I find impossible to swallow' (2001a: 167).

Kureishi's subsequent play, *Borderline*, focused specifically on the predominantly Sikh Asian community in Southall, west London. It was also notable as the first play by a British Asian writer writing about the British Asian community to be given a mainstream, albeit 'radical' mainstream, venue. *Borderline* was performed at the Royal Court Theatre in 1981 and created in line with the Joint Stock theatrical methodology, which involved a number of months of joint research by cast, writer and director, followed by writing, improvisation, rehearsal and rewriting.

Rather than speaking from the margins, Kureishi candidly admitted that he 'knew the subject was there but we couldn't get at it, not from the outside – it was too big, too vague – and not from the inside, either: we didn't know enough' (Kureishi 1992: xix). In this statement Kureishi calls into question not only the effectiveness of the company's journalistic methodology but also his own ability to speak from the perspective of the Asian community, rather than about it. While Kureishi obviously had an 'inside' view in the respect that he himself was a British Asian his knowledge of the Asian community in Southall was obviously extremely limited, which was exemplified by his admission that 'the research helped me to begin to see the diversity and drama of the Asian community' (Kuresihi 1992: xix).

Kureishi's and the company's position in relation to the Asian community is reflected by one of the white characters in the play, Susan, a journalist 'intent on making a radio programme about the predominantly Sikh community in London's Southall [...] [because] her research mirrors the research undertaken by the mixed race company that was assembled before the play was written' (Peacock 1999: 117). Kureishi recognised the importance of the Asian voice in the mainstream of British theatre and dramatised his anxieties concerning the representation and 'ownership' of that voice. In *Borderline* Susan, the white journalist who comes to do a story on the Asian Youth Movement, is warned by one of its members that she should not 'think you can represent us truly [...] you take our voice. Use our voice. Annex our cause' (Kureishi 1992: 132), which might be read as a warning to the British theatre not to exclude British Asian theatre practitioners.

Perhaps, either because there may have been a fear of 'excluding' the largely white, non-Asian speaking audience of the Royal Court, or as a result of the company's inability or unwillingness, there are no Asian languages employed in the text so that apart from a 'slight hint of formality in the speech of the first generation immigrants [...] Kureishi makes no attempt to convey Asian English' (Peacock 1999: 118). The decision not to employ Asian languages or accents may have been exacerbated by the methodological implications of the integrated cast. If the white actors adopted Asian accents or languages the performance may have become subsumed within a racist discourse that appropriates and stereotypes portrayals of non-white people.

Borderline responded to, and was based on, actual events that occurred in west London. In 1979 the National Front, a neo-fascist group that, in the 1970s and 1980s 'became increasingly visible in British inner cities' (Smith 1994: 149) decided to hold a rally in Southall. Their decision to hold a rally in a constituency in which they 'had virtually no support [...] and had not fielded a candidate there since 1970 [...] was seen as a calculated act of provocation' (Brah 1996: 44) by the large, local Asian community. The subsequent protest by the Asian residents was met by a massive police presence, including members of the notoriously aggressive Special Patrol Group. The resultant violent confrontation left many protestors injured and a white schoolteacher, Blair Peach, dead.

The increasing militancy of this Asian resistance became visible once again in 1981 when it was alleged that on their way to a concert at the

Hanborough Tavern in Southall white skinheads with National Front banners launched an unprovoked attack on an Asian shopkeeper. In response, the Southall Youth Movement mobilised young Asians onto the streets and the Hanborough Tavern was set ablaze. As Avtar Brah and other cultural commentators such as Dilip Hiro in *Black British, White British* (1973) point out, these organised outbursts of resistance by British Asian youth groups marked a generational shift in thinking so that 'however much they may be constructed as "outsiders", they contest [...] psychological and geographical spaces from the position of insiders' (Brah 1996: 47), and articulate and include themselves within a discourse of 'Britishness'.

Borderline attempted to dramatise these social developments by focusing on two issues, firstly the resistance of the 'second generation' British Asians to the racist treatment they encounter and secondly the intergenerational cultural negotiations within the Asian community. The main protagonists of the play were four 'second generation' British Asians, members of the Asian Youth Movement modelled on the Southall Youth Movement discussed above. The play examined how they negotiated their hybrid cultural identity within a racist British society exemplified by the increasing attacks on the community by a neo-fascist group. *Borderline* was certainly ambitious in its scope to represent the intra- and inter-community tensions of the Asian community in west London.

The central debate staged in the play is between two routes of possible resistance for 'second generation' British Asians, which were either to become the 'worm in the body' (Kureishi 1992: 117) of the British establishment, espoused by the university-educated Haroon, or go for the more separatist agenda espoused by Anwar. The dramatisation of Haroon's approach to be 'the black mole under the lawns and asphalt of England' (Kureishi 1992: 159) brought him into conflict with the more militant members of the Asian Youth Movement who disagreed with this individualistic approach and believed in a politics of opposition and active resistance.

Amina's mother is concerned that her daughter has become anglicised, symbolised in the play by her clothes changing from wearing *salwar kameez*[1] to jeans and a t-shirt. However, while Amina may reject Asian dress she is committed to protecting, and allies herself within, the Asian community and is instrumental in the battle to protect it from racist attack. Indeed, Kureishi's final image of the play of a light left burning in the offices of the Asian Youth Front, like a beacon 'so people know we're here' (Kureishi 1992: 168) as the characters go to protest against the meeting held by the neo-fascists symbolised both defiance and solidarity in the play as well as signalling the arrival of British Asian drama on a mainstream stage.

There were some methodological choices taken by Joint Stock, exemplified in their casting policy, which did not assist their credibility in addressing their Asian subject matter. In contrast to Tara who had maintained a strict policy of using all-Asian casts, Joint Stock employed integrated casting for *Borderline* with a cast of seven actors, four white and three Asian, playing 13 characters. While Tara's all-Asian casting approach foregrounded and positively insisted on the recognition of the cultural difference of the performers in respect of being non-white, Joint Stock's 'experiments in integrated casting aim to make the unfamiliar (Asian and Black faces amidst White) *acceptable*' (Verma 1996a: 200) but crucially neglect issues of representation and difference.

These tensions were apparent in an article in the *Asian Digest*, 'Tara: An Asian Perspective', which drew a clear distinction between Tara Arts who 'offer a perspective on Asian life in Britain today....[and] Joint Stock, through Hanif Kureishi's play [*Borderline*] depicting contemporary Asian "problems" – rather like some of the more popular dailies who, every so often find Asians "newsworthy"'(Asian Digest 1982).

Parv Bancil

Parv Bancil joined Hounslow Arts Co-Operative (HAC) as a stage manager in 1987 alongside the other key members Ravinder Gill, Preet Bancil, Shakiel Khan and later Neran Persaud, but it was not long before he became, to all intents and purposes, their resident writer. HAC was the methodological antithesis of companies such as Tara and was described by Jatinder Verma as 'the only Asian theatre company I ever saw which [...] deliberately sought to defy memory (and history) by having no reference at all to the Indian subcontinent – whether in language, in the story, in its costume and scenic detail or music' (Verma 1994: 4). In this respect HAC actively reacted against Tara's theatrical experiments in 'Binglish', which drew on Asian forms that they perceived as 'about vacuous pledges to the powers that be of providing so called "culture" ' (Gill 1987: 2).

HAC's raison d'être was to portray what they felt were the authentic experiences of second generation Asians in plays such as *The Curse of the Dead Dog* (1987) co-written by Parv Bancil and Ravinde Gill where 'there were three characters we'd never seen represented before on TV or stage [...] what you'd term now as British Asian' (Bancil, 1999). *The Curse of the Dead Dog* focused on three teenage Asian boys who are on the dole and spend their days causing trouble in the local park and getting drunk and was described as a 'play for the new generation of Asians who have been brought up in this country pointing a tentative finger as to what direction this generation will take' (Govinda 1987).

The work seemed to sit uncomfortably with funding bodies that expected the onus of the work to be on the 'Asian' rather than 'British' element in 'British Asian':

> the company was in the process of receiving transitional funding from Hounslow council [...]. the opening night was attended by councillors and the mayor of Hounslow, who seemed very supportive of new, multicultural theatre. I remember that some of the councillor's wives even wore saris; I think they wanted us to feel at home. We were told afterwards that they had expected to see a spot of Kathak dancing and traditional south-Asian costume. Instead, they watched a play about three disaffected British Asian boys looking for a way out of a dead-end town. The characters spoke like me and my friends: a concoction of cockney slang, Jamaican patois and Punjabi. Like most kids from that part of the world, they swore, smoked cigarettes and played hip-hop. By the interval, most of the councillors and the mayor left in disgust; we received a letter from them, complaining that 'we had let our parents and our culture down'.
>
> (Bancil 2008)

HAC was formed in 1981 as a community group who had initially based their plays on Indian classics yet had a radical change of direction from 1985 as it aimed to be 'a reaction against the stereotypes and alienation that as young Asians we felt at that time' (Bancil 2008). HAC was one of a number of new black and Asian theatre companies formed in the 1980s as 'Temba, Tara Arts, the Black Theatre Cooperative, and Talawa were joined by the British Asian Theatre Company, Hounslow Arts Co-operative, the Asian Theatre Co-operative, Double-Edged Theatre, Carib Theatre and Tamasha' (Peacock 1999: 183).

In subsequent plays such as *Ungrateful Dead* (1993), depicting gang wars, rape and drugs in Southall, and *Crazyhorse* (1997), peopled with petty criminals, Parv Bancil was 'unique because he avoids the normal Asian subject, be it the relationship with India, be it mixed marriages [...] he's the only one among Asian writers who's looking at the seamier side, at the alienated youth of London' (Verma 2002).

Crazyhorse (1997)

Jas, a small-time crook, hangs out with his two friends, Nobby and Ronnie, in his father's lock-up garage behind the house. Jas has just been released from prison and is working for his father as a mechanic but Ronnie wants him to return to his criminal ways and strip down stolen cars. Mr Jutla has plans to ask Linda, his new girlfriend, to marry him and make Jas move out. When Jas discovers his father's plan he agrees to steal a car for Ronnie. During the robbery Jas accidentally runs Linda over and hides her body in the garage.

Crazyhorse began as a short play written for the Paines Plough Writers Group season of rehearsed readings 'The Wild Lunch' at the Bridewell Theatre, London, in March 1977. Crazyhorse was a co-production between Paines Plough and Tara Arts and was first performed on 1 October 1997 at the New Vic Studio, Bristol Old Vic.

The characters in *Crazyhorse* were as far away from the stereotypical Asian shopkeepers or doctors as Parv Bancil would want, featuring a cast of drug-taking petty criminal misfits. *Crazyhorse* depicts a world in which the cultural certainties of Asian family life where 'sons should respect their father's' (17) have broken down, topless models have replaced the Sikh calendar and Jas is reduced to eating boiled potatoes rather than 'all that curry an ting you people eat' (30).

Jas, the central character, is an inept thief who, with his accomplice Nobby, contrived to steal a broken toaster instead of a jewellery box full of gold on his last burglary, then spent three months in prison for a crime he didn't commit. Jas and his father are attempting, and failing, to keep their backstreet garage business going. Since Jas came out of prison relations between father and son are extremely strained as his father not only holds him responsible for the collapse of the business but also for the loss of his wife who died in childbirth.

> MR JUTLA: 'I've given the last twenty-three years over to you, do you know that? Twenty three shit fucking years, and what do I get?
> *Mr Jutla points to Jas*
> This.
> (56)

Parv Bancil also created the character of Nobby, Jas's friend, as a means of both satirising and celebrating the fluidity of cultural identity.

Nobby was a precursor to Sacha Baron Cohen's popular television creation 'Ali G', 'a product of London now [...] a white guy who [...] wants the South London side, he likes dreadlocks, the ganja, the heavy dub base' (Bancil 1999). Bancil lampoons Nobby, and those like him, for their belief that cultural identity is something completely mutable:

> NOBBY: You want to get out to India. They love us black guys out there.
> RONNIE: But you ain't black.
> NOBBY: What you talking' about Rasta? Don't be racist. I hate racists. It ain't about colour, black comes from within. I ain't being funny Ronnie. But I think I'm blacker than you. (39)

While Bancil recognises these characters do share a fluid hybrid cultural space that is not predicated on discrete cultural borders, in the case of Nobby this premise is taken *ad absurdam* so that 'one minute you're a skinhead and the next this Indian [...] Rasta' (39).

While the first half of the play depicts the casual criminality, drug taking and banter of the three culturally diverse friends, the second half of the play inhabits more metaphysical territory. Firstly, the dramatic temperature is raised considerably as Jas, Nobby and Ronnie find themselves in a 'murder situation' (45) after Jas knocks down and kills Mr Jutlas' girlfriend, Linda, and brings her body back to the garage in the car he has stolen for Ronnie. Secondly, *Crazyhorse* increasingly becomes infused with a magic realism dramatised in the unexplained flickering lights and buzzing sounds, which culminate in the resurrection Mr Jutla's dead wife.

While the three friends are busy hiding Linda's dead body in the garage pit, Mr Jutla returns from his aborted attempt to propose to her. Mr Jutla is left alone in the garage with the body, which is now possessed by the spirit of his dead wife. In a macabre twist, symbolic of a futile attempt to return to the past, Mr Jutla then has sex with the lifeless body:

> Mr Jutla lies the woman down. She does not respond. He has sex with her. She lies still. Jas enters. (70)

While this bleak image is slightly redeemed by the reconciliation of father and son as Mr Jutla apologises there is no disguising Bancil's preoccupation with a second generation that has not only lost its way but has also been abandoned.

Made in England (1998)

Kes, Mick and Bally are members of *Death Row*, a post-punk band on the cusp of finishing their new album. The band seem poised for success when Bally is offered, and accepts, a solo record deal that leads to an acrimonious split in the band. In order to achieve success with his new record label Bally is forced to 'sell out'; changing his name and donning a turban and sitar to surf the popular wave of 'Asian cool'. When Bally's success begins to wane he returns to make peace with Kes and Mick.

Made in England was a direct engagement by Parv Bancil with what 'cool Britiannia' meant for British Asians as the recently elected Labour Party led by Tony Blair invited the cream of 'Britpop' to Downing Street. Bancil took a critical look at the cultural zeitgeist and its hunger for all things Asian, from *balti* to Bollywood and took a sceptical position on the appropriation of Asian culture by the mainstream:

> when you're lifting Hindi film songs and this and that and the other you're sort of exotic [...] that's why you're being recognised [...]. Kes comes from a generation where he had to fight for a stake in this country [...] we're not just these Indians who come from India because we haven't had that experience [...] we were brought up in this country, on British food, on British TV on British pop music and now we're playing this music that we denied all this time [...] that's Kes' perspective.
>
> (Bancil 1999: 4)

He interrogates the very different responses to that perceived appropriation within the 'second generation' as the 'term spans from British Asians who are now in their late 30s to British Asians who are in their mid 20s' (Bancil 2000: 90). *Made in England* was initially commissioned as a 15-minute piece for the Red Room Theatre Company produced to be part of the Seeing Red Festival at the Battersea Arts Centre. It was first performed as a full-length play at Waterman's Arts Centre on 21 October 1998.

The play opens as the band prepare to rehearse at Mick's tattoo parlour and as Kes, the driving force behind the band, bemoans the fact that 'music isn't saying anything these days. It's got no message' (94) in contrast to the politics of his band, *Death Row*:

> He lays the flag out on the floor. The Union Jack is defaced and has 'Death
> Row - Made In England' sprayed onto it with car paint
> MICK: That used to wind people up no end. Especially when they
> saw you.
> KES: A Paki made in England. They didn't get the joke.
> (94)

As the latest recruit, Bally, arrives for rehearsal he accidentally steps on the flag prefiguring what he is symbolically going to do the ethics of the band. Bally has been seduced by Blue Max record label who want to sign him as Asians are 'in' and have given him a sitar, which he can't play, in order that he looks and sounds appropriately 'exotic'. Kes remonstrates that 'a sitar's a complex instrument [...] you can't just play it like a guitar [...] it doesn't mean anything' (102), symbolic of Bancil's belief that British Asians are being exoticised.

Bancil stages a debate on ethnicity in Act Two with the arrival of a journalist at Bally's hotel room. It is six months later in California and Bally has split from the band and anglicised his name to Billy India. He is on a world tour having successfully released his debut single 'Youth in Asia' – a comical song about an Asian shopkeeper with a Welsh-sounding accent – achieving the commercial success he craved, but at a cost to his credibility and his anti-racist politics. Bally believes that in order for him to achieve commercial success he must disavow his ethnicity, even taking care that he does not step out onto his hotel balcony in case he gets a suntan. Bancil points out that it is not the disavowal of Bally's ethnicity but its exoticisation that has led to his popularity and that is why the record company make him 'play a sitar, use an Asian sounding name and make constant references to Asians in your song titles' (111).

The cyclical structure of the play returns Bally to the tattoo parlour where *Death Row* rehearse in Act Three as Mick and Kes are about to celebrate New Year's Eve. Kes wants to disband *Death Row* as a result of Bally 'selling out', and his anger that 'he didn't only fuck himself, he fucked us. He put us back ten years' (118) can be read as an admonishment to those in the British Asian community prepared to play into exoticised stereotypes.

KES: I wanted something people would be scared of. I saw the potential in you. Death Row should have been fronted by a hard-core Paki with a guitar.

BALLY: That's what I am!

KES: You were. Now you're just a passive Paki with a sitar.

Kes contends that. Bally is simply adhering to stereotype because he has denied his real musical influences:

BALLY: Hip hop. Dub. Reggae. Punk. Some heavy rock [...] Nirvana [...] House and Garage [...] A bit of drum and bass. Some techno. A bit of the Indie stuff [...]

KES: You listen to any Indian pop records?

BALLY: Fuck off!

KES: Any classical stuff?

BALLY: Only the stuff my dad plays, but I don't like it much. Never really listened to it.

KES: Then why play a sitar?

(125)

Bancil clearly sympathises with the character of Kes who, like many of the older 'second generation', 'had some very bitter experiences that shaped them when they were growing up on the front line. They were the ones went in, got all the shit [...] and whatever we got now they created. The music scene [...] the arts scene [...] everything. They also don't have a credit for it' (Bancil 1999).

This clear divide in the experiences within the 'second generation' is graphically symbolised in *Made in England* by the Union Jack. For Bally the Union Jack is simply a flag he wants tattooed on his arm because it looks 'cool' whereas for Kes and Mick it symbolises the National Front, racist violence and class oppression; this is their rationale for it being defaced.

Gurpreet Bhatti's *Behzti (Dishonour)*

Gurpreet Kaur Bhatti's play, *Behzti (Dishonour)*, precipitated a national debate on the issue of 'freedom of speech' and catapulted British Asian theatre into the headlines. The play opened at Birmingham Repertory Theatre on 9 December 2004 and was forced to close on Saturday 18 December as a result of violent protests from some members of the Sikh community who attempted to storm the stage and disrupt the performance.

For the first time since Jim Allen's play *Perdition* was abandoned by the Royal Court Theatre in 1987 after protests from the Jewish community, the cancellation of *Behzti* was precipitated on the grounds that the theatre could no longer guarantee the safety of the audience. The artistic director of the National Theatre at that time, Nick Hytner, led the calls of the theatre community with a very public plea made on BBC Radio Four's *Today Programme* for artists to be allowed 'freedom of the imagination' (2004). This sentiment was endorsed by the executive director of the Birmingham Repertory Theatre, responsible for cancelling the remaining performances of *Behzti*, who was quoted in *The Independent* that it was 'a matter of great concern to us that [...] freedom of speech can be curtailed by violent acts' (2004).

The national press were divided on the matter with the *Independent* (above) reprinting one of the most controversial scenes in the play on their front page and its leader clearly determined that 'the threat of mob violence should not curtail the right of artistic expression' (2004), while locating the debate in the wider context of the increasing tensions between secularism and religious fundamentalism. Stephen Glover of the *Daily Mail*, however, was keen to express his 'sneaking admiration for those who, unlike us, fight to defend their faith' (2004: 12).

Perhaps, with hindsight, the Birmingham Repertory's attempt to liaise closely with representatives of the Sikh community from an early stage, even to the extent of putting on a private performance of the show for them was a miscalculation because it unwittingly seems to have given the impression that they had some right of veto over artistic decisions. It became clear that the focus of animosity towards *Behzti* from some sections of the Sikh community was aroused not so much by the portrayal of Sikh characters committing acts of rape and violence in the play but the setting of these acts in the Sikh place of worship, the *gurdwara*. Indeed, the central plank of the early negotiations between the playwright and the representatives of the Sikh community was to relocate the action to a community centre, a concession the writer and the theatre were not prepared to make.

The director of the Sikh Human Rights Group, Dr Jasdev Singh Rai, pointed out the reason why this was at the heart of the protest:

> *Behzti's* theme is sexual and financial abuse using Sikh characters. Most Sikhs could not care less about this. But by setting the play – unnecessarily – in a *gurdwara*, Bhatti disrespected the sanctity of the Guru. An offended Sikh can of course stay away from the play but most Sikhs feel they have to maintain the *gurdwara's* sanctity.
>
> (2005)

The argument as to whether the play should be performed raged as keenly within the Sikh community as without, with the defence of the play exemplified by playwright Ash Kotak who believed 'the idea that whole [Asian] communities are homogenised is bollocks especially as we go through generations. The people who are campaigning are the ones who oppressed us in the first place' (2004: 3).

The strength of the protest came as something as a surprise to the wider community as Sikhism is widely regarded as a tolerant and progressive religion with its rejection of caste and espousal of gender equality, while still valuing its traditions. However, when Bhatti broke her silence for the first time since the play had been cancelled in an article in the *Guardian* on 13 January 2005 she drew a distinction between the action of the demonstrators and their faith.

While condemning the violence directed at herself and her play she was at pains to defend Sikhism and point out that 'there can never be any excuse for the demonisation of a religion or its followers' (2005: 25). Indeed, in the foreword to *Behzti* she makes an impassioned defence of Sikhism, which has 'propagated values of egalitarianism and selflessness' (2004: 17). However, while she sets out her admiration for the Sikh values of egalitarianism and selflessness she also 'finds herself drawn to that which is beneath the surface of triumph [...] that is anonymous and quiet, raging, despairing, human, inhumane, absurd and comical' (Bhatti 2004: 17).

Behzti (Dishonour) (2004)

Balbir is determined to find a husband for her daughter, Min, and turns to Mr Sandu, a temple elder and old friend of her deceased husband, to help find a suitable candidate from his 'list'. Balbir and Min go to the *gurdwara* to meet Mr Sandhu. Elvis, Balbir's carer, has feelings for Min but when he accompanies them to the gurdwara is seduced by one of Balbir's old friends, Polly. Mr Sandhu agrees to help Min but when they are alone he rapes her. When Min goes to Balbir, Polly and Teetee for help they beat her. Min is then forced to apologise to Mr Sandhu who offers himself as a prospective husband. Min and Elvis are reunited but when Balbir finds out that Mr Sandhu has raped Min she kills him.

In the arresting opening image of *Behzti* we see Balbir, Min's mother, sitting naked on a stool in the bath as Min washes her and gets her ready for their trip to the *Gurdwara*. Min is a full-time carer for her disabled and incontinent mother and in this opening scene we soon gain an insight into their claustrophobic and dysfunctional relationship in which Balbir warns her daughter that 'if I had a knife I'd stick it up your arse' (40) and Min sellotapes her mother's mouth shut. The plot is driven by Balbir's insistence on arranging a marriage for her daughter through Mr Sandhu at the *gurdwara* because 'it's not pleasant watching a fat virgin becoming infertile' (46).

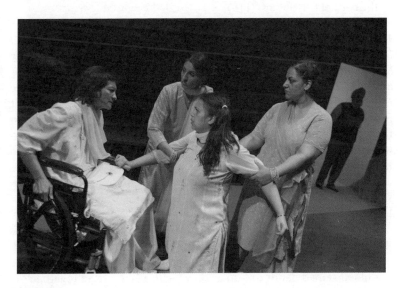

Behzti 2004
© Robert Day.
Yasmin Wilde (Min) being held by Pooja Kumar (Polly) and Harvey Virdi (Teetee) in front of Shelley King as Balbir in her wheelchair, as Madhav Sharma (Mr Sandhu) looks on from the doorway.

While Min romanticises the egalitarian principles and practicalities of the *gurdwara* the reality is shown to be very different. Corruption reigns at the *gurdwara* from the comedic double act of Teetee and Polly who steal the shoes of the worshippers while they are at prayer and their jewellery during *sayva*[2] to the more malign form of Mr Sandhu, an elder of the *gurdwara*, a local councillor and head of the renovation committee.

Bhatti's real focus of attack is on those who favour '[...] outward appearance, wealth and the quest for power' (Bhatti 2004: 17) in the form of Mr Sandhu. When Blabir's husband died Mr Sandhu bought their property, turned it into flats and had Balbir and Min evicted. Mr Sandhu shocks Min with the revelation that he and her father were lovers and tells her 'you remind me of my Tej [...] he [...] he used to kiss me [...] on the lips [...] so fucking hard' (109) as he then rapes Min to the accompaniment of the *aardass*.[3] Although this takes place offstage the audience are left in no doubt what has occurred by the stage directions for the next scene:

> Min hobbles off. As she walks, we see a terrifying patch of blood staining the back of her clothes. (113)

The complicity of the female characters is a key theme for Bhatti in *Bezhti*. Under the watchful gaze of Mr Sandhu, Polly and Teetee accuse Min of disrespectfully entering the *gurdwara* when she has her period and refuse to listen to her claim that Mr Sandhu 'put himself inside me' (120). Teetee colludes with Mr Sandhu in covering up his assault on Min in the hope he awards her son Billu the contract to build the new extension for the *gurdwara*. They gag and beat her, even forcing her mother, Balbir, to join them, as Min is made to apologise to her attacker. However, this collusion is shown to have consequences as Polly and Teetee reveal to Balbir that Mr Sandu's marriage list is simply a ruse 'so that girls go up and see him. So he can force them [...]' (125).

Behzti comes to a final bloody end worthy of a revenge tragedy as Balbir murders Mr Sandhu, rather fittingly with his own kirpan [dagger], and we are left with a tableau of Min, Elvis and Balbir. Balbir is showing her bloodstained hands to Min as they recite a Sikh prayer together:

> MIN: Vaheguruji kha khalsa..[God be with you, the members of the Khalsa belong to God]
> BALBIR: Vaheguruji khi fateh [All victories are God's] (139)

There is a shared motif between *Behzti* and *Behsharram*, Gurpreet Bhatti's first play, as both their main protagonists, Min and Jaspal, respectively, have relationships with black characters. Both Elvis in *Behzti* and Patrick, the would-be boxer, in *Behsharam*, are sympathetic and supportive characters that face racism from the Asian characters. Min rejects Elvis's declaration of love but even so he remains loyal insisting 'you've moved me Min [...] Maninder, you've made me feel like I'm flesh and blood and bone and hair. And [...] and [...] I love you [...] ' (111). Indeed,

Bhatti makes sure that Elvis and Min are 'the only two characters associated with undistorted human values [...]. the one completely outside
Sikh culture, the other almost entirely marginalised within it' (Crow
2007. 215) and it is their relationship that provides a sense of hope.

While *Behzti* gained Gurpreet Bhatti notoriety her first play *Behsharam*
(*Shameless*), which first performed at the Soho Theatre on 11 October
2001 broke the theatre's box office records at that time. The idea driving
the play was to 'look at dysfunctionalism in a family and how [...]
secrets in a family [...] could destabilise it' (Bhatti 2003), which gave
Bhatti an opportunity to dissect what she perceived to be the idealised
representations of the extended Asian family. An early draft of the idea
was sent to Birmingham Repertory Theatre in 1998 and she was invited
to join the attachment scheme for new writers in order to develop the
play. There are, similarly to *Behzti*, two female characters at the centre
of the play, in this case Jaspal, the older sister who has been thrown out
of the family home, and her 16-year-old sister, Sati, who remains.

Behsharam (Shameless) (2001)

The play opens in 1998 as Jaspal prepares to take the stage of a
down-at-heel nightclub with her tribute act as Kiran, rather than
Karen, Carpenter and is reunited with her sister Sati after four
years. We then go back to 1994 when the sisters were still in contact and Jaspal lived with her long-suffering Jamaican boyfriend,
Patrick, a would-be professional boxer. Sati spends her time working in her uncle's shop with her grandmother and talking to a
life-size cut-out of the footballer Ian Wright. When Sati realises
her mother, Mummy One, has not been on a religious pilgrimage
to holy shrines in India and Pakistan for the past seven years but
is in a care home nearby suffering from mental health problems
she too leaves home.

The critical reception to the play recognised Bhatti's aim to expose 'the
pre-occupation of British-Asian mothers with their male issue, and the
treatment of daughters as disposable assets' (Billington 2001b), as Bhatti
provocatively suggests that within the Asian community 'educating
your daughter is like watering another man's field' (Bhatti 2001: 43).

Structurally, Bhatti was accused by critics of belying her roots as a
scriptwriter for the soap opera *EastEnders* and letting 'situations take

precedence over ideas' (Billington 2001), suggested by 12 scenes in five locations in *Besharam*. The first two scenes take place in 1998 and the plot then flashes back to 1994 to explore the reason behind the rift between the two sisters and why Jaspal left home. The domestic realism of that genre was further exemplified in the detailed set design of Jaspal's flat:

Very messy bedsit – two chairs and a beanbag in the middle of the room [...] there is a messy packed coffee table, covered with tobacco, rizzla papers, bits of food, old make-up and empty takeaway containers [...] (Bhatti: 30)

Bhatti does not spare either the Asian or black communities in their response to the inter-ethnic relationship between Jaspal and Patrick. Although Patrick is a sympathetic character who tries to wean Jaspal off drugs he is continually abused and stereotyped by the Asian characters who refer to him either as a 'black bastard' (Bhatti 45) or believe all black people are pimps or drug dealers. Like Elvis in *Behzti*, Patrick has remained loyal to Jaspal and kept 'faith in you and me, even when I had to drag you back home when you were off your face fucking strangers on the streets, I always had faith' (Bhatti 55). However, his friends from the black community are equally vociferous in warning him against having a relationship with an Asian woman on the grounds that Asians think themselves superior and may 'pollute his race' (69).

While both *Behsharam* and *Behzti* could be categorised as examples of British Asian 'In-yer-face' theatre in which 'the language is usually filthy, characters talk about unmentionable subjects, take their clothes off, have sex, humiliate each other, experience unpleasant emotions, become suddenly violent' (Sierz 2001: 5), they are also leavened by humour and ultimately optimistic. From the tyrannical grandmother, Beji, who makes abusive phone calls to her son's new wife, drinks, shoplifts and generally abuses her son, to the quirkiness of Sati who spends her time speaking to a cardboard cut-out of the footballer Ian Wright. Indeed, while Bhatti's vision is often bleak it is always finally redemptive.

Behsharam ends with the sisters' reconciliation and a sense of hope as Jaspal performs her Kiran Carpenter act to a rapturous audience. However, it is also clear that there has been lasting 'damage' done to them both.

At this point, both their reflections can be seen in all three mirrors, gradually their reflections overlap and it is hard to make one out from the other.
Do you see now?

JASPAL: Yeah. It's the same old damage. Right pair of old cunts aren't we? Who would have thought it?
SATI: What?
JASPAL: You. You turned out as bad as me. Worse by the looks of you.

(Bhatti 95)

The religious protest over *Behzti* can be read as a further sign of the increasing fragmentation of Asian identity as a result of the privileging of religion, most obviously in relation to the Muslim faith. This started with the demonstrations against Salman Rushdie's book *The Satanic Verses* in the late 1980s and was further polarised in the wake of the events of 11 September 2001[4] and the subsequent 'war on terror' and its geopolitical ramifications. As Sarfraz Manzoor has pointed out, the critical question this poses 'is this new religious identity part of an overarching plural identity, or is it exclusive and separate?' (2005) The response to *Behzti* suggests that any homogenising constructions of identity, be they predicated on race or religion, will be heavily contested within and without ethnic minority communities.

A pertinent contribution to the dispute was made by Trevor Phillips, the chairman of the Commission for Racial Equality when he suggested on BBC Radio 4's *Today Programme* that the issue is less about the particular depiction of Sikhs in *Behzti* and more a result of a lack of representation of Sikh characters on the stage and screen; *Bend It Like Beckham* (2002) excepted.

Gurpreet Bhatti explained in the foreword to the play that she wanted to generate a debate and 'wrote *Behzti* because I passionately oppose injustice and hypocrisy' (2004: 18), but perhaps she did not envisage that this debate would be on a national scale. However, in spite of the play being cancelled, and not subsequently being performed in this country, the writer has remained uncowed, insisting that 'this warrior is fighting on' (2004).

Ayub Khan-Din

Ayub Khan-Din repeated the 'crossover' success of *East is East* (1996) and proved that British Asian theatre could still find a mainstream audience and a main stage at the National Theatre with *Rafta Rafta* (2007).

Rafta Rafta (2007)

Newlyweds Atul and Vina move into his parents' small terraced house in Bolton after the wedding. The domineering presence of Atul's father, Eeshwar, and the pranks played by the family on the couple's wedding night means that six weeks after their wedding the marriage has still to be consummated. When Vina confides in her mother and father the situation gets worse as soon news spreads to the wider circle of family and friends. Atul finally snaps when he is taunted by his boss for his lack of success in the bedroom and attacks him, resulting in the sack. However, all is happily resolved when Atul and Vina finally consummate the marriage and their parents buy them a new house on return from their honeymoon.

Rafta Rafta, appropriately translated as 'slowly slowly', was adapted by Ayub Khan-Din from Bill Naughton's play *All in Good Time* (1963) and was first performed on 26 April 2007 in the Lyttelton auditorium of the National Theatre. Khan-Din describes seeing *The Family Way*, the film version of *All in Good Time* and thinking 'it would work perfectly with two Asian families because, especially with soaring house prices, people are still living with their parents after marriage' (Khan-Din in Sierz 2007).

The critics believed 'Khan-Din's success lies in integrating Naughton's plot into a vivid portrait of Indian family life' (Billington 2007) that might allow the, rather dated, central premise of the play to ring true for a contemporary audience. In order to make the 1963 plot function Khan-Din made the character of Atul a little 'old fashioned' in his insistence on adhering to the custom of the bride moving in with the groom's parents. Having utilised this Asian cultural context in order to trap the newlyweds in the small house Khan-Din allows the situation, running gags, comic characters, slow burns and double entendres go to work. The production was aided by a critically acclaimed 'two up two down', open dolls-house set by Tim Hatley, which allowed the audience to see the upstairs and downstairs simultaneously.

The father of the groom, Mr Dutt, a first generation Indian immigrant was played by Bollywood star Harish Patel with a 'magnificent mixture of vanity and pathos' (Billington 2007: 38). The relationship between Mr Dutt and Atul is strained, as a son who would rather read a book than *bhangra* bemuses the father. Proceedings even take a Freudian turn for the worse after the wedding as father and son engage in a bout of arm wrestling and Mr Dutt beats Atul in front of all the wedding guests, including Atul's new bride, much to the dismay of his mother, played by Meera Syal.

While there are elements of the play specific to the new Asian context, Khan-Din also exploits the situation for all of its scatological comic worth irrespective of the ethnicity of the family. As the newlyweds finally make it up to the bedroom:

> (*He approaches her and holds her. He reaches up and takes her face in his hands. He leans in to kiss her again. We hear the toilet flush in the bathroom*)
> JAI   (*Offstage*) Bog's free! (43)
> (*It breaks the mood. Vina suddenly becomes shy*)

Further interruptions follow as Eeshwar, in his pyjamas, reassures Atul that if he needs anything he just needs to tap on the wall as he is a very light sleeper. This leads to the comic climax of Scene One as the bed collapses just as the newlyweds are about to consummate the marriage. This prank organised by his brother, is the final straw for Atul who turns on Vina:

> ATUL: Just shut up! You're as bad as the bloody rest of 'em.
> *Vina stops laughing, shocked at the state he has got himself into.*
> (47)
> The running gag of the couple being interrupted every time they are about to consummate their marriage resumes in Scene Two, set six weeks later:
> *They move over to the bed. Atul gets on top of her and starts to push up her nightgown.*
> VINA: Ohhh, gently [...] here [...].
> *He's a bit clumsy, and Vina reaches down and tries to help. The landing light goes on. She sees it and is not sure whether to stop Atul. We hear Eeshwar coughing. He clears his throat loudly outside the door.*
> Atul [...] Atul [...] No, don't, your dad [...] Ohhhhh..your dad's gone to the toilet.
> *We hear Eeshwar urinating loudly and then he passes wind.*
> (51)

As the respective sets of parents get together to discuss their children's 'problem' skeletons come tumbling out of the closet and the difficulties of starting married life are aired. It is here the particularities of the Asian migrant experience are more fully explored. Firstly, it is revealed that in common with many immigrants Eeshwar came to England with his male friend from his village rather than his wife. When Lota, his bride, did arrive from India for her honeymoon in Blackpool she was to have the company not only of her new husband but also his best friend, Brijesh.

Khan-Din allows Eeshwar to describe the understandably close bond between himself and his friend with some pathos and of course no little humour. Eeshwar describes how he and Brijesh would leave his newly married wife at the hotel and go for walks along the promenade together in their newly purchased 'lightweight, non-crease, built-in-belt' (79) safari suits like the Bollywood stars Amitabh Bachhan and Rajesh Khanna.

However, this was a totally innocent ménage a trois even though:

> LOPA: Then I stood and watched them on the bumper cars, the Big Dipper, the ghost train, the waltzers ... the tunnel of love.
> [...]
> EESHWAR: We thought they were speed boats. (78)

Indeed, the play touches on the migrant experience as Eeshwar recounts how they would send all the money they made back to the family in India.

Khan-Din does not shy away from detailing the racism experienced by Eeshwar and Brijesh at that time and the importance of the validation that friendship brought:

> EESHWAR: You could be walking down the street minding your own business, and one person would give you that look [...]. I tell you how it made me feel, it made me feel like I was nothing.
>
> *He shakes his head as he remembers, and sips his whisky*
>
> I'm not ashamed to say it upset me. Deeply. I could never understand how people could be so cruel [...] I still don't. It's as if [...] as if it wasn't just me they were looking at. It was my family, my life, my whole world, they were dismissing [...] But Brijesh was there, he knew [...] he knew who I was [...]. (27)

The plot is finally resolved not by the interference of the parents but as a result of an argument between Atul and Vina because she has told her mother about their problem:

> ATUL: Did you tell 'em everything, did you? All the gory details! Tell'em how you always put me off! How you laughed at me on our wedding night! Did you say that, did you! Did you? Well, did you? *Vina suddenly slaps him across the face. Atul is shocked. He grabs hold of her roughly.* You bloody bitch, I'll [...]
> VINA   (*defiantly*) You'll what?
> *They stand there looking at each other.*

By the time they come back downstairs they have not only consummated the marriage but find that their respective parents have bought a house for them when they come back from their honeymoon. In spite of the old-fashioned plot and conveniently happy ending the critics were 'overcome by the brio of Nicholas Hytner's production and the vivacity of the cast' (Billington 2007) in Khan-Din's successful adaptation.

Conclusion

This book took as its historical starting point Naseem Khan's report 'The Arts Britain Ignores' in 1976 because it revolutionised the way the Arts Council conceptually and financially engaged with the work of artists from ethnic minorities. The report initiated the first steps which enabled companies such as Tara Arts and, subsequently, Tamasha, Kali and a host of new British Asian writers since that time to gain official acceptance as British theatre practitioners. The report was the first to document the contribution of Asian theatre practitioners to the cultural life of Britain at that time and pointed out the emerging role of 'second generation' British Asian artists who might respond to the British location. The work discussed is testimony that there has indeed been a powerful response not only in terms of content in relation to the experience of Asians in Britain but also in relation to form, dramaturgy, process and, of course, performance.

Tara Arts' first play, *Sacrifice*, was performed in 1977 and over 30 years later their production of Hanif Kureishi's *The Black Album* (2009) opened at the Cottesloe Theatre at the National Theatre. As the longest-running Asian Theatre Company in Britain, Tara Arts have had three distinct artistic phases. The first phase, from 1977 to 1984, examined the 'second generation' British Asian experience, recovered the hidden histories of Asians in Britain long before postwar immigration and sought connections between colonial histories from the subcontinent and the position of the Asian migrant in contemporary Britain. The discussion of Tara's work in Chapter 2 also focuses on the methodological implications of the representation of the Asian subject within the confines of text-based realism and the limits of that form.

The second phase of Tara's artistic development led to the creation of their innovative 'Binglish' theatre praxis that 'aimed to directly challenge or provoke the dominant conventions of the English stage' (Verma 1996: 194) and contest the marginal position of the British Asian subject. This was achieved by drawing on Eastern as well as Western dramaturgies, such as the *natyasastra*, using 'other' languages alongside English, employing all-Asian casts and applying this 'Binglish' methodology to classical European and Asian texts. The discussion of *Tartuffe* (1990), *The Little Clay Cart* (1984/86/91) and *Cyrano* (1995) in Chapter 3 explores how and why the creation of a 'Binglish' performance praxis was to take Tara Arts from the margins to the 'centre' of British theatre.

The *JTW* trilogy (2002) marked a clear change of direction for Tara as they attempted to align their 'Binglish' methodology with an overtly postcolonial agenda. Chapter 7 explores how the *JTW* trilogy mapped an Indian diaspora to Kenya and Britain over the course of the last century. The trilogy was not only an attempt to recover and make visible an Asian history overwritten by and inextricably linked with colonial power but also as a means of reconnecting with the company's constituent Asian audience. Tara's work post-trilogy has largely been marked by a return to a scaled-down approach to 'Binglishing' European classics, which unfortunately precipitated a severe cut in their Arts Council funding in 2008. It is to be hoped that Tara's return to the National Theatre with *The Black Album* will mark the beginning of a new artistic chapter for the company.

While the work of Tamasha has largely been predicated on a performative quest for 'authenticity' through realism there have also been a number of quite radical experiments in form. Chapter 4 examined the company's adaptations of Asian novels, their application of a research-based methodology to new writing and their experimentation with intercultural[1] performance in *Women of the Dust* (1992). Tamasha describe their theatre practice as *intra*[2] cultural and draw on Rustom Bharucha's definition as the 'dynamics between and across specific communities and regions within the boundaries of the nation state' (2000: 6) in the context of the regional differences within India. In the British context, Tamasha apply the term as it relates to the dynamics between different ethnic communities as opposed to geographical regions.

Tamasha are perhaps best known for the critical and popular success of Ayub Khan-Din's *East is East* discussed in Chapter 5. However, they have also have made a number of forays into the musical theatre form beginning with the innovative staging of a Bollywood film in *Fourteen Songs, Two Weddings and A Funeral* (1998, 2001), the dance-led drama *Strictly Dandia* (2004) and, more recently, a musical version of Emily Bronte's *Wuthering Heights* (2009) set in the deserts of Rajasthan.

Further experiments include applying the verbatim form to the Asian experience in *The Trouble with Asian Men* (2005) and the genesis of a methodology for cultural inclusion and representation in *Lyrical MC* (2007), which draws on the 'cultural context'[3] of the actor and inscribes the particularities of their ethnicity into performance.

Tamasha's commitment to training Asian theatre artists is clearly demonstrated by their 'Developing Artists' programme which was launched in 2004 and now caters for directors, designers, writers and actors.[4] Indeed, one of the new writers, Emteaz Hussain, was offered a full commission as a direct result of her participation in the 'Developing Artists' programme, and her play *Sweet Cider* was produced by Tamasha at the Arcola Theatre in 2008.

In this respect, the role played by the Kali Theatre Company since their inception in 1990 in supporting British Asian women playwrights has also been sustained and vital. The company, like Tamasaha, has been running its own development programmes, as discussed in Chapter 6. The murder of Balwant Kaur at a woman's refuge was the imperative for the creation of Kali and their first production *Song for a Sanctuary* (1990) by Rukhsana Ahmad, sharing a parallel with the formation of Tara Arts in response to the racist murder of Gurdeep Singh Chaggar.

The range of work produced by Kali, and the selection examined in Chapter 6, gives credence to their aim 'to present the distinct perspective and experience of Asian women to people from all backgrounds and to celebrate that richness and diversity'.[5] Kali's work ranges from an examination of communal violence in Rukhsana Ahmad's *River on Fire* (2000) to little-known cultural corners of the subcontinent in Shelley Silas's comedy *Calcutta Kosher* (2004) portraying the declining Jewish Indian community, and an unflinching view of Asian family life in contemporary northern England in Amber Lone's *Deadeye* (2006).

There is also a sign of increasing ambition at Kali as they aim at commissioning mid-scale as well as studio work. Janet Steel is to work with Gurpreet Kaur Bhatti for the first time since their collaboration on the controversial *Behzti* (2004). The new work *AD 2050* examines a future world in which global warming, religious extremism and rampant neo-conservatism have taken their toll. In this production the company are aiming not only to increase the scale of production but also search for a theatrical vision beyond 'kitchen sink' realism.

Gurpreet Kaur Bhatti's *Behzti* (2004) is explored in detail in Chapter 7 alongside her earlier work *Behsharaam* (2001). This chapter examines a small selection of new writing by British Asian writers since 1976 including the groundbreaking work of Kureishi's *Borderline* (1981), Bancil's representation of the British Asian 'underclass' in *Crazyhorse* (1997) and examination of the mainstream appropriation of British Asian culture in *Made in England* (1998) as well as the continued mainstream success of Khan-Din with *Rafta Rafta* (2008).

A very notable omission is Tanika Gupta who has written widely for television as well as the stage over the past 15 years. Her work includes *The Waiting Room* (2000) and *Sanctuary*[6] (2002) at the National Theatre, an adaptation of *Hobson's Choice* (2003) at the Young Vic, *Fragile Lands* (2003) at Hampstead Theatre, *Gladiator Games* (2005) at Stratford East Theatre Royal, *Sugar Mummies* (2006) at The Royal Court and *White Boy* (2008) at the National Youth Theatre and Soho Theatre.

Further British Asian playwrights with plays in print include Maya Chowhdry's *Monsoon*, exploring female sexuality and the 'return' of a British Asian woman to India; drug dealing and pretty criminality on the streets of London in Shan Khan's *The Office* (2000); Ash Kotak *Hijra* (2000), a comedy which looks at gay relationships; Dolly Dhingra's *Unsuitable Girls* (2001), an amusing take on British Asian relationships from a female perspective; Nirjay Mahindru's *The Hot Zone* (2005) a response to 'extraordinary rendition'[7] as part of the US response to the attacks on September 11 2001; as well as the majority of Tanika Gupta's plays discussed above. There are also two collections of plays that feature work by British Asian writers, *Black and Asian Women Writers*[8] (1993), edited by Kadija George, and *Black and Asian Plays Anthology* [9] (2000).

A key aim of this book is to make visible a range of British Asian theatre work since 1976 and explore the diversity of approaches, dramaturgies, themes, theatrical forms, processes, languages, social and political contexts, performance methodologies and productions. The companies and playwrights discussed have not only facilitated the dramatisation of the Asian subject onto the British stage but also redressed the lack of representation of Asian characters and actors. While British Asian theatre has found myriad ways of performing the particularities and heterogeneous cultural differences, histories and diasporas of the Asian communities in Britain they have one clear commonality and that is to insist on its inclusion as a part of British theatre. In this way British Asian theatre has been a powerful force not only for inscribing 'difference' on the British stage but also contesting homogeneous constructions of national cultural identity and theatrically attempted to 'disturb those ideological manoeuvres through which "imagined communities" are given essentialist identities' (Bhabha 1994: 149).

Notes

1 Introduction: British Asian Theatre on the Map

1. The Theatre Museum is now housed at the V & A. Go to http://www.vam.ac.uk/collections/theatre_performance for further information.
2. Salidaa website can be found at: http://www.salidaa.org.uk/salidaa/site/Collections/Theatre.
3. Tara Arts website: http://www.tara-arts.com.
4. The Macpherson report was published in February 1999 and can be obtained in full from: http://www.archive.official-documents.co.uk/document/cm42/4262/4262.htm.
5. For further information on this traditional Indian dance drama that originated in the state of Kerala in the seventeenth century and other traditional Asian performance forms see *The Cambridge Guide to Asian Theatre*, ed. James R. Brandon. Cambridge: Cambridge Press: 1993.
6. Refers to the Second World War. For initial background see http://www.bbc.co.uk/history/worldwars/wwtwo.
7. For initial background on the *Windrush* see http://www.bbc.co.uk/history/british/modern/windrush_01.shtml.
8. British rule of India was established in 1858 and lasted until the Indian independence in 1947.
9. Jimmy Akingbola as Jimmy Porter in *Look Back in Anger* at the Jermyn Street Theatre (2008); Jenny Jules as Ruth in Pinter's *The Homecoming* at The Almeida (2008); and even Sanjeev Bhasker as King Arthur in *Spamalot* (2008).
10. On 11 September 2001 four aeroplanes were hijacked. Two of the planes were crashed into the World Trade Centre, one into the Pentagon and one landed in a field in Pennsylvania resulting in the loss of almost 3,000 lives. See http://www.bbc.co.uk/history/recent/sept_11.
11. On 7 July 2005 four suicide bombers attacked a number of transport locations in London killing 52 people and injuring hundreds more. http://news.bbc.co.uk/1/hi/in_depth/uk/2005/london_explosions/default.stm.

2 Tara Arts 1977–1984: Creating a British Asian Theatre

1. See Heywood (2007: 52–3).
2. *Look Back in Anger* by John Osborne at The Royal Court heralded a new realism on the British stage and gave rise to the term 'angry young men' to describe a new generation of playwrights. See Roberts (1999) and Dan (1999).
3. The term *subaltern* is drawn from a group of scholars known as the Sub-altern Studies Group who focused on those outside of the colonial elite as the agents of Indian independence rather than the passive objects. See

Ranjit Guha's seminal 1998 essay 'On Some Aspects of the Historiography of Colonial India' in *Selected Subaltern Studies*. Oxford University Press.
4. Margaret Thatcher was Conservative Prime Minister from 1979 to 1990.
5. For a fascinating discussion of 'colonial mimicry' see Homi Bhabha (1994) 'Of mimicry and men: the ambivalence of colonial discourse' in *The Location of Culture*. London: Routledge, pp. 85–92.
6. On 13 April 1919 a large group of demonstrators gathered in the Jallianwala Bagh, Amritsar, for a public meeting. General Dyer, who had issued orders prohibiting such meetings, ordered his troops to fire on the unarmed crowd. Official British sources estimated that 379 people were killed.
7. For a seminal discussion of racial politics in postwar Britain see Gilroy (1987).
8. Kristeva (1980).
9. For a seminal critique of how the West constructs the East see Said (1995).
10. It should be noted that professional level training for Asian directors has only recently been addressed, most notably by Tamasha Theatre Company, as discussed in Chapter 5.
11. For a discussion of agitprop in Britain see Kershaw (1992).

3 Tara Arts 1984–1996: Creating a 'Binglish' Theatre

1. Indian classical dance form from Northern India.
2. Ayub Khan-Din went on to write the very successful *East is East* (1996) for Tamasha Theatre Company, discussed in Chapter 4 and *Rafta Rafta* (2007) discussed in Chapter 8.
3. See Stanislavsky's seminal work *An Actor Prepares*.
4. In February 1989 the Supreme Leader of Iran, Ayatollah Ruhollah Khomeni, issued a *fatwa*, or death sentence on Salman Rushdie, as his book *The Satanic Verses* was deemed to be blasphemous against Islam.

4 Tamasha Theatre Company 1989: Authenticity and Adaptation

1. Shared Experience was originally founded in 1975 by Mike Alfreds and has been run by Nancy Meckler and Polly Teal since 1987. The company are best known for their adaptations of classic texts privileging the physicality of the actor in their process. http://www.sharedexperience.org.uk.
2. See Stephen Lacey's (1995) for an excellent discussion of *The Kitchen* and its wider cultural and theatrical context.

5 Tamasha Theatre Company 1989 – *East is East*: From Kitchen Sink to Bollywood

1. Kitchen sink drama was a term coined for work by playwrights such as Arnold Wesker and John Osborne in the 1950s. For further discussion see Rebellato, D. (1999) and Roberts, P. (1999).
2. See 'Of mimicry and man: The ambivalence of colonial discourse' in Homi K. Bhabha's seminal postcolonial work *The Location of Culture* (1994: 85–92).

3. These five articles, or the five 'Ks' as they are known, are the *kesh*, meaning hair which is a symbol of faith and should not be cut; *kangha*, a comb; *karra*, a steel bracelet; *kachha*, which are shorts or underwear; and *kirpana*, sword or dagger.
4. See Bharucha (2000).
5. Further information of the Developing Artists Programme, which was launched in 2004, can be found on the Tamasha website at http://www.tamasha.org.uk/developing-artists.

6   Kali Theatre Company 1990–2007: Producing British Asian Women Playwrights

1. *Ghazal*: A poetic meditation on love normally consisting of five or six couplets, the second of which is often repeated.

7   Tara Arts 1997–2007: Mapping a 'Binglish' Diaspora

1. *Henna* – A non-permanent plant dye used to decorate the body, especially the hands and feet.
2. *Rangoli* – drawings of plants, flower motifs or geometrical designs, which are traditionally made to decorate the courtyards or walls of houses at a time of festival.

8   New Writers from 1977: Kureishi, Bancil, Bhatti and Khan-Din

1. *Shalwar kameez* is traditional dress worn in South Asia by men and women. The *Shalwar* are loose pyjama-style trousers and the *kameez* a long tunic.
2. *Sayva* – Service to God, which in this context means helping in the kitchen.
3. *Aardas* – Sikh prayers of the day.
4. On this day two airliners, highjacked by the terrorist organisation al-Quaeda, crashed into the Twin Towers of the World Trade Centre in New York City causing catastrophic loss of life. A third plane crashed into the Pentagon and a fourth in a field near Shanksville, Pensylvannia.

Conclusion

1. For a discussion of intercultural theatre see Pavis (1996).
2. Intracultural is defined in Bharucha (2000: 63) as allowing for 'new possibilities of interaction and exchange within and across a wealth of living traditions from vastly different time frames and cultural contexts'.
3. For further reading see Hingorani (2009).
4. For further information see http://www.tamasha.org.uk/developing-artists/.
5. Visit the Kali website at http://www.kalitheatre.co.uk/about/about.htm.
6. For an incisive discussion of *Sanctuary* see Griffin (2003: 228–32).

7. 'Extraordinary rendition' is often referred to as 'torture by proxy' and is the illegal detention and transportation of a suspect from one state to another 'third party' state – where torture is routinely used.
8. George (1993).
9. *Black and Asian Plays Anthology* (2000).

Bibliography

Ahmad, R. (1993) 'Song for a sanctuary', *Six Plays by Black and Asian Writers*. Ed. Kadija George, London: Aurora Metro Press.

Ahmad, R. (2000) *River on Fire* Salidaa [South Asian Diaspora Literature and Arts Archive] http://vads.ahds.ac.uk/collections/SALIDAA.html (accessed 21 April 2010).

Ahmad, R. (2008) Personal Interview with Dominic Hingorani at the British library, 16 December.

Ahmed, R.Z. (2004) 'Calcutta is Kosher in times of hate' *Sunday Times of India*, 22 February.

Ahmed-Fall, Nadia (2003) Education Co-ordinator Tara Arts. Personal Interview. Royal National Theatre, 10 September.

Akbar, A. (2002) 'Theatre industry is guilty of institutional racism, managers admit' *The Independent*, 19 April.

Alfree, Claire (2006) Rev. 'Trouble with Asian Men' *Metro* Monday, 11 September.

Allfree, Claire (2007) 'Bollywood? Pah!' *The Metro*, 10 January.

Ali, Naqi (1984) 'The excruciating pain of chilli in your eyes' Review of Chilli in Your Eyes *Asian Herald*.

Alibhai-Brown, Yasmin (2000) *Who Do We Think We Are? Imagining the New Britain*. London: Allen Lane & Penguin.

—— (2001) *Mixed Feelings the Complex Lives of Mixed-Race Britons*. London: The Women's Press.

Anderson, Benedict (1983) *Imagined Communities – Reflections on the Origin and Spread of Nationalism*. London: Verso.

Arditti, Michael (1991) Rev. of *Little Clay Cart*. Adapted by Jatinder Verma. 'Constant reversals of fortune' *The Evening Standard*, 6 December.

Armitstead, Claire (1992) Rev. of *Women of the Dust* by Ruth Carter *The Guardian*, Tuesday 17 November.

Arnot, Chris (2000) Rev. of *Balti Kings* by Sudha Bhuchar, Kristine Landon-Smith, Shaheen Khan. 'Stand by your nan' *The Guardian*. Wednesday 5 January, p. 14.

Arora, Keval (1994) Rev. of *Women of the Dust*. 'In search of a voice' *The Pioneer* (Delhi), 3 February.

Arts Council of Great Britain. *Grants for the Arts – Stabilisation and Recovery*. http://www.artscouncil.org.uk/funding/stabilisation.html (accessed 5 March 2006).

—— (2002) 'The Eclipse Report – Developing Strategies to Combat Racism in Theatre'. http://www.artscouncil.org.uk/publication_archive/eclipse-developing-strategies-to-combat-racism-in-theatre/ (accessed 12 April 2010).

—— (1997) *'The Landscape of Fact' – Towards a Policy for Cultural Diversity for the English Funding System: African, Caribbean, Asian and Chinese Arts*. London: Arts Council.

Arts Council of Great Britain (1998a) *Correcting the Picture – New Perspectives on Cultural Diversity in Arts Management*. London: Arts Council.
——— (1998b) *Cultural Diversity Action Plan*. London: Arts Council.
Ashcroft, Bill. Griffiths, Gareth. Tiffin, Helen. Eds (2002) *The Empire Writes Back*. 2nd edition. London: Routledge.
——— Eds (2004) *The Post-colonial Studies Reader*. London: Routledge.
Ashworth, Pat (2002) Rev. of *JTW* Trilogy. 'How the West was Wonderful' *The Stage*, 28 March.
Asian Women's Writers Collective. 'AWWC Membership Information' http://www.salidaa.org.uk/salidaa/site/Collections?adlib_id=400000003&image_index=0 (accessed 4 February 2009).
Attwood, Brian (1991) 'Tara Studio closes' *The Stage and Television Today*, 7 March.
Aurora, Keval (1994) Rev. of *Women of the Dust* by Ruth Carter. 'In search of a voice' *The Pioneer* (Delhi), 3 February [Tamasha Archive].
Bajeli Singh, Diwan (1988) Rev. of *Untouchable* by Kristine Landon-Smith. 'Untouchability still relevant' *Indian Express*, 19 September.
Baker, Nick (1984a) 'Avoiding artistic apartheid' *Arts Express – London Supplement*, August, Issue 4.
——— (1984b) 'Indian flavour' Rev. of *Miti Ki Gadi* by Jatinder Verma *The Times Educational Supplement*, Friday 28 December, No. 3574.
Bancil, Parv (1987) *Crazyhorse*. London: Faber and Faber.
——— (1999) Personal Interview with Dominic Hingorani at The National Theatre, 9 September.
——— (2000) 'Made in England' in *Black and Asian Plays*. Introduced by Afia Nkrumah. London: Aurora Metro Press.
——— (2009) 'What have multi cultural arts practices done for us?' Posted by Parv Bancil, *The Guardian* Tuesday 16 December 2008, 11.13 GMT.http://www.guardian.co.uk/stage/theatreblog/2008/dec/16/arts-funding-theatre-multicultural-policy (accessed 16 February).
——— (2009) Exeter University conference British Asian theatre project. http://spa.exeter.ac.uk/drama/research/batp/conference_abstracts.shtml#parvbancil (accessed 18 January 2009).
Barber Susan, Torrey (1993) 'Insurmountable difficulties and moments of ecstasy: Crossing class, ethnic, and sexual barriers in the films of Stephen Frears' *Fires Were Started – British Cinema and Thatcherism*. London: UCL.
Barker, Clive (2000) *Twentieth Century Actor Training*. Ed. Alison Hodge London: Routledge.
Batten, Rhiannon (2003) 'Crossing cultures and the dance floor' *The Sunday Times*, 24 August.
Baumann, Gerd (1996) *Contesting Culture Discourses in Multi-Ethnic London*. Cambridge: Cambridge University Press.
Bayley, Claire (1995) Rev. of *Cyrano*. Adapted by Jatinder Verma *The Independent*, Friday 27 October.
Berthoud, Richard, Modood, Tariq (1997) *Ethnic Minorities in Britain – Diversity and Disadvantage*. London: Policy Studies Institute.
Best, Katy (1982) 'Creating a theatre tradition for Asians' *Stage and Television Today*, 19 August 1982, No. 5288.
Bhabha, Homi K. (1986) 'The other question' *Literature Politics and Theory*. London: Methuen.

Bhabha, Homi K. (1990) *Nation and Narration*. London: Routledge.

―――― (1994) *The Location of Culture*. London: Routledge.

Bharucha, Rustom (1993) *Theatre and the World*. London: Routledge.

―――― (2000) *The Politics of Cultural Practice – Thinking through Theatre in an Age of Globalisation*. London: Athlone Press.

Bhatti (2003) Interview with Gurpreet Bhatti clickwalla.com (accessed 21 March 2003).

Bhatti, Gurpreet Kaur (2001) *Behsharam (Shameless)*. London: Oberon.

―――― (2004) *Behzti (Dishonour)*. London: Oberon.

Bhatti, Gurpreet Kaur (2005) 'This warrior is fighting on' *The Guardian*, Thursday 13 January.

Bhavnani, E. (1979) *The Dance in India*. Bombay: D.B. Taraporevala Sons & Co.

Bhegani, B. Rev. (1981) of *Diwaali* by Tara Arts *City Limits*.

Bhuchar, Sudha (1990) 'Double helping of Indian classic tale is a "first" ' *Leicester Mercury*, Friday 5 January.

―――― & Khan, Shaheen (1999) *Balti Kings* Unpublished 1999 [Tamasha Archive].

―――― & Khan, Shaheen & Landon-Smith, Kristine (1999) 'The Making of Balti Kings' Video [Tamasha Archive].

―――― & Landon-Smith, Kristine (1989a) 'Untouchable misery 50 years after Gandhi' *The Independent*, 11 December.

―――― (1998b) *Tamasha Theatre Company – into the Millennium* [Tamasha Archive].

―――― (1991a) Foreword, *House of the Sun* Programme [Tamasha Archive].

―――― (1992a) Foreword, *Women of the Dust* Programme [Tamasha Archive].

―――― (1999a) *Untouchable*. London: Nick Hern Books.

―――― (1999b) *House of the Sun*. London: Nick Hern.

―――― (1999c) *A Tainted Dawn*. London: Nick Hern Books.

―――― (1999d) Personal Interview with Dominic Hingorani Tamasha Theatre Company Office, 22 January.

―――― (2001) *Fourteen Songs, Two Weddings and A Funeral*. London: Methuen.

―――― (2004a) *Strictly Dandia*. London: Methuen.

―――― (2004b) Tamasha Theatre Company Gala Programme. 15'th Anniversary Fundraising Gala. 12 February [Tamasha Archive].

―――― (2006) Interview by Claire Allfree. 'Bollywood? Pah!' *The Metro* Tuesday 10 January.

―――― (2007a) *A Fine Balance*. London: Methuen.

―――― (2007b) *Lyrical MC* [Tamasha Archive].

―――― & Landon-Smith, K. & Wallinger, L. (2005) *The Trouble with Asian Men* [Tamasha Archive].

Billington, Michael (1989a) Rev. of *Ala Afsur (The Government Inspector)* by Jatinder Verma and Anuradha Kapur *The Guardian*, 21 January.

―――― (1989b) Rev. of *Blood* by Harwant Bains. *The Guardian*, 1 September.

―――― (1990) Rev. of *Tartuffe*. Adapted by Jatinder Verma. *The Guardian*, 26 February.

―――― (1991) Rev. of *Little Clay Cart* 'Role of the dice' *The Guardian*, Monday 9 December.

―――― (1995) Rev. of *Cyrano*. Adapted by Jatinder Verma. Additional songs by Ranjit Bolt. 'Cerebral brew's medium mix-up' *The Guardian*, Thursday 26 October.

―――― (1996) Rev. of *East is East* by Ayub Khan-Din 'East is best' *The Guardian*, Tuesday 26 November.

Billington, Michael (1998) *The Guardian*. Thursday 19 November, p. 12.
—— (2000a) Rev. of *Balti Kings* by Sudha Bhuchar, Shaheeen Khan. 'Curryoke night' *The Guardian*, Saturday 15 January, p. 23.
—— (2000b) 'White out' *The Guardian*, Wednesday 18 October.
—— (2001) Rev. of *Fourteen Songs*...Adapted by Sudha Bhuchar and Kristine Landon-Smith. 'Krishna saves the day' *The Guardian*, Tuesday 20 February.
—— (2001a) *One Night Stands*. London: Nick Hern Books.
—— (2001b) 'Review of Behsharaam' by Gurpreet Kaur Bhatti *The Guardian*, Monday 15 October.
—— (2002) 'Life in a box' *The Guardian*, 4 December.
—— (2003) Rev. of *A Taste for Mangoes*, *The Guardian*, Saturday 22 November.
—— (2006) 'A history lesson but where's the story?' *The Guardian*, Tuesday 17 January.
—— (2006a) 'Comic timing – How do you get a British audience to laugh at a 200 year old French joke? Michael Billington finds out from writer and translator Ranjit Bolt' http://www.guardian.co.uk/stage/2006/16/theatre1 (accessed 2 February 2009).
—— (2007) 'Northern folk comedy gets to grips with Asian family life' *The Guardian*, Friday 27 April.
Biswas, Neil (1998d) Tara Arts Company *Exodus III* Script [Trilogy Background File # TB20. Tara Arts Archive].
Black and Asian Plays Anthology (2000) London: Aurora Metro.
Black, Ian (2000) 'Europe 'should accept' 75m new migrants' *The Guardian*, 28 July, p. 1.
Brace, Marianne (1994) 'After bollywood, Binglish' *The Independent*, Wednesday 9 November.
Brandon, James Ed. (1993) *The Cambridge Guide to Asian Theatre*. Cambridge: Cambridge University.
Brah, Avtar (1996) *Cartographies of the Diaspora – Contesting Identities*. London: Routledge.
Brahmachari, Sita (2007) *Lyrical MC* [Tamasha Archive].
—— (2008) Personal Interview with Dominic Hingorani.
Brahmachari & Landon-Smith (2001) Time 2001 'placing teachers' voices at the centre of intercultural debate' *Drama Magazine*, Summer Edition. http://www.dramamagazine.co.uk (accessed 12 June 2008).
Brown, Georgina (1989) Rev. of *Untouchable*. Adapted by Sudha Bhuchar and Kristine Landon-Smith. 'Untouchable misery 50 years after Gandhi' *The Independent*. Ed. Penny Jackson, 11 December.
Caplan, Betty (1989) Rev. of *Untouchable*. Adpated by Sudha Bhuchar and Kristine Landon-Smith. *The Guardian*, December.
—— (1991) Rev. of *House of the Sun*. Adapted by Sudha Bhuchar and Kristine Landon-Smith. *The Guardian*, 20 April.
Carter, Ruth (1999a) *Women of the Dust*. London: Nick Hern Books.
—— (1999b) *A Yearning*. London: Nick Hern Books.
Cavendish, Dominic (2006) 'A powerful indictment is neutered' *The Daily Telegraph*, 18 January.
Cavendish, Dominic (1998) 'A force to be reckoned with' *The Independent*, 21 October, p. 12.
Chandra, B. & Mukherjee, A. & Panikkar, K.N. & Mahajan, S. (1988) *India's Struggle for Independence*. London: Puffin.

Chaudhuri, Anita (1989) Rev. of *Untouchable*. Adapted by Sudha Bhuchar and Kristine Landon-Smith. *Bazaar*. November, Issue 11.

Christopher, James (1990) Rev. of *Tartuffe*. Adapted by Jatinder Verma. *Time Out*. 25 April.

Clapp, Susannah (2002) Rev. of *JTW* trilogy by Jatinder Verma. 'It's all Gujarati to me' *The Observer*. 31 March.

Clarke, Anthony (2001) Personal Interview at The Royal National Theatre. March [Tara Arts Archive].

Clews, Wayne (2001) Rev. of *River on Fire*. *The Metro*, Monday 12 March.

Cook, William. (1990) Rev. of *Ala Afsur* (*The Government Inspector*). Adapted by Anuradah Kapur. *City Limits*. 29 March–5 April. Issue 443.

——— (1991a) *The Independent*. 23 April.

——— (1991b) Rev. of *Little Clay Cart*. Adapted by Jatinder Verma and Ranjit Bolt. 'Indian Summer' *City Limits*, 21–28 November, p. 6.

Cooper, Neil (2006) Rev. Tara Arts 'Enemy of the people' *The Herald*, 27 April.

Correspondent (1989) Rev. of *Untouchable* by Kristine Landon-Smith. *The Asian Herald*, Friday 17 November, p. 9.

Counsell, C., Wolf, L. (2001) *Performance Analysis*. London: Routledge.

Coveney, Michael (1990) Rev. of *Tartuffe*. Adapted by Jatinder Verma. *The Observer*, 25 February.

——— (1992) Rev. of *Little Clay Cart*. Adapted by Jatinder Verma. Additional Verse Ranjit Bolt. 'Golden ages revived' *The Observer*, Sunday 5 January.

Crow, Brian (2007) 'The *Behzti* affair revisited: British multiculturalism, audiences and strategy' *Theatre and Performance*, Vol. 27, No. 3. Bristol: Intellect.

Curtis, Nick (1990) Rev. of *Ala Afsur* [The Government Inspector] Adapted by Jatinder Verma. *Time Out*, 28 March.

——— (1992) Rev. of *Women of the Dust*. Adapted by Ruth Carter. *Time Out*, 11–18 November.

——— (1998) Rev. of *Exodus* by Tara Arts 'Making a meal of it' *The Evening Standard*, Monday 26 October, p. 53.

——— (2004) 'Family in a pickle' ES Review *The Evening Standard*, Tuesday 15 June.

Dadswell, S. (2010) 'Kali Theatre Company' *British South Asian Theatres: A Documented History*. Eds. Ley, G. and Dadswell, S. Exeter: Exeter University Press.

Davis, G. & Fuchs, A. Eds (2006) *Staging New Britain – Aspects of Black and South Asian British Theatre Practice*. Brussels: Peter Lang.

De Jongh, Nicholas (1995) Rev. of *Cyrano*. Adapted by Jatinder Verma and Ranjit Bolt. 'A nose for the ironic' *The Evening Standard*, Thursday 26 October, p. 48.

Delgado, Maria, M. Heritage, Paul (1996) *In Contact With the Gods – Directors Talk Theatre*. Manchester: Manchester University.

Denford, Antonia (1991) Rev. of 'Song for a Sanctuary' *City Limits*, 20 May.

Desai, Jigna (2004) *Beyond Bollywood – The Cultural Politics of South Asian Diasporic Film*. London: Routledge.

Deschampsneufs, Peta (1968) '600 Shuttlecock Asians in test for Callaghan' *The Sunday Times*, 24 March, p. 1.

Dibden, Thom (2003) Rev. of *Strictly Dandia* 'Out of Step actors give show an amateur feel' *Edinburgh Evening News*, 28 August.

Dickson, Andrew (1986) Rev. of *Miti Ki Gadi* [*The Little Clay Cart*]. Adapted by Jatinder Verma. *City Limits*, 17–23 January.

Eccles, C. (1984) Rev. 'Chilli in Your Eyes' by Tara Arts. *City Limits*, 15–21 June.

Edwardes, Jane (1991) Rev. 'The Little Clay Cart'. Adapted by Ranjit Bolt and Jatinder Verma. *Time Out*, 11 December.

—— (1998) Rev. of *Exodus* by Biswas and Company. *Time Out*, 21–28 October.

—— (2000) Rev. of *Balti Kings* by Sudha Bhuchar and Shaheen Khan. *Time Out*, January.

Esslin, Martin (1998) *Plays International*. December 1995, pp. 20–21, Rev. of *Exodus* by Biswas and Company. Battersea Arts Centre. *Eastern Eye*, 30 October.

Evans, Lloyd (2006) Rev. of *The Trouble with Asian Men* 'Audience participation' *The Spectator*, 23 Saturday September.

Fanon, Frantz (1967) *The Wretched of the Earth*. London: Penguin.

—— (1986) *Black Skin White Masks*. London: Pluto Press.

Feay, Suzi (1991) Rev. of *House of the Sun* by Sudha Bhuchar and Kristine Landon-Smith. *Time Out*, 24 April.

Fisher, Phillip (2006) Rev. 'Trouble with Asian Men' *The British Theatre Guide*.

Foucault, M. (1980) *Power/Knowledge*. London: The Harvester Press.

Gaier, C. (1983) Rev. of *Lion's Raj* by Jatinder Verma. 'The Lion's Raj – A triumph of the imagination'. *The Coventry Standard*, 29 January.

Ganatra, Ravin (2001) Personal Interview. Tara Arts' 25'th Anniversary Report, 21 April [Tara Arts Archive].

Gardner, Lyn (1992). *The Independent*, Tuesday 10 November.

—— (2006a) Rev. of *The Trouble with Asian Men*. 'Rambling comedy lets men off the hook' *The Guardian*, Saturday 9 September.

—— (2006b) Interview with Tanika Gupta ' Write about arranged marriage? No way!' *The Guardian*, 25 July.

—— (2006c) Review *Deadeye The Guardian*, Tuesday 21 November.

Gardner, Lynn (1982) Rev. of *The Shape of Dreams* by Tara Arts. 'Theatre: New reviews' *City Limits*, 3–9 December.

George, G. (1994) Rev. of *Women of the Dust* by Ruth Carter. 'Path-breaking women of the dust' *The Statesman* (Delhi), 3 February [Tamasha Archive].

—— Ed. (1993) *Six Plays by Black and Asian Women Writers*. London: Aurora Metro Press.

Gilbert, John (1985) Rev. of *Miti Ki Gadi*. Adapted by Jatinder Verma. 'Tara Arts Group' *The Birmingham Post & Mail*, Saturday 23 February.

Gilby, Liz (1990) 'Combining the cultures' *What's On*, 21 March, p. 35.

Gill, Ravinder (1987) Interview 'Hounslow' *Bazaar*, Issue 2.

Gilroy, Paul (1987) *There Ain't No Black in the Union Jack*. London: Hutchinson.

—— (1992) 'The end of anti-racism', *Race Culture and Difference*. Ed. J. Donald, A. Rattansi, London: Sage.

—— (2000) *Between Camps – Nations, Cultures and the Allure of Race*. London, Penguin.

Glover, Stephen (2004) *The Daily Mail*, Tuesday 21 December, p. 12.

Godiwala, Dimple Ed. (2006) *Alternatives within the Mainstream – British Black and Asian Theatres*. Newcastle: Cambridge Scholars.

Govinda, Manick (1987) Rev. of *The Curse of the Dead Dog* by Parv Bancil. *Bazaar*, Issue 8.

Govinda, Manick (1988a) 'Playwright in progress' Interview with Harwant Bains. *Bazaar*. Issue 4, p. 2.

——— (1988b) *Bazaar.* October. Issue 8.

——— (1988c) 'Doing the write thing' *Bazaar,* November, Issue 9, p. 6.

Green, Tim (1990) Rev. of *Tartuffe*. Adapted by Jatinder Verma. *What's On,* 14 March.

Grier, Christopher (1990) Rev. of *Tartuffe*. Adapted by Jatinder Verma. *The Evening Standard*, 30 April.

Griffin, G. (2003) *Contemporary Black and Asian Women Playwrights in Britain.* Cambridge: Cambridge University Press.

Grimley, Terry (2002a) Rev. of *JTW Part 1* by Jatinder Verma. 'Journey Through History' *The Birmingham Post*, 25 April [*JTW* Production File. Tara Arts Archive].

——— (2002b) Rev. of *JTW Part II* by Jatinder Verma. 'Alternative perspective on "Rivers of Blood"' *The Birmingham Post*, 26 April [*JTW* Production File. Tara Arts Archive].

——— (2002c) Rev. of *JTW Part III* by Jatinder Verma. 'Works of a rare visual beauty' *The Birmingham Post*, 27 April [*JTW* Production File. Tara Arts Archive].

Grimley, Terry (2006a) 'Familiar story of abuse and depression' *The Birmingham Post*, Thursday 19 October.

——— (2006b) 'The Lone arranger' *The Birmingham Post*, Tuesday 17 October.

Gross, John (1990) Rev. of *Tartuffe*. Adapted by Jatinder Verma. *The Sunday Telegraph*, 22 April.

Grossberg, Lawrence (2000) 'Identity and cultural studies: Is that all there is?', *Questions of Cultural Identity*. Ed. S. Hall, & P. du Gay, London: Sage, pp. 87–107.

Gupta, Chandra Bhan (1991) *The Indian Theatre*. New Delhi: Munshiram Manoharlal.

Hall, Catherine (2000) *Cultures of Empire*. Manchester; Manchester University.

Hall, Fernau (1986) Rev. of *The Little Clay Cart* by Jatinder Verma. 'Tara Arts Group' *The Daily Telegraph*, Saturday 11 January.

Hall, Stuart (1992a) 'New ethnicities', *'Race', Culture and Difference*. Ed. J. Donald and A. Rattansi, London: Sage.

——— (1992) 'The question of cultural identity', *Modernity and its Futures*. Ed. S. Hall, D. Held, T. McGrew, Cambridge: Polity.

——— (1995) 'New ethnicities' *The Post-colonial Studies Reader*. Eds., Ashcroft, B., Griffiths, G., Tiffin, H. London: Routledge.

——— (1996) *Questions of Cultural Identity*. Ed.S. Hall, & P. du Gay, London: Sage.

——— (1996a) 'When was the postcolonial? Thinking at the limit', *The Postcolonial Question*. Ed. I. Chambers, L. Curti, London: Routledge, pp. 242–60.

——— (1996b) 'The politics of identity', *Culture Identity and Politics – Ethnic Minorities in Britain*. Ed. T. Ranger, Y. Sarmad, O. Stuart, Hants: Avebury.

——— (1996c) *Critical Dialogues in Cultural Studies*. Ed D. Morley, Kuan-Hsing Chen, London: Routledge.

——— (1997) *Representation: Cultural Representations and Signifying Practices*. Ed. Stuart Hall, London: Sage.

Halliburton, Rachel (2006) Rev. of *The Trouble with Asian Men Time Out* 13–20 September.

Hameed, Ambreen (1989) Rev. of *Ala Afsur (The Government Inspector)* 'Less play more truth' *New Life*, Friday 10 February.

Hardwick, Viv (2002) Rev. of the *JTW* trilogy by Jatinder Verma. 'The best in the West' *The Northern Echo*, Thursday 2 May.

Harvie, Jen (2005) *Staging the UK*. Manchester: Manchester University.

Hassell, Graham (1991) Rev. of *The Little Clay Cart* by Jatinder Verma and Ranjit Bolt. *What's On*, 11 December.

—— (1990) Rev. of *Tartuffe*. Adapted by Jatinder Verma. *What's On*, 25 April.

Hattenstone, Simon (1997) 'What country friend, is this' *The Guardian*, 29 January.

Hattersley, R. (2001) 'Immigrants should learn our language' *The Guardian*, 27 August, p. 14.

Hay, Malcolm (1984) Rev. of *Miti Ki Gadi*. Adapted by Jatinder Verma. *Time Out* [*Miti Ki Gadi* Production File 1986, Tara Arts Archive].

Hepple, Peter (1986) 'Tara Arts set the black cart rolling' Rev. of *The Little Clay Cart* by Jatinder Verma. *The Stage and Television Today*. 23 January.

Hepple, Stuart (2005) Rev. 'The trouble with Asian men' *The Stage*, Wednesday 23 November.

Hewison, Robert (1989) 'Experiments with fringe benefits' *The Sunday Times Review*, Sunday 22 January.

Heywood, A. (2007) *Political Ideologies – An Introduction*, 4th edition. Basingstoke: Palgrave.

—— (1989) Rev. of *Ala Afsur* (*The Government Inspector*) by Jatinder Verma and Anuradha Kapur. *The Listener*, 2 February.

—— (1989a) 'The Molliere Wallah' *The Independent*, Monday 11 September.

Hiley, Jim (1990) Rev. of *Tartuffe* Adapted by Jatinder Verma. *The Listener*, 8 March.

—— (1991) Interview with Jatinder Verma. *The Late Show*. February BBC 2 [Tara Video Archive # VHSTARA 0061].

Hingorani, D. (2009) 'Ethnicity and actor training: A british asian actor prepares'. *South Asian Popular Culture*. 7 (3), October, pp. 165–79, Oxfordshire: Routledge.

Hiro, Dilip (1973) *Black British, White British*. London: Pelican Books.

Hoyle, Martin (1989) Rev. of *Ala Afsur* [*The Government Inspector*] by Jatinder Verma and Anuradha Kapur. *The Financial Times*, 23 January.

—— (1991) Rev. of *Song for a Sanctuary* 'Flat song with sharp lines' *The Times*, Saturday 12 October.

—— (1995) Rev. of *Cyrano*. Adapted by Jatinder Verma and Ranjit Bolt. 'Cyrano goes to Bollywood' *The Financial Times*, 16 October.

Hughes, David (1990) Rev. of *Tartuffe*. Adapted by Jatinder Verma. 'National-ised Asian' *The Birmingham Post*, Thursday 10 May.

Hundal, Sunny (2004) Rev. of *Strictly Dandia* by Sudha Bhuchar and Kristine Landon-Smith. 'Tamasha wows audiences with Strictly Dandia' AsiansMedia.org, Wednesday 21 January. http://www.asiansinmedia.org/news/printable.php?article=269.

Hussein, Iqbal (1999) *I Will Be a Text*. Dramaturgical Notes [Tara Arts Archive] Trilogy Background Files, ref # TB28, p. 1.

—— (2001) Interview with Sarah Butler. 30 March [Tara Arts Archive].

Hytner, Nick (2004) *The Today Programme*, Interviewed by J. Naughtie BBC Radio Four, Tuesday 21 December.

James, Lawrence (1997) *Raj – The Making and Unmaking of British India*. London: Little Brown and Company.

Javed, Khalid (1989) 'Review of untouchable'. *What's On*. Listings Magazine.

Johnson, Christopher (1997) *Derrida*. London: Phoenix Press.

Jones, R., Gnanapala, W. Eds (2000) *Ethnic Minorities in English Law*. Stoke-On-Trent: Trentham.

Joshi, Abhijat (1999) *A Shaft of Sunlight*. London: Nick Hern Books.

Judah, Hettie (1999) 'Out of India' *The Evening Standard*, 18 November , p. 58.

Kali (1992) *Song For A Sanctuary* Programme [Kali Theatre Archive].

Kali Theatre Company Website (2009) http://www.kalitheatre.co.uk.

Kalsi, Barinder (1984) Rev. of *Miti Ki Gadi* by Jatinder Verma. *City Limits* [*Miti Ki Gadi* Production File,1986. Tara Arts Archive].

Kemp, Peter (1989) Rev. of *Ala Afsur* [*The Government Inspector*] by Jatinder Verma and Anuradha Kapur. *The Independent*, 23 January.

Kershaw, Baz (1992) *The Politics of Performance – Radical Theatre as Cultural Intervention*. London: Routledge, pp. 78–92.

Khan, Naseem (1976) *The Arts Britain Ignores – The Arts of Ethnic Minorities in Britain*. Report sponsored by The Arts Council Of Great Britain, Calouste Gulbenkian Foundation and The Commission for Racial Equality. London: The Commission For Racial Equality.

—— (1979) Rev. of *Sacrifice*. Adapted by Jatinder Verma. *Time Out*, 13–19 November, No. 586.

—— (1980) 'Ethnic theatre', *Dreams and Deconstructions Alternative Theatre in Britain*. Ed. Sandy Craig, Derbyshire: Amber Lane Press, pp. 69–75.

—— (1984) Review of *Miti Ki Gadi*. Adapted by Jatinder Verma. *The New Statesman*, 8 June.

Khan, Naushaba (2001) Personal Interview, 30 March [*Summary Of Research Into Tara's History 1977–2001*. Tara Arts Archive].

Khan, Shaheen (1999) 'The Making of Balti Kings' Video [Tamasha Archive].

Khan-Din, Ayub (1996) *East is East*. London: Nick Hern Books.

—— (1999) 'I speak English, not Urdu . . .' Feature on *East is East. The Observer Review*, 31 October, p. 6.

—— (1999) *Last Dance at Dum Dum*. London: Nick Hern Books.

—— (2004) *Notes on Falling Leaves*. London: Nick Hern Books.

—— (2007) *Rafta Rafta*. London: Nick Hern Books.

Khilnani, Sunil (1997) *The Idea of India*. London: Penguin.

Kingston, Jeremy (1986) Rev. of *Miti Ki Gadi*. Adapted by Jatinde Verma. *The Times*, Friday 10 January.

—— (1989) Rev. of *Untouchable* by Sudha Bhuchar and Kristine Landon-Smith. *The Times*, 9 December.

——(1990) Rev. of *Ala Afsur* [The Government Inspector] Adapted by Anuradha Kapur. *The Times*, 24 March.

—— (1991a) Rev. of *The Little Clay Cart* by Jatinder Verma and Ranjit Bolt 'India with an odd accent' *The Times*, Monday 9 December.

—— (1991b) Rev. of *House of the Sun* Adapted by Sudha Bhuchar and Kristine Landon-Smith. 'Too many people, too much time' *The Times*, Saturday 20 April.

—— (1997) Rev. of *East is East* by Ayub Khan-Din 'Zipped-Up culture clash' *The Times*, 11 February.

—— (2002) 'A passage to India packed with pleasure' *The Times*, 26 March.

Kirkley, Paul (2002) Rev. of the *JTW* Trilogy by Jatinder Verma. 'The true stories of' *The Reading Weekender*, Thursday 23 May.

Kristeva, Julia (1980) *Desire in Language: A Semiotic Approach to Literature and Art*. New York: Columbia University Press.

Koenig, Rhoda (2003) 'Review a taste for mangoes' *The Independent*, Monday 1 December.

Kotak, Ash (2004) 'Tale of rape at temple sparks riot at theatre *The Guardian*, Monday 20 December.

Kureishi, Hanif (1986) *My Beautiful Launderette and the Rainbow Sign*. London: Faber and Faber.

—— (1992) *Outskirts and Other Plays*. London: Faber and Faber.

Kyle, Keith (1999) *The Politics of the Independence of Kenya*. Basingstoke: Macmillan.

Lacey, Stephen (1995) *British Realist Theatre – The New Wave in its Context 1956–1965*. London: Routledge, pp. 106–108.

Lahiri, Shompa, Dr 'The Grunwick dispute' *Moving Here Migration Histories*. http://www.movinghere.org.uk/galleries/histories/asian/politics/grunwick.htm (accessed 5 March 2006).

Landon-Smith, Kristine (1991) 'House of the sun opening – 2nd play by Asian theatre group' Interview with a Staff Writer. *India Abroad – Britain*. 12 April, p. 21.

—— (1994) Interview with Gayatri Sinha. 'A British view of migrant workers' *The Times of India*, 28 January [Tamasha Archive].

—— (1998) Foreword. *Fourteen Songs, Two Weddings and A Funeral* [Tamasha Archive].

—— (2004) 'Spotlight Asian theatre' *The Independent*, Friday 16 January, p. 30.

—— (2006) 'Right of reply' *The Guardian*, Wednesday 25 January, p. 21.

—— (2008a) 'Actor Training and Multiculturalism' Paper at Exeter University Conference on Asian Theatre [Tamasha Archive].

—— (2008b) Interview with Dominic Hingorani at Tamasha Offices, 14 July.

Lathan, Peter (2005) Rev. of *The Merchant of Venice*. 2005 *The British Theatre Guide*, 16 December. http://www.britishtheatreguide.info/reviews/merchanttara-rev.htm (accessed 10 April 2010).

Lawson, Peter (1992). Rev. of *Women of the Dust* by Ruth Carter. *City Limits*, 12–19 November.

Lemos, Gerald (1998) *Correcting the Picture*. London: Arts Council Of Great Britain.

Lewis, Peter (1991) Rev. of *The Little Clay Cart*. Adapted by Jatinder Verma and Ranjit Bolt 'Where the sitar meets the shamrock' *The Times*, 4 December.

Ley, G. & Dadswell, S. Eds (2010) *British South Asian Theatres: A Documented History*. Exeter: Exeter University Press.

—— Eds (2010) *Critical Essays on British South Asian Theatre*. Exeter: Exeter University Press.

Livingstone, K. (2007) 'India now' *Time Out*.

Lodge, David. Ed (1988). *Modern Criticism and Theory – A Reader*. Harlow: Longman.

Logan, Brian (2006a) Rev. 'A fine balance' *Time Out*, 25 January–1 February.

—— (2006b) Rev. 'Marriage of Figaro', *The Guardian*.

Logan, Brian (1998) Rev. of *Fourteen Songs, Two Weddings and A Funeral*. Adapted by Sudha Bhuchar and Kristine Landon-Smith. *Time Out*, 17 November.

Lone, Amber (2006a) *Deadeye*. London: Oberon.

—— (2006b) Programme 'Asian women talk back' Soho Theatre, p. 3.

Loomba, Ania (1998) *Colonialism/Postcolonialism*. London: Routledge.

Lucy, Niall (2004) *A Derrida Dictionary*. Oxford: Blackwell Publishing.

Lustig, Vera (1990) Rev. of *Tartuffe*. Adapted by Jatinder Verma. 'Pigeons and parallels' *The Times*, Thursday 19 April.

——— (1990a) 'Plundering tradition' *Plays and Players*, May, pp. 14–16.

McAfee, Annalena (1991) Rev. of *House of the Sun*. Adapted by Sudha Bhuchar and Kristine Landon-Smith 'Block Tactics' *The Evening Standard*, 17 April.

Macaulay, Thomas (1995) 'Minute on Indian education' *The Post-colonial Studies Reader*. Ed Bill Ashcroft, Gareth Griffiths, Helen Tiffin, London: Routledge.

MacLeod, Tracy (2000) Rev. of *Balti Kings* by Sudha Bhuchar and Shaheen Khan. 'Curry on at your convenience' The Wednesday Review *The Independent*, 12 January, p. 11.

McGinn, Caroline (2008) Rev. Tara Arts 'The Tempest' *Time Out*, 16–22 January.

McLeod, John (2000) *Beginning Postcolonialism*. Manchester: Manchester University.

McMasters, B. (2008) 'Supporting excellence in the arts – from measurement to judgement'. http://www.artscouncil.org.uk/publication_archive/mcmaster-review-supporting-excellence-in-the-arts-from-measurement-to-judgement/ (accessed 10 January 2010).

McMillan, Joyce (2003) Rev. of *Strictly Dandia* by Sudha Bhuchar and Kristine Landon-Smith. 'Dance of pure life-enhancing pleasure' *The Scotsman*, Thursday 28 August.

McMillan, Joyce (2006) Rev. Tara Arts 'Enemy of The People' *The Scotsman*, 27 April.

MacPherson, W, Sir (1999) 'The Stephen Lawrence Enquiry'. http://www.archive.official-documents.co.uk/document/cm42/4262/4262.htm (accessed June 21 2007).

Mcpherson, Douglas (1998) Rev. of *Exodus* by Biswas and Company *What's On*, 21–28 October.

Mahindru, Nirjay (2002) Personal Interview, 12 February [*Summary Of Research Into Tara's History 1977–2001*. Tara Arts Archive].

Majumdar, Krishnendu (1998) 'Killing that set off a career in the theatre' Backstage with the Post *Mauri-Asia Post*. 10 April.

Manzoor, Sarfraz (2005) 'We've ditched race for religion' *The Guardian*, Tuesday 11 January, p. 22.

Marlowe, Sam (2006) Rev. 'The trouble with Asian men' *The Times*, Monday 11 September.

——— (2008) Rev. Tara Arts 'The tempest' A stiff breeze is not a storm' *The Times*, Tuesday 15 January.

Marmion, Patrick (1989) Rev. of *Ala Afsur* (*The Government Inspector*). Adapted by Anuradha Kapur. *What's On*, 25 January.

Maxwell, Dominic (2006) 'A grim tale compellingly told with wit and warmth' *The Times*, 18 January, p. 27.

Millard, Rosie (2007) 'Tailor-made for the stage' *The New Statesman*, 23 April.

Miller, Carl (1990) Rev. of *Tartuffe* Adapted by Jatinder Verma. *City Limits*, 26 April.

Milne, Kirsty (1991) Rev. of *The Little Clay Cart* by Jatinder Verma and Ranjit Bolt. *The Sunday Telegraph*, 8 December.

Mishra, Vijay (2002) *Bollywood Cinema – Temples of Desire*, London: Routledge.

Modood, T. (1997) *The Fourth National Survey of Ethnic Minorities – Ethnic Minorities in Britain – Diversity and Disadvantage.* Ed. R. Berthoud, T. Modood, London: Policy Studies Institute.

Morley, Sheridan (1989) Rev. of *Ala Afsur [The Government Inspector].* Adapted by Anuradha Kapur *The Herald Tribune*, 8 February.

Mountford, Fiona (2006) 'Uneasy passage to epic India is out of balance' *The Evening Standard*, Tuesday 17 January.

Mousawi, Dina (2002) Rev. of the *JTW* Trilogy by Jatinder Verma. *Leicester Mercury*, 8 March.

Murdin, Lynda (1986) Rev. of *The Little Clay Cart* 'Doing the Delhi glide' *The London Standard* Monday, 13 January.

Myerson, Jonathan (2001) Rev. of *Fourteen Songs, Two Weddings and A Funeral* by Sudha Bhuchar and Kristine Landon Smith. 'A load of old bollywood' *The Independent*, 20 February.

N.B. (1984) 'Eastern Optimism' *Times Educational Supplement*, 15 June.

Nagpal, Kavita (1994a) 'Indian woes in English' 6 February [Tamasha Archive].

—— (1994b) Rev. of *Women of the Dust* by Ruth Carter. 'Poignant moments in women of the dust' *The Hindustani Times* (Delhi), 6 February [Tamasha Archive].

Nightingale, Benedict Rev. of *Tartuffe*. Adapted by Jatinder Verma. *The Times*, 23 February 1990.

—— (1995) Rev. of *Cyrano*. Adapted by Jatinder Verma. Additional Verse Ranjit Bolt. 'Hapless loser by a long nose' *The Times*. Friday 27 October.

O'Toole, Fintan (1990) Rev. of *Ala Afsur [The Government Inspector]*. Adapted by Anuradha Kapur. 'A passage to India' *The Irish Times*, 23 June.

Ohbi, Harjinder (2002) Rev. of the *JTW* Trilogy by Jatinder Verma. 'Brilliant and epic work' *Leicester Mercury*, 25 March.

Onwardi, Sylvester (1990) Rev. of *Ala Afsur [The Government Inspector]*. Adapted by Anuradha Kapur. *What's On*, 28 March.

Osborne, Charles (1990) Rev. of *Tartuffe*. Adapted by Jatinder Verma. *The Daily Telegraph*. 20 April.

Owusu, Kwesi (1986) *The Struggle for Black Arts in Britain – What Can We Consider Better than Freedom.* London: Commedia Press.

Paddock, Terri (2008) 'Arts council must come clean, says Cut Tara Arts' *The Stage*, 1 February.

Pandey, Vibha (1988) Rev. of *Untouchable* by Kristine Landon-Smith. 'Anand's 'Untouchable' comes alive' *The Patriot* (New Delhi), 28 September.

Parker, Mike (2004) Rev. of *Calcutta Kosher* 'Touching, comic clash of cultures' *The Morning Star*, Thursday 1 July.

Parks, Diane (2006) Interview with Amber Lone. *Birmingham Mail*, Friday 13 October.

Parry, Jann (2003) Rev. of *Strictly Dandia* 'Would you like a lift' *The Observer Review*, 31 August .

Paz, Anjana (1984) 'A despair we know – Tara Arts' *New Life*, Friday 8 June.

Pavis, Patrice (1996) *The Intercultural Performance Reader*. London: Routledge.

Peacock Keith, D. (1999) *Thatcher's Theatre – British Theatre and Drama in the Eighties*. New York: Greenwood Press.

Pearson, G. (1981) Rev. of *Vilayat* by Jatinder Verma 'Just like us.... ' *Croydon Advertiser*, Friday 17 July.

Pearson, G. (1982) Rev. of *Lion's Raj* by Jatinder Verma. 'A Guru or a betrayer' *Croydon Advertiser*, Friday 8 October.

Pestonji, Meher (1994) Rev. of *Women of the Dust* by Ruth Carter. 'Anger trapped within' *The Statesman* (Delhi), 29 January.

Peter, John (1996) Rev. of *East is East* by Ayub Khan-Din. 'Crossed countries' *The Sunday Times*, 1 December.

Peter, John (2006) Rev. 'A fine balance' *Sunday Times*, 15 April.

PL. (1991) Rev. of *Song for a Sanctuary* by Rukhsana Ahmad *Yorkshire Post*, 21 June.

Plastow, Jane (2004) 'Jatinder Verma: Encounters with the epic – an interview' *Contemporary Theatre Review*. London: Routledge, Volume 14, Issue 2.

Porter, Cedric (1982) Interview with Jatinder Verma. 'Closing the culture gap' *South London Press*, Tuesday 28 September [*Lion's Raj* Production File, 1982. Tara Arts Archive].

Powell, Enoch (1968) 'Explosive race speech by Powell' *The Sunday Times*, 21 April, pp. 1–2.

Powell, Lucy (2007) 'Review the tempest' *Time Out*, 3–9 October.

Rai, Jasdev, Singh (2005) 'Behind *Behzti*' *The Guardian*, 17 January.

Rana, Vijay (1998) Interview with Jatinder Verma. 'Search for space' *India Today International*, 2 November.

Rangacharya, Adya (1996) *The Natyasastra*. New Delhi: Munshiram Manoharlal.

——— (1998) *Introduction to Bharata's Natyasastra*. New Delhi: Munshiram Manoharlal.

Rea, Kenneth (1984) Rev. of *Miti Ki Gadi* by Jatinder Verma. *The Guardian*, Thursday 13 December.

——— (1990) Rev. of *Tartuffe* Adapted by Jatinder Verma. 'Moliere in a dhoti' *The Guardian*, Thursday 12 April.

Reade, Simon (1990) 'The Asian viewpoint' *Plays International*, May, p. 13.

Rebellato, D. (1999) *1956 and All That: The Making of Modern British Stage*. London: Routledge.

Renton, Alex (1987) Rev. of *The Lost Ring*. Adapted by Prof. P. Lal. *The Independent*, 14 March.

Rewrite (2008) [http://www.rewrite.org.uk/about_rewrite.html].

RL (1980) 'Indian history comes to life' *Ipswich Evening Star*, 29 September.

Roberts, P. (1999) *The Royal Court Theatre and the Modern Stage*. Cambridge: Cambridge University Press.

Rojek, Chris (2003) *Stuart Hall – Key Contemporary Thinkers*. Cambridge: Polity.

Rubin, Gareth. Rev. of the *JTW* trilogy 'Last jokes on the road to nowhere' *The Daily Telegraph*, 26 March 2002.

Rushdie, Salman (1991) *Imaginary Homelands*. London: Granta Books.

Said, Edward (1978, 1995) *Orientalism – Western Conceptions of the Orient*. London: Penguin.

Schechner, Richard (1994) *Performance Theory*. London: Routledge.

——— (1983) *Performative Circumstances – From the Avant Garde to Ramlila*. Calcutta: Seagull Books.

Scott, Adam (2004) Rev. of *Strictly Dandia* by Sudha Bhuchar and Kristine Landon-Smith *The Independent*, Tuesday 27 January.

Sen, Devdan (1987) 'First steps at theatre royal' *Bazaar*, March. Issue 1.

Shah, Devi (1992) 'The spotlight's on blacks' arts & style section *The Independent*, Friday 24 July.

Shelley Silas in Interview with Martha Carney Friday 6 February 2004b Broadcast http://www.bbc.co.uk/radio4/womanshour/2004_05_fri_04.shtml (accessed 29 January 2009).

Shore, Robert (2004) Rev. of *Calcutta Kosher, Time Out*, 11–18 February.

Shore, Robert (2006) Rev. *The Marriage of Figaro Time Out.*

Shulman. Milton (1989) Rev. of *Blood* by Hawant Bains. *The Evening Standard*, 1 September.

Shuttleworth, Ian (1991) *City Limits*, 25 April.

—— (1996) Rev. of *East is East* by Ayub Khan-Din 'Mixed race family conflict' *Financial Times.*

Sierz, Aleks (2000) Rev. of *River on Fire*. 'Bravely Bollywood' *Tribune*, 24 November.

—— (2001) *In-Yer-Face Theatre – British Drama Today*. London: Faber and Faber.

—— (2007) 'Funny peculiar' *The Times*, 21 April.

Silas, Shelley (2004) *Calcutta Kosher*. London: Oberon.

Silas, Shelley (2004a) 'Oy Calcutta' *Jewish News*, Friday 4 June.

Sinha, Gayatri (1994) Rev. of *Women of the Dust* by Ruth Carter. 'A British view of migrant workers' *The Times of India*, 28 January [Tamasha Archive].

Smith, Anna Marie (1994) *New Right Discourse on Race and Sexuality – Britain 1968–1990*. Cambridge: Cambridge University.

Snell, Rupert (2004) *Teach Yourself Hindi – Dictionary*. London: Hodder & Stoughton Educational.

Special Correspondant (1998) Rev. of *Exodus* by Biswas and Company. 'Exodus: Asians are here to stay' *The Asian Age*, 29 October, p. 1.

Spencer, Charles (1989) Rev. of *Blood* by Harwant Bains *The Daily Telegraph*, 2 September.

—— (1991) 'Hotch-potch Indian treat' *The Daily Telegraph*, Thursday 12 December, p. 19.

—— (1995) Rev. of *Cyrano* Adapted by Jatinder Verma. Additional Verse Ranjit Bolt. 'A Cyrano within sniffing distance of success' *The Daily Telegraph*, Friday 27 October.

—— (1996) Rev. of *East is East* by Ayub Khan-Din 'Rich mix of culture and comedy' *The Daily Telegraph*, 25 November.

—— (2000) Rev. of *Balti Kings* 'American treacle has its moments, but a night in this curry house really stays with you' *Daily Telegraph*, 21 January.

—— (2001) Rev. of *Fourteen Songs* ... Adapted by Sudha Bhuchar and Kristine Landon-Smith 'Bollywood lends hilarity to a tale of love' *The Daily Telegraph*, Tuesday 20 February.

—— (2004) Rev. of *Strictly Dandia* by Sudha Bhuchar and Kristine Landon-Smith. 'Dance floor romance is far from Fine and Dandia' *The Daily Telegraph*, 21 January.

—— (2006) Rev. of *The Trouble with Asian Men*. 'Asian drama with a fundamental flaw' *The Daily Telegraph*, Monday 11 September.

St. George, Andrew (1991) Rev. of *The Little Clay Cart* by Jatinder Verma and Ranjit Bolt 'Strange fable from India' *The Financial Times*, 7 December.

Staff Reporter (1994) Rev. of *Women of the Dust* by Sudha Bhuchar and Kristine Landon-Smith 'A British portrayal of Indian lives' *The Statesman* (Delhi), 26 January.

Stansfield, Keith (1991) Rev. of *The Little Clay Cart*. Adapted by Jatinder Verma. *City Limits*, 12 December.

Stokes, John (1995) 'Bollywood babylon' *TLS Arts*, 2 November.

Stratton, Kate (1995) Rev. of *Cyrano*. Adapted by Jatinder Verma and Ranjit Bolt. *Time Out*, 1 November.

Subramaniam, Arundhathi (1994) Rev. of *Women of the Dust* by Ruth Carter. 'A nation polluted with saviours' *The Statesman*, 29 January.

Correspondent. 'Tara – an Asian perspective'. *Asian Digest*, January/February 1982, p. 46.

Taylor, Paul (1991) 'On delivering the good' *The Independent*, 7 December.

'The Asians who were forced to say "TARA" to East Africa' *Mauri-Asia Post*, October 1998.

The Independent (2004) 'The threat of mob violence should not curtail the right of artistic expression', Tuesday 21 December.

Thorpe, Vanessa (1999) Interview with Venu Dhupa. 'Theatre cast as villain by black actors'. *The Observer*, 2 May, p. 8.

Unattributed (1983) Rev. of *Ancestral Voices* by Tara Arts Company. 'Awaaz Puraani' – the ancestral voices from young Asians past' *New Life*, 11 March, p. 15.

Unattributed (1982) *The Asian Digest*. January/February, p. 46.

Vaish, Arti (1994) Rev. of *Women of the Dust* by Ruth Carter 'Labouring hard to construct reality' *The Economic Times* (Delhi) 5 February.

Varadpande, V.S. (1979) *Traditions of Indian Theatre*. New Delhi: Abhinav Publications.

—— (1987) *Invitation to Indian Theatre*. New Delhi: Arnold Publishers.

Vatsyayan, Kapila (1987) *Traditions of Indian Folk Dance*. New Delhi: Clarion Press.

Vaughan, Tom (1984a) Rev. of *Chilli in Your Eyes* by Jatinder Verma *Morning Star*, 7 June.

—— (1984b) Rev. of *Miti Ki Gadi* by Jatinder Verma. 'Between Brecht and Peking Opera' *The Morning Star*, Friday 28 December.

—— (1992) 'Close-Up on women of the South' *The Morning Star*, 3 November [Tamasha Archive].

—— (1991) Rev. of *Song for a Sanctuary*. 'Perceptive look at the truth of tragedy' *The Morning Star*, Friday 25 October.

Verma, Deepak (2001) *Ghostdancing*. London: Methuen.

Verma, Jatinder (1976) *The Uganda Railway and Migrant Labour, 1895–1905*. M.A. Thesis [*Jatinder Verma* Production File. Tara Arts Archive].

—— (1977a) *Sacrifice* Script Unpublished [*Sacrifice* Production File, 1977. Tara Arts Archive].

—— (1977b) *Sacrifice*. Programme. [*Sacrifice* Production File, 1977. Tara Arts Archive].

—— (1978a) *Fuse* Script Unpublished [*Fuse* Production File, 1978. Tara Arts Archive].

—— (1978b) *Fuse* Programme [*Fuse* Production File, 1978. Tara Arts Archive].

—— (1978c) *Playing The Flame* Unpublished Script [*Playing The Flame* Production File, 1978. Tara Arts Archive].

—— (1979a) *Yes, Memsahib* Script Unpublished [*Yes, Memsahib* Production File, 1979. Tara Arts Archive].

—— (1980a) *Inkalaab, 1919* Script Unpublished [*Inkalaab, 1919* Production File, 1980. Tara Arts Archive].

Verma, Jatinder (1980b) *Inkalaab, 1919* Programme [*Inkalaab, 1919* Production File, 1980. Tara Arts Archive].

——— (1980c) *Jhansi* Script Unpublished, [*Jhansi* Production File, 1980. Tara Arts Archive].

——— (1980d) *Diwaali* Script Unpublished [*Diwaali* Production File, 1980. Tara Arts Archive].

——— (1981a) *Vilayat or England, Your England* Unpublished Script. [*Vilayat* Production File, 1981. Tara Arts Archive].

——— (1981b) *Vilayat or England, Your England* Programme [*Vilayat* Production File, 1981. Tara Arts Archive].

——— (1981c) *Fuse* Script Unpublished [*Fuse* Production File, 1978. Tara Arts Archive].

——— (1982) 'Creating a theatre tradition for Asians' *Stage and Television Today*, 19 August 1982. No. 5288.

——— (1982a) *Lion's Raj* Script Unpublished [*Lion's Raj* Production File, 1982.Tara Arts Archive].

——— (1982b) *Lion's Raj* Production Programme [*Lion's Raj* Production File, 1982. Tara Arts Archive].

——— (1982c) *Scenes in the Life of* [*Scenes in the Life of* Production File,1982. Tara Arts Archive].

——— (1982d) 'Closing the culture gap' *South London Press*, Tuesday 28 September.

——— (1983a) *Ancestral Voices* Script [*Ancestral Voices* Production File, 1983. Tara Arts Archive].

——— (1983b) *The Passage* Script [*The Passage* Production File, 1983. Tara Arts Archive].

——— (1984a) Interview with Rick Banot. 'Staging the Asian Experience'. *Ilea Contact Magazine*. 20 January, pp. 9–10.

——— (1984b) *Miti Ki Gadi* Rehearsal Notebook [*The Little Clay cart* Production File 1984, Tara Arts Archive].

——— (1984c) *Miti Ki Gadi* Script 1984a [*Miti Ki Gadi* Production File 1984, Tara Arts Archive].

——— (1984d) *Chilli in Your Eyes*. Unpublished Script [*Chilli in Your Eyes* Production File, 1984. Tara Arts Archive].

——— (1985a) *Miti Ki Gadi* Performance, 24 February. Videocassette. Video Archive # 120. Tara Arts Archive]

——— (1985b) 'Indian folk theatre in Britain' *Asian Theatre Newsletter*, September 1985 Issue 4.

——— (1985b) *The Little Clay Cart* Rehearsal Notebook Arts Theatre Production, December 1985b [*The Little Clay Cart* Production File 1986, Tara Arts Archive].

——— (1985c) *The Little Clay Cart* Script [*The Little Clay Cart* Production File 1986, Tara Arts Archive].

——— (1986a) 'Indian Theatre and Tara Arts' [*The Little Clay Cart* Production File, 1986. Tara Arts Archive].

——— (1986b) *The Little Clay Cart* Programme for the Black Theatre Season [*The Little Clay Cart* Production File, 1986. Tara Arts Archive].

——— (1987) Rev. of *The Lost Ring* Adapted by Prof. P. Lal. *Bazaar*. Issue 2. pp. 3, 28.

——— (1989a) 'Doing the write thing' *Bazaar*, September, Issue 9, pp. 4–5.

Verma, Jatinder (1989b) 'Transformations in culture: The Asian in Britain' The Sir George Birdwood Memorial Lecture Speech delivered to the Society on Wednesday 22 March 1989. Reproduced in *RSA Journal* November, pp. 767–78.

—— (1990a) *Tartuffe* Script [*Tartuffe* Production File 1990, Tara Arts Archive].

—— (1990b) Interview with Nick Smurthwaite. 'Bound By Traditions' *The Stage and Television Today*, 12 April. No. 5687.

—— (1990c) Interview with Tony Palmer. *Kaleidoscope* Prod. Nicki Paxman. Radio Four. 7 February 21.15 p.m.–21.45 p.m.

—— (1991a) Interview with Jim Hiley. *The Late Show*. BBC2, 2 February [Tara Arts Video Archive # VHSTARA 0061].

—— (1991b) Bolt, Ranjit. *The Little Clay Cart* No script.

—— (1991c) Bolt, Ranjit. *Little Clay Cart* Programme. [Little Clay Cart Production File 1991. Tara Arts Archive].

—— (1994a) 'Cultural transformations', *Contemporary British Theatre*. Ed. Theodore Shank, Basingstoke & London: Macmillan.

—— (1994b) Keynote Speech. 'Asian theatre in Britain: Historical developments and contemporary identity'. Asian Theatre Conference. Birmingham Rep. Theatre, Birmingham, 20–21 October 1994. [http://www.tara-arts.com].

—— (1995) Bolt, Ranjit. *Cyrano* Script [*Cyrano* Production File, 1995. Tara Arts Archive].

—— (1996) 'The challenge of Binglish: Analysing multi cultural productions', *Analysing Performance: A Critical Reader*. Ed. Patrick Campbell, Manchester: Manchester University. pp. 193–203.

—— (1996a) *In Contact With the Gods*. Ed. Maria M. Delgado & Paul Heritage, Manchester: Manchester University Press, pp. 277–298.

—— (1996b) 'The Binglish imperative'. Conference. Aberystwyth. 5 September [http://www.tara-arts.com].

—— (1996c) 'Punjabi theatre in Britain: Context and challenge', Conference. W. Hounslow, London, 25 September 1996c. [http://www.tara-arts.com].

—— (1996d) 'Asian writers in English', 'Mother Tongue' Conference. Oldham, April [http://www.tara-arts.com].

—— (1997a) 'Advertisement for Interviewees' [Tara Arts Archive] Trilogy Background File ref # TB 19.

—— (1997b) Actor Briefing Document, August [Tara Arts Archive] Trilogy Background File ref # TB 19.

—— (1997c) Actor Briefing Document, October [Trilogy Background File ref # TB 19. Tara Arts Archive].

—— (1997d) *Exodus 1* Schedule Phase 1 Document B, August [Trilogy Background File ref # TB 19. Tara Arts Archive].

—— (1997e) *Exodus 1* Recorded Tara Arts Studio. 8 November [Video Archive #VHS0053. Tara Arts Archive].

—— (1998a) 'Killing that set a career in the theatre' – Backstage with the Post. The Mauri-Asia Post. Interview Krishnendu Majumdar. April, p. 10.

—— (1998b) 'Binglishing the stage: A generation of Asian theatre in England', *Theatre Matters: Politics and Culture on the World Stage*. Ed. Richard Boon and Jane Plastow, Cambridge: Cambridge University, pp. 126–134.

—— (1998c) 'The show must go on' *Eastern Eye*, 17 July.

—— (1998d) *Exodus III* Script [Trilogy Background File # TB20. Tara Arts Archive].

Verma, Jatinder (1998e) *Exodus* Update, March [Trilogy Background File # TB20. Tara Arts Archive].

—— (1998f) *Exodus* Joining instructions to Actors [Trilogy Background File # TB20. Tara Arts Archive].

—— (1999) *Genesis* Work in Progress Production. Filmed at Warwick University 10 March [Tara Arts Archive].

—— (2001a) 'Salaam Bombay' Interview for Krishnendu Majumdar *The Guardian*, 21 February.

—— (2001b) 'Braids and Theatre Practice'. Address. British Braids Conference. Brunel University, Twickenham Campus, 20 April [http://www.tara-arts.com].

—— (2002) *The Bone in the Kebab* Interview with prod. Mukti Jane Campion. BBC Radio 4, 11.30 a.m., Thursday 21 February.

—— (2002a) *Journey to the West Part I* [Tara Arts Archive].

—— (2002b) *Journey to the West Part II* [Tara Arts Archive].

—— (2002c) *Journey to the West TW Part III* [Tara Arts Archive].

—— (2003a) 'Asian Arts in the 21'st Century' Keynote Address at the DNAsia Conference, Watermans Arts Centre, 24 March [http://www.tara-arts.com].

—— (2003b) *A Taste for Mangoes* [Tara Arts Archive].

—— (2004) 'Encounters with the Epic – An Interview' *Contemporary Theatre Review*. Interview with Jane Plastow. Vol. 14 (2), pp. 82–87.

—— (2006a) 'It could be you…'*The Guardian*. Section G2 22 February p. 22.

—— (2006b) 'The shape of the heart', *Alternatives within the Mainstream-British Black and Asian Theatre*. Ed. Dimple Godiwala, Newcastle: Cambridge Scholars.

Verma, Jatinder & Kapur (1989a) Anuradha. *Ala Afsur* Script [*Ala Afsur* Production File 1989, Tara Arts Archive].

—— (1989b) *Ala Afsur* Programme [*Ala Afsur* Production File 1989, Tara Arts Archive].

Visram, Rozina (1986) *Ayahs Lascars and Princes: Indians in Britain 1700–1947*. London: Pluto Press.

Wainwright, Jeffrey (1990) Rev. of *Tartuffe*. Adapted by Jatinder Verma. *The Independent*, 8 March.

Walker, Lynne (2003) Rev. of *Strictly Dandia* by Sudha Bhuchar and Kristine Landon-Smith 'This thin offering is strictly amateur fare' *The Independent*, 28 August.

Walker, Tim (2007) Rev 'A fine balance' *The Sunday Telegraph*, 15 April.

Walsh, Maeve (2000) Rev. of *Balti Kings* by Sudha Bhuchar, Kristine Landon-Smith & Shaheen Khan. 'A bit too much on their plate' *The Independent on Sunday*, 16 January.

Wardle, Irving (1991) Rev. of *The Little Clay Cart* by Jatinder Verma and Ranjit Bolt. *The Independent on Sunday*, 8 December.

Woddis, Carole (1989) Rev. of *Untouchable* by Sudha Bhuchar and Kristine Landon-Smith. *City Limits*, 9 December.

Woddis, Carole (2006) Rev. of *The Trouble with Asian Men*. Whatsonstage.com, Friday 8 September.

Wolf, Matt (1997) 'East heads off west' *The Times*, 25 March.

Wolf, Rita (1989) 'Doing the write thing' *Bazaar*, September, Issue 9, p. 4.

Woods, Richard (1991) Rev. of Little Clay Cart *The Tribune* in *The Theatre Record*, 3–31 December.

Wright, Michael (1995) 'Britain's Asian culture comes of age' *The Daily Telegraph*, Saturday 14 October.

Young, Hugo (1989) *One Of Us* London: Pan Books Ltd.

Young, Robert. (1990) *White Mythologies – Writing History and the West.* London: Routledge.

Zahno, Kamila (1991) Interview Rita Wolf Dircts Song for a sanctuary *Spare Rib*.

Zarilli, P., Swann, Darius L., Richmond, Farey P. Eds (1990) *Indian Theatre Traditions of Performance.* Honolulu: University of Hawaii Press.

Index

aardass, 180
Abhinaya, 46, 53
abrogation, 12–13
Achut, 73
agitprop, 42
Aharya, 46
Ahmad, Rukhsana, 16, 120–3
alaap, 51
Allen, Jim, 177
All in Good Time, 184
Amritsar, 82
Ancestral Voices, 35
Anderson, Benedict, 9
Angika, 46
appropriation, 13
*Arts Britain Ignores: The Arts of Ethnic
    Minorities in Britain, The*, 2–8, 18,
    188
Arts Council, 5, 9, 18, 73, 131, 165
Arts Theatre, 164
Ashcroft, 28, 49
Asian language, 12–14, 22–3
Asian Women's Writing Collective,
    120–1
Asian Youth Movement, 169
ATC (Asian Theatre Co-operative),
    122, 171
authenticity, 49, 76–7, 93, 109, 118

Balidaan, 20
Balti Kings, 15, 71, 82–8
Bancil, Parv, 170–6
Battersea Arts Centre, 131, 147, 174
Behsharaam, 17, 190
Behzti, 6, 10, 17, 176–83
Bells, 123
Bend It Like Beckham, 183
Bhabha, Homi K., 101
Bhangra dance, 37, 43
Bharucha, Rustom, 15
Bhatti, Gurpreet Kaur, 10, 17,
    176–83

bhavai, 45, 65
Bhuchar, Sudha, 15, 71, 92
    see also Landon-Smith, Kristine
Binglish language, 47–49, 66–70,
    145–6
Binglish theatre, 45–70, 143–166
    Miti Ki Gadi, production of, 49–51
Birmingham Repertory Theatre, 10,
    97, 137, 176
Black Album, The, 69–70, 188
Black and Asian Women Writers, 1
Black Theatre Cooperative, 171
Black Theatre Season, 50
Bollywood, 1, 101–105
Bolt, Ranjit, 60
Bombay Dreams, 105
Borderline, 122, 167–70
Brah, Avtar, 7, 11, 169
Brahmachari, Sita, 114, 115, 118
Brahmins, 65, 72
British colonialism, 9
British Council, 72
'Britishness', 100
British Raj, 9, 120
Brook, Peter, 11, 103
Buchner, 62
Bush Theatre, 132

Calcutta Kosher, 16, 131–6
*Called to Account. The Indictment of
    Anthony Charles Lynton Blair for the
    Crime of Aggression Against Iraq-A
    Hearing*, 109
Cambridge Guide to Asian Theatre,
    46, 65
Captain's Malt, 120
Carib Theatre, 171
Carter, Ruth, 89
Centre of Indian Arts, The, 24
chaandi, 152
Chaggar, Gurdip Singh, 14, 16, 120,
    159

Chand, Meira, 76
Chandran, V., 163
Chaos, 123
Chapman, Gerald, 34
Chekhov, Anton, 62, 72
Chilli in Your Eyes, 14, 20, 36–44
Civil Rights movement, 8
Clarke, Anthony, 30
colonialism, 13
colonial mimicry, 25
colour blind casting approach, 3, 9–10, 21
Colour of Justice, The, 109
Commission For Racial Equality, 18, 183
Common Stock, 122
Commonwealth Immigrants Act, 143
community theatre, 19
Coronation Street, 122
CrazyHorse, 17, 171–4
cultural authenticity, 117
cultural context, 12, 16, 116–19
cultural diversity, 7
culture clash, 7, 98
culture of hybridity, 7, 13
Curse of the Dead Dog, The, 170–1
Cyrano De Bergerac, 15, 49, 68–70

dalit, 72, 76
Deadeye, 16, 136–42
Decibel initiative, 4, 6
Devanagari script, 13
diaspora, 13, 15, 145
    see also Binglish diaspora
diaspora space, 11
Diwaali, 20, 33–4, 105, 107

EastEnders, 181
East is East (Khan-Din), 17, 71, 95–119
Eclipse Report – Developing Strategies to Combat Racism in Theatre, The, 4–5, 6
Enemy of the People, An, 163, 164
England Your England, 14
English language, 12, 23, 27–9, 48
ethnic arts, 2–6, 4
ethnicity, 6–11

ethnic minority communities theatre, 2–3
Exodus, 145, 146–7
Eyre, Richard, 59

Falling, 132
Family Way, The, 184
fatwah, 68
Fine Balance, A, 15, 71, 78–80
Forest, Waltham, 59
Fourteen Songs, Two Weddings and A Funeral, 15, 95, 101–5
Fuse, 20, 34–6

garba, 65, 105–6
Genesis, 145, 148
ghazal, 139–40
Gill, Ravinder, 170
Government Inspector, Ala Afsur (Gogol), 68, 69
Greater London Arts Association, 18, 73
Griffin, Gabrielle, 1, 126
Gupta, Tanika, 166
gurdwara, 177–80

Hall, Stuart, 7, 8, 13
Harijaans, 72–3
Heer Ranja, 67
henna artists, 152
Hindi language, 12, 13, 14, 47
"hot seat" exercise, 84, 113–14
Hounslow Arts Co-Operative (HAC), 170–1
House of the Sun, 15, 71, 76–7, 81
Hum Aapke Hain Koun (Who Am I to You), 101, 104
Hussein, Iqbal, 144, 146
Hytner, Nicholas, 177, 187

Imagined Communities (Anderson), 9
Inkalaab, 23, 26–7, 29
institutional racism, 5
intracultural, defined, 15

jamadar, 92
Jeyasingh, Shobana, 55, 61
Joint Stock, 167, 170
Journey to the West trilogy, 143–60

Kali Theatre Company, 16, 120–42
Kapoor, Shobu, 92
Kapur, Anuradha, 62, 68
Kathak, 55, 65
Kathakali, 7, 163
Kaur, Balwant, 16, 120–1
Khan, Naseem, 8, 19, 188
Khan, Shaheen, 83, 86
Khan-Din, Ayub, 183–7
Kiddush, 135
King and Me, The, 167
Kitchen, The, 88
kitchen sink drama, 95
Kotak, Ash, 178
Kshatriyas, 72
Kureishi, Hanif, 166–70, 188

Labour Government, 143, 174
Landon-Smith, Kristine, 12, 15–16,
    71–120, 189, 190
language theatre, 23
Lion's Raj, 19, 22, 23, 30, 31–2, 35
Little Clay Cart, The, 14, 57–62
    sutradhar in, role of, 58–9
    see also Miti Ki Gadi
Lone, Amber, 16, 136–42
Look Back in Anger, 22
Lyrical MC, 16, 95, 113–19

Macaulay, Thomas, 9
Macpherson report of 1999, 4
Made in England, 17, 174–6
Mahabharata, 32, 156
Manzoor, Sarfraz, 183
Marriage of Figaro, The, 163
Mayes, Sue, 83, 85, 90
mazdoors, 91–4
McMasters, Sir Brian, 6, 105
Merchant of Venice, The, 163
Milan Centre, 19
mimicry, 101
Minority Art Advisory Service
    (MAAS), 4
Mistry, Rohinton, 78
Miti Ki Gadi, 14, 22, 49–57

National Front, 37, 168, 169, 176
National Theatre, 2, 15, 59, 163, 184
Natyasastra, 45, 53–6, 66

Naughton, Bill, 184
Navratri, 105
New Constitution, 120
Newham Monitoring Project, 37
Non-Fiction Theatre Company, 107

Odyssey-Ramayan, The, 148
Orientalism, 9
Osborne, John, 22
Outskirts, 167

Patel, Harish, 184
Powell, Enoch, 143
prakrits, 56
psychological realism, 103
pundit, 130
Punjabi language, 12, 13, 23, 37, 47–8
purvaranga, 66

Rafta Rafta, 17, 183–7
Ramayana, 33–4
Ram Lila folk, 62
rangapuja, 65–6
rangoli artists, 152
REACT youth theatre, 115
Revelations, 148
River on Fire, 16, 128–31
Riverside Studios, 73, 88, 122, 148
Rostand, 15, 68–9
Rowlatt Act, 26
Royal Court Theatre, 97, 122, 167, 168
Royal Court Young People's
    Theatre, 30
Royal National Theatre, 49, 50, 59, 62,
    64, 144
Rushdie, Salman, 68, 183

Sacrifice, 20–2, 23, 188
Saggar, Sunil, 19
Said, Edward, 9
Salidaa, 2
salwar kameez, 169
Sanskrit language, 13, 56
Satanic Verses, The, 68, 183
Sattvika, 46
'second generation' Asians, 19, 33–44,
    37, 169
Sepoy's Salt, 120
Shabbat, 135–6

Shah, Naseeruddin, 68–9
Shudraka, 22
Sikh Human Rights Group, 177
Silas, Shelley, 16, 131, 132
Sock'em With Honey, 131
Soho Theatre's Writers Attachment
    Programme, 137
Song for a Sanctuary, 16, 120, 121,
    123–8
Southall Youth Movement, 169
South Asian language, 13, 47, 124
Special Patrol Group, 168
Staging the UK, 1, 101
Steel, Janet, 16, 131
Stephen Lawrence Inquiry, 5
Strictly Dandia, 15, 95, 105–7
stylised gestures, 54
Sulkin, David, 30
*Supporting Excellence in the Arts-From
    Measurement to Judgment*, 6
sutradhars, 58–9, 62, 155

tabla, 52
Tagore, Rabindranath, 20
Tainted Dawn, A, 105
Talawa, 171
Talking to Terrorists, 109
Tamasha Theatre Company, 15–16,
    71–120, 189, 190
Tara Arts Theatre Company, 14–15,
    18–71, 143–166
    see also Binglish theatre
Tara-In-The-Sky, 15, 160
Tartuffe, 15, 59, 62–8
Taste for Mangoes, A, 15, 160–1
Temba, 171
Tempest, The, 163, 164
Thatcher, Margaret, 25
Theatre Royal Stratford East, 76, 77, 97
Throw of the Dice, A, 161

TIME (Tamasha Intercultural
    Millennium Education)
    Conference, 113–14
translated man, *see* Verma, Jatinder
Tricycle Theatre, 109
Trouble with Asian Men, The, 15, 95,
    107–13
Tully, Mark, 82
Tulsidass, 33
twinspronged stance, Tara Arts, 39

Uganda Railway and Migrant
    Labour, 24
Ungrateful Dead, 171
Untouchable, 15, 71, 72–8
Urdu, 13, 47, 66, 67
Urnful of Ashes, An, 128

Vacika, 46
Vaishayas, 72
verbatim theatre, 15, 107–19
    see also Lyrical MC; *Trouble with
        Asian Men, The*
Verma, Jatinder, 2, 11, 12
    see also Tara Arts
Vilayat, 14, 35

Wallinger, Louise, 107
Waterman's Arts Centre, 163, 174
Webber, Andrew Lloyd, 105
Wesker, Arnold, 88
West Midlands Arts Association,
    The, 18
Wilton's Music Hall, 160, 161
Windrush, 7
Wolf, Rita, 16, 122, 123
Women of the Dust, 15, 71, 88–94

Yes Memsahib, 19, 23, 24–5, 28–9